THE CASE AGAINST THE DEMOCRATIC HOUSE IMPEACHING TRUMP

Also by Alan Dershowitz

THE CASE AGAINST THE DEMOCRATIC HOUSE IMPEACHING TRUMP

ALAN DERSHOWITZ

HOT BOOKS

Hot Books may be purchased in bulk at special discounts for sales promotion, corporate gifts, fund-raising, or educational purposes. Special editions can also be created to specifications. For details, contact the Special Sales Department, Skyhorse Publishing, 307 West 36th Street, 11th Floor, New York, NY 10018 or info@skyhorsepublishing.com.

Hot Books® and Skyhorse Publishing® are registered trademarks of Skyhorse Publishing, Inc.®, a Delaware corporation.

Visit our website at www.hotbookspress.com

10 9 8 7 6 5 4 3 2 1

Library of Congress Cataloging-in-Publication Data is available on file.

Cover design by Brian Peterson

ISBN: 978-1-5107-4770-8
Ebook ISBN: 978-1-5107-4771-5

Printed in the United States of America

Dedication

This book is respectfully dedicated to an endangered species: genuine civil libertarians who pass the "shoe on the other foot" test.

Acknowledgments

―――――――

My appreciation to my wife, Carolyn Cohen, who reads, reviews, and corrects everything I write, and to Elon Dershowitz, Jamin Dershowitz, Ella Dershowitz, and others who critiqued my words. Also, thanks to Harvey Silverglate and Alan Rothfeld for reviewing and critiquing the manuscript.

This book could not have been written without the valuable assistance of my research team, Aaron Voloj Dessauer, Jennifer Barrow, and Hannah Dodson, who researched and contributed to the text and footnotes, and my assistant, Maura Kelley, who deciphered and typed my handwritten drafts and provided her usual invaluable assistance. You all know how much I appreciate your extraordinary efforts. A special thanks to my agent, Karen Gantz, who guided me through the process.

Also, my thanks to Michael Campbell, Tony Lyons, and Bill Wolfsthal of Skyhorse Publishing for their speed and professionalism in getting the book ready for print.

Author's Note

——————

Part I of the following text was originally printed in *The Case Against Impeaching Trump* (Hot Books, an imprint of Skyhorse Publishing, 2018). In the months since the original publication, I have only seen the issues discussed therein worsen. In hopes of contributing to a more tolerant, less extreme, more nonviolent, and more critical America, I've added to, updated, and revised my arguments and published them here. For the sake of democracy, I hope they are widely read.

Contents

THE CASE
AGAINST THE
DEMOCRATIC
HOUSE
IMPEACHING
TRUMP

Part I:

The Constitutional Case Against Impeaching Trump Doesn't Pass the *Legal* Test

As a liberal democrat who worked hard to try to win back the House of Representatives, I urge my fellow Democrats not to shoot themselves in the foot by trying to impeach President Trump. As soon as it was announced that the Democrats had won control of the House, radical leftists were urging them to impeach President Trump. In an op-ed in the *New York Times* entitled "Why Democrats Must Impeach the President," billionaire Democratic activist Tom Steyer demanded that "the new Democratic House majority must initiate impeachment proceedings against him as soon as it takes office in January." Some newly elected Democratic members of Congress who ran on the promise to impeach President Trump are also demanding that articles of impeachment be prepared, as are some in the media.

There are several reasons why this would be a mistake. The first is constitutional: it would be unconstitutional to impeach Trump unless there was substantial evidence that, while in office, he committed treason, bribery, or other high crimes and misdemeanors. Second, it would be a costly political blunder for the Democratic members of Congress who now control the House to fritter away their hard-earned mandate by engaging in a futile effort to remove President Trump. The effort would almost certainly fail unless dramatic new evidence of high crimes and misdemeanors were to emerge, because it would be impossible to secure the two-thirds supermajority in the Senate that is required to remove a sitting president. Finally, it would be hypocritical in the extreme for Democrats to do to President Trump what the Republicans did to President Bill Clinton: namely, impeach him for conduct that did not constitute a constitutionally impeachable offense.

Democrats, including me, railed against Republicans for impeaching Bill Clinton, as we did when Republicans threatened to impeach and/or "lock up" Hillary if she became president. Impeaching President Trump would not pass what I call the "shoe on the other foot test," which I explain in Part II of this book.

The decision to impeach and remove a duly elected president is a momentous constitutional event. It has never occurred in our history as a nation, though the House of Representatives impeached both President Andrew Johnson (whose removal by the Senate was only one vote short of the two-thirds required for conviction) and President Bill Clinton (the Senate divided 50-50 along largely partisan lines). President Richard Nixon probably would have been impeached and removed had he not resigned.

If the formal process of removal is to have legitimacy, it must be done in strict compliance with the provisions of the Constitution. Despite frequent claims that the impeachment and removal process is entirely *political*, that is not the case. Removing a president requires that *legal* criteria, set out explicitly in the Constitution, must first be satisfied before *political* considerations can come into play. The impeached president must be found guilty and convicted by two-thirds of the Senate of "treason, bribery, or other high crimes and misdemeanors."

I will argue in this book that if a president has not committed any of these specified crimes, it would be unconstitutional to remove him,[1] regardless of what else he may have done or may do. If and only if he has committed at least one of these crimes may the House and Senate consider the political implications of impeaching and removing him. In other words, the commission of an impeachable crime is a *necessary* but not *sufficient* condition for a president's removal. Put another way, the Constitution does not *empower* Congress to remove a president who has not committed an enumerated crime, and it does not *require* Congress to remove him even if he has committed such a crime. To that extent, and only to that extent, impeachment and removal are political in nature.

Those who argue that because the process is *legislative* rather than *judicial*, that it must be entirely *political* rather than also *legal*, ignore an important structural aspect of our constitutional system of separation of powers and

---

1   I was hoping to use the female pronoun after the 2016 election, but sadly that is not how it turned out.

checks and balances: namely, that all three branches of our government are bound by our Constitution.

The case against (or for) the impeachment of President Trump (or any other president) must, therefore, begin with the text of the Constitution. There are at least fifteen provisions of the Constitution and its twenty-six amendments that are relevant to impeachment. Some are directly on point, such as the criteria for impeaching a president (which are the same for all federal government officials). Also directly on point are the procedures governing the trial of an impeached president, which are different in only one important respect from those of other impeached officials. The chief justice must preside at the trial of the only government official who is not, in the words of Professor Akhil Amar, "fungible"[2]—that is, whose duties are capable of being performed by another official. Other provisions are implicit or arguably relevant, but they, too, must be considered in making a case regarding impeachment.

Let us begin with what should be uncontroversial: the Constitution sets out explicit criteria for impeaching and removing "the President, Vice President, and all civil officers of the United States." These criteria, as articulated in Article II, §4, are the following: "Treason, bribery, or other high crimes and misdemeanors." Only one of those crimes—treason—is defined in the Constitution. It "shall consist only in levying war against [the United States] or in adhering to their enemies, giving them aid and comfort." The critical words—"levying," "war," "adhering," "enemies," "aid" and "comfort"—are not further defined. Three procedural prerequisites for conviction of treason are enumerated: (1) "the Testimony of two Witnesses"; (2) "to the same overt act"; (3) or a "confession in open court."[3]

The other specifically enumerated crime—bribery—is not defined in the Constitution, but Article I, §9, provides that no federal official "shall, without the consent of the Congress, accept any present emolument, office, or title of any kind whatever, from any King, Prince, or foreign state." And Article II, §1, precludes the president from receiving "other emoluments from the United States or any of them." Violation of these provisions was not explicitly made a crime or a ground for impeachment. Under the common law at the time of the Constitution, merely *giving* or *accepting* something of value did not constitute the crime of bribery unless it was specifically intended

---

2   Akhil Amar. "On Impeaching Presidents." 28 *Hofstra Law Review* 291, 293 (1999).
3   *Id.*

to influence a public official's action. So it is unclear whether the word "brib-ery," as used in the constitutional criteria for impeachment and removal, incorporates the "emoluments" clauses or is limited to the crime of bribery as defined at the time of the Constitution or by subsequent statutory enactments.

The remaining criteria for impeachment—"other crimes and misde-meanors"—are not defined. Nor are procedural requirements for conviction of these crimes set out, except insofar as the Constitution and the Bill of Rights establish procedural requirements for conviction of all crimes in the courts of law.

The Constitution is not explicit as to whether the procedural require-ments for conviction of treason apply only to criminal trials in courts of law, or as to trials in the Senate for impeachment. Nor is it clear from the text of the Constitution whether the general procedural protection in criminal trials for bribery or other high crimes and misdemeanors are required for an impeachment trial based on those crimes in the Senate. These general pro-cedural protections include the privilege against self-incrimination contained in the Fifth Amendment and the right to be "confronted with the witnesses against him" as required by the Sixth Amendment. It is clear that other pro-cedural safeguards—such as indictment by grand jury and trial by petit jury—are not applicable to impeachment since the Constitution provides that impeachment, which is the counterpart of indictment, is by the House of Representatives and the "trial" is by the members of the Senate. Article III, §3 explicitly states that the "trial of all crimes, except in cases of impeach-ment, shall be by jury. . . ."

The procedures for impeaching and trying a president are incompletely articulated in the Constitution. Remarkably, the text says nothing at all about the procedures for impeachment by the House. It does not even tell us whether impeachment requires a simple majority of House members or the kind of supermajority—two-thirds—required for removal by the Senate. By implication and precedent, a bare majority can impeach. The substantive *criteria* for impeachment are the same as for removal—treason, bribery, or other high crimes and misdemeanors—but the *standards* for establishing these criteria are not set out in the Constitution. Nor is it set out whether standards for impeachment are the same as for removal. If impeachment by the House and conviction by the Senate were to be analogized to indictment by a grand jury and conviction by a trial judge or a petit jury, the standards would be significantly different: probable cause for impeachment, and beyond a reasonable doubt for conviction. But it isn't clear whether this analogy is apt.[4]

Nor is it clear whether the subject of the impeachment—the president or other official—has any procedural rights in the House. May he, or his lawyer, cross-examine adverse witnesses? May he testify—or refuse to testify if subpoenaed? May his lawyer file legal briefs, argue orally, or make motions? Compel the production of favorable witnesses? Submit documentary evidence?

Although the text of the Constitution provides little guidance as to the rights of the impeached official when he is on trial in the Senate, the fact that the Constitution speaks in terms of "try" ("The Senate shall have the sole power to *try* all impeachments") and "conviction" ("No person shall be *convicted* without the concurrence of two thirds of the members present")—suggests that at least some of the basic rights and procedural safeguards traditionally required when a person is tried and convicted of crimes must be accorded to the defendant in an impeachment trial. But the text does not explicitly tell us which, if any, of these safeguards are applicable in Senate removal trials.

Precedent suggests that the impeached "defendant" has the right at his Senate trial to retain counsel, to produce and confront witnesses, to testify on his own behalf, and to have the benefit of a presumption of innocence (despite his impeachment by the House). It is unclear whether other procedural safeguards such as the privilege against self-incrimination, the Fourth Amendment exclusionary rule, and the protection against ex post facto laws—laws that criminalize acts that were not criminal at the time they were committed—are applicable. It is clear that the protection against bills of attainder is not applicable since impeachment and removal are the functional equivalents of a bill of attainder: they are legislative actions directed against a *single* individual. Moreover, the Constitution explicitly provides partial protection against the consequences traditionally associated with attainder: Article I, §2 provides: "Judgment in cases of impeachment shall not extend further than to removal from office, and disqualification to hold [other federal office]."

---

4   During the Clinton impeachment, senators were frequently referred to as "jurors." Chief Justice William Rehnquist ruled that "the Senate is not simply a jury; it is a court in this case." 145 Cong. Rec. 5, 279 (1999).

There is one intriguing provision of the Constitution, applicable *only* "when the President of the United States is tried." In such cases, and only in such cases, "the chief justice shall preside." (Article II, §3)

This provision is intriguing because it introduces a judicial element into what is otherwise (and in all cases of non-presidential impeachments and trials remains) a *legislative* check and balance on the executive and judicial branches (yes, judges and even justices are subject to legislative impeachment and removal). Hamilton characterized the decision to have the chief justice preside as a compromise between a trial in front of the Supreme Court and a trial in front of the Senate:

> Would it have been an improvement of the plan, to have united the Supreme Court with the Senate, in the formation of the court of impeachments? This union would certainly have been attended with several advantages; but would they not have been overbalanced by the signal disadvantage, already stated, arising from the agency of the same judges in the double prosecution to which the offender would be liable? To a certain extent, the benefits of that union will be obtained from making the chief justice of the Supreme Court the president of the court of impeachments, as is proposed to be done in the plan of the convention; while the inconveniences of an entire incorporation of the former into the latter will be substantially avoided.[5]

The very concept of a compromise suggests that the inclusion of the chief justice was supposed to introduce some sort of judicial element into the Senate trial. But what is the nature of this judicial element, and what is the precise role of the chief justice at a Senate trial of the president? Is it merely symbolic? Is the presence of a robed justice (actually "judge"—the Constitution doesn't speak of justices) supposed to lend solemnity to the trial of a president? Does he rule on the admissibility of evidence? And if so, by what criteria? Common law? Rules that govern the courts? Special rules established by the Senate? Is he supposed to rule on motions submitted by the president and his lawyers? By the prosecution? Are his rulings subject to challenge and vote by the Senate? The Constitution provides no guidance.

The most fundamental and difficult question is whether the chief justice is empowered to rule on a motion to dismiss the charges on the ground that

---

5   Alexander Hamilton, *The Federalist Papers*, No. 65.

the Bill of Impeachment passed by the House does not charge an impeachable offense. Imagine a situation in which a president were to be impeached not for treason, bribery, or other high crimes and misdemeanors, but rather for "malpractice or neglect of duty"—a standard explicitly rejected by the Framers—or some other violation of the public trust not included among the enumerated criteria. Indeed, one does not have to imagine such a situation, because that is essentially what occurred with regard to our first presidential impeachment and removal trial. President Andrew Johnson was impeached in 1868 for dismissing Secretary of War Edwin Stanton without the approval of the Senate as required in the Tenure of Office Act[6] and for attacking congressional policies on the Reconstruction of the South.[7]

Now imagine what would have happened if Johnson's lawyers had made a motion to dismiss the charges in the Bill of Impeachment on the ground that they did not meet the constitutional criteria for impeachment and removal because they did not accuse the president of committing an act of treason, bribery, or any other high crimes and misdemeanors.[8]

What options, obligations, or powers would the chief justice have if faced with such a motion? Once again, if we analogize a Senate trial to an ordinary criminal trial, a judge would be obligated to rule on the motion, and if he concluded that the indictment did not charge a crime under the federal criminal code—for example, if a defendant had been indicted for sexual harassment, which is a civil tort but not a crime—he would be obligated to dismiss the charges. Could a chief justice presiding at the Senate trial of a president do that? Would he be obliged to? If he did, could his dismissal be overruled by the Senate? Could the Senate simply refuse to accept the chief justice's ruling? Could it be appealed to the full Supreme Court?

---

6   *Proceedings of the Senate Sitting for the Trial of Andrew Johnson President of the United States: On Articles of Impeachment exhibited by the House of Representatives*, Art. I.

7   *Id.* at Art. X.

8   "The primary claim was that Clinton's conduct, even if constituting perjury and obstruction, did not fall under the definition of high crimes and misdemeanors because this standard was restricted to conduct related to his office. White House lawyers argued that this conduct would not be indictable in a conventional case due to technical definitions of perjury and obstruction. Historically, a similar argument had been raised in the Johnson trial." Jonathan Turley, Senate *Trials and Factional Disputes: Impeachment as a Madisonian Device*, 49 Duke L.J. 1, 102 (1999). "Johnson's defenders argued both that an offense must be indictable and that it must be related to the office." *Id.* at n. 484 (citing Michael Les Benedict, *The Impeachment And Trial Of Andrew Johnson* 28 [1973]).

We don't know the answers to these and other hypothetical questions, because the Framers of our Constitution did not provide textual answers. Nor did they provide much in the way of interpretative information in contemporary debates or discussions. Neither the debates over the Constitution nor *The Federalist Papers* give much guidance as to the anticipated role of the chief justice.

There are, however, several textual provisions of the Constitution that are relevant to the claim made frequently and stridently by scholars, commentators, and advocates with regard to the impeachment and removal process: that it is entirely a "political" process, ungoverned by the rule of law or legal constraints.[9]

The most extreme and reductionist articulation of this position was made by former President Gerald Ford, on April 15, 1970, when he served as Minority Leader of the House: "An impeachable offense is whatever a majority of the House of Representatives considers it to be at a given moment in history; conviction results from whatever offense or offenses two-thirds of the other body considers to be sufficiently serious to require removal of the accused from office." This view, which was expressed in the context of an unsuccessful effort to impeach liberal Supreme Court Justice William O. Douglas, simply picks and chooses among the provisions of the Constitution that govern impeachment and removal. It accepts the two-thirds requirement for removal, while ignoring the explicitly enumerated substantive requirements. In this respect, it would be no different from saying that a president (or other official) could be removed on the basis of a *majority*— rather than two-thirds—vote by the Senate for conviction on charges of treason or bribery.

Imagine a case of a tyrannical president who committed numerous high crimes and misdemeanors that endangered our nation greatly and that

---

9   See, e.g., Edwin B. Firmage and R. Collin Mangrum, *Removal of the President: Resignation and the Procedural Law of Impeachment*, Duke L.J. 1023, 1027 (1974) ("Being a political process, impeachment should not be viewed as a duplication of the criminal process. The impeachment process was designed to be neither a criminal proceeding, nor, in a strictly technical sense, a juridical trial. Removal from office cannot be viewed as criminal punishment or its equivalent."); Notes: Bribery and Other Not So "Good Behavior": Criminal Prosecution as a Supplement to Impeachment Of Federal Judges, 94 *Columbia Law Review* 1617, 1620 (1994) ("The delegates to the Constitutional Convention designed the impeachment mechanism to be an essentially political process"); *id.* at 1672. ("Impeachment is a political process, designed to be cumbersome and to require the expenditure of political capital.")

clearly justified impeachment—but the Senate vote to remove him fell a few votes short of the required two-thirds. No reasonable construction of the constitutional text would justify removal. How would ignoring the two-thirds requirement be different than ignoring the substantive criteria? The whims of Congress cannot overrule the actual words of the Constitution.

Nor is Ford the only member of Congress to have expressed this extreme view. Recently, Congresswoman Maxine Waters, in demanding Trump's impeachment, said the following: "Impeachment is whatever Congress says it is. There is no law."[10]

Other commentators have taken less extreme positions, but still ones that largely ignore the criteria expressly enumerated in the Constitution. The distinguished American University history professor Allan Lichtman, for instance, argues that Trump could be impeached based on his "war on women," as well as on his climate change policy, which Lichtman considers a "crime against humanity" worthy of impeachment.[11] It would be dangerous to the stability of our system of government—and in direct defiance of the constitutional text and debates—if we could impeach a president based on mere policy disagreements. The founding fathers considered criteria of abuse of office and flatly rejected it. At the Philadelphia Convention, James Madison objected to a proposal that would have made "maladministration" sufficient grounds for impeachment. The term was "so vague," he said, that it would be "equivalent to a tenure during pleasure of the Senate."[12]

These expansive views of the criteria for impeachment ignore several provisions of the constitutional text. These provisions include the following: (1) the articulation and listing of explicit criteria for impeachment and removal; (2) the requirement that all senators "when sitting for a removal trial shall be on Oath or Affirmation," (Article II, §3); and (3) and the requirement that the chief justice preside at the trial of a president.

Let us begin with the first provision—the listing of specific criteria for impeachment and removal.

10　Congressional Black Caucus, September 21, 2017.

11　Allan J. Lichtman, *The Case for Impeachment*. 2017. Dey Street Books. New York, NY.

12　Many renowned constitutional law scholars, such as Noah Feldman and Akhil Amar, also take the position that impeachable offenses do not have to be necessarily criminal. See, e.g., Akhil Amar, "On Impeaching Presidents," 28 *Hofstra Law. Review* 291, 295 (Winter 1999). Noah Feldman and Jacob Weisberg, "What are Impeachable Offenses?" *The New York Review of Books*, Sept. 28, 2017.

Not surprisingly, my colleague and friend Laurence Tribe and his coauthor Joshua Matz make a brilliant case in their book *To End a Presidency* for a more expansive view of the criteria for impeachment based on their concept of a "living Constitution" that must adapt to changing times and new developments. ("Now and as always, the Constitution belongs to the living."[13]) I agree with the living Constitution approach when it comes to open-ended terms that *invite* changing interpretations. These terms include "due process of law," "equal protection" of the laws, "freedom of speech," "cruel and unusual punishments," "establishment of religion," and others. There are, however, certain provisions of the Constitution that are not "living" and subject to changing interpretation. There is no lawful basis, for example, for changing the age criteria for serving as president, senator, or representative, or for changing the life tenure of judges, just because we live longer. There are provisions in the Constitution that fit the late Antonin Scalia's pithy term "dead Constitution"—words that cannot be altered or reinterpreted except by amendment. The question is whether the enumerated criteria for impeachment and removal are *alive* or *dead*. Surely the definition of treason is dead, because the constitutional protection against ex post facto laws would preclude expanding the constitutional definition and applying it retroactively to a public official in the context of a criminal prosecution. (It might be different if Congress enacted a broader definition of treason and applied it prospectively, though the defendant could claim reliance on the constitutional limitation: "Treason shall consist *only* . . ."). I believe that the Constitution would also preclude expanding the constitutional definition of treason in the context of impeachment and removal. Congress may be free to interpret the words of the definition of treason more expansively—words such as "adhering" or "giving aid and comfort"—but it would not be free to ignore them. Professor Richard Painter, who ran for the Democratic nomination for senator from Minnesota on an "Impeach Trump" platform, absurdly argued that it is "treason" for a president or his campaign to "collude" with a foreign power to gain electoral advantage.[14] Painter should read the words of the Constitution, rather than making up crimes for partisan and personal

---

13   *Id.* at 16.

14   Chris Riotta, "Will Trump Be Impeached? His Aides Committed 'Treason and Betrayal,' Ex-White House Ethics Chief Says." *Newsweek*, July 12, 2017. http://www.newsweek.com/will-donald-trump-be-impeached-or-resign-russia-scandal-white-house-ethics-635458

advantage. Members of Congress (or candidates) are not free to expand the constitutionally limited definition of treason any more than they could ignore the requirement of a two-thirds vote.

Nor would Congress be free, in my view, to ignore the words of the other criteria, "bribery or other high crimes and misdemeanors," though it could reasonably interpret them in accordance with the rule of law.

When the Constitution speaks in clear terms, its plain meaning must prevail over other considerations. It's hard to imagine a clearer set of words than those governing impeachment: "The President, Vice President, and all civil officers of the United States shall be removed from office on impeachment for, and conviction of, treason, bribery, or other high crimes and misdemeanors." The text speaks clearly of *crimes*, enumerating treason, bribery, and other high crimes and misdemeanors. It requires a trial in the Senate and *conviction* of one or more of those crimes. Moreover, Article III, §2(3) says that "the trial of all *crimes*, except in cases of impeachment, shall be by jury" (emphasis added). This surely implies that cases of impeachment require *crimes*. Finally, Article II, §2(1) authorizes the president to grant pardons "for offenses against the United States, except in cases of impeachment." Since the president's pardon power extends only to *crimes* (including criminal contempt), this, too, would suggest that impeachment requires crimes. It is difficult to argue reasonably from the text that these words can be interpreted to mean that a person can be impeached for anything less than a crime.

Professors Tribe and Matz make a clever textual argument employing the Latin phrase *ejusdem generis*. Here is their argument:

> In thinking about what types of offenses those might be, it's useful to invoke *ejusdem generis*. While this may sound like a spell from Harry Potter, the reality is no less exciting: it's a canon of legal interpretation. (Okay, maybe that's less exciting.) *Ejusdem generis* says that if we list a series of items and then include a catchall phrase at the end, that phrase includes only things similar to the items that precede it. Courtesy of Justice Antonin Scalia and his co-author Bryan A. Garner, here's a helpful example of *ejusdem generis*: "If one speaks of 'Mickey Mantle, Rocky Marciano, Michael Jordan, and other great competitors,' the last noun does not reasonably refer to Sam Walton (a great competitor in the marketplace) or Napoleon Bonaparte (a great competitor on the battlefield). It refers to other great *athletes*."

In our case, the relevant list is "Treason, Bribery, or other high Crimes and Misdemeanors." Invoking *ejusdem generis*, we can presume that "high Crimes and Misdemeanors" are offenses of the same general type as treason and bribery. Treason causes the gravest possible injury to the nation and reflects a betrayal of the first order. Bribery is the ultimate corruption of office—and exercise of power for private benefit, not public good. Both offenses drastically subvert the Constitution and involve an unforgiveable abuse of the presidency. It's inconceivable that someone who committed these misdeeds could ever again be trusted with "the Executive Power." Both offenses are also momentous they have the capacity to inflict extraordinary harm on the nation, and the discovery that they occurred could disqualify any president as a viable national leader. To qualify as impeachable, offenses must share close traits.

Treason and Bribery have one more thing in common: they require proof of *intent*.[15]

The logical fallacy of their argument, as applied to the constitutional criteria for impeachment and removal, should be clear to everyone. Yes, the categories have several things in common, including the requirement of intent, betrayal, and serious misconduct. But the authors leave out the most obvious and most salient element that every component of the enumerated list shares: namely, that the impeached person must be convicted, after a trial, of a *crime*. Treason is a crime; bribery is crime; high crimes are crimes; and misdemeanors are crimes. Indeed, Blackstone, whose commentaries were canonical to the founding lawyers, wrote of a category of crimes that were "capital misdemeanor[s]." "To steal a pig or a fowl, which is easily done, was a capital misdemeanor, and the offender was punished with death."[16]

---

15   Tribe and Matz, *To End a Presidency*, pp. 38–39. 2018. Basic Books. New York, NY.

16   *Commentaries on the Laws of England* (1765–1769), Sir William Blackstone, Book 4, Chapter 1, Of the Nature; and Their Punishment:

A CRIME, or misdemeanor, is an act committed, or omitted, in violation of public law, either forbidding or commanding it. This general definition comprehends both crimes and misdemeanors; which, properly speaking, are mere synonymous terms: though, in common usage, the word "crime" is made to denote such offenses as are of a deeper and more atrocious dye; while smaller faults, and omissions of less consequence, are comprised under the gentler name of "misdemeanors" only.

It is especially important that we not ignore words in the Constitution that are there to protect the rights of individuals, even if those individuals are government officials who are being subjected to impeachment and removal. It is one thing to use the concept of a living constitution to *expand* or *create* rights that were not explicitly included in the text. That is how it has generally been employed in recent times—e.g., gay rights, a woman's right to choose, restrictions on capital punishment. It is quite another thing to use this concept to *diminish* or *ignore* constitutional protections accorded individuals, even government officials. Advocates of eliminating the requirement of a crime for impeachment may argue that this extends the *rights* of all Americans to honest government officials. But that is dangerous sophistry, which, if accepted, would permit diminution of all constitutional rights for accused individuals, since these rights—such as the privilege against self-incrimination and the right to be secure against unreasonable searches—often make all Americans less safe.

There is simply no way around this textual limitation. A noncrime no more fits into the exclusive list cited by Tribe and Matz than a nonathlete would fit into the Scalia list they quoted. Tribe and Matz use this rule of construction to argue that a president can be removed for conduct that does not constitute a crime. But words have meanings and crime means crime, not something else. They try to escape the unavoidable consequences of a plain reading of the text by subtly substituting the words "offenses" and "misdeeds" for the specific word used in the Constitution: "crimes." But it doesn't work. The Constitution specifies "high crimes and misdemeanors," not "offenses and misdeeds."

As I've said, I do not believe that the text permits totally ignoring the requirement of a "crime." It may, however, permit inclusion of state crimes, which were the dominant crimes at the time of the framing. It may also permit "common law" crimes, which were permissible until 1812.[17] The text would not, however, permit the inclusion of bad, even dangerous, "misdeeds" that did not fit the definition of "crime."

The common law distinction between felony and misdemeanor has been eliminated in most modern criminal codes. Blackstone's broader example of a high misdemeanor—"mal-administration"—was expressly rejected by the Framers as a ground for impeachment.

17   *United States v. Hudson and Goodwin*, 11 U.S. (7 Cranch) 32 (1912).

To their credit, Tribe and Matz urge caution in deploying the nuclear weapon of impeachment:

> While evaluating alleged presidential misconduct, Congress must care-fully avoid crying wolf. If legislators are quick on the trigger in urging impeachment—or in suggesting that possibility—each subsequent call may be taken less seriously. A nation constantly warned that the pres-ident is a despot can grow numb to those accusations especially if prophesies of doom aren't immediately realized. That's why Congress should always tread carefully around references to removing the presi-dent. When impeachment talk is normalized as an aspect of partisan discourse, it is easily trivialized. Promiscuous invocation can thus pre-vent the impeachment power from achieving its purpose.[18]

But Tribe himself did not follow this sage advice when he tweeted in December 2016, less than a month after Trump had won the election, that impeachment should begin "on Inauguration Day." A week after inaugura-tion, Tribe tweeted that "Trump must be impeached for abusing his power and shredding the Constitution more monstrously than any other President in American history." Relatively soon after that Tribe wrote an op-ed enti-tled, "Trump Must Be Impeached," just four months into the Trump presi-dency. He insisted that "the time has come for Congress to launch an impeachment investigation of President Trump for obstruction of justice."[19] This would seem inconsistent with the cautionary approach he and his coauthor later suggested. I suspect that he reconsidered his position while researching and writing the book. This is commendable.

But despite the newfound caution, I fundamentally disagree with apply-ing "living constitution" interpretation to erase the explicit words in Article I, §4, that require conviction of a specified crime as a prerequisite to impeach-ment. Sometimes the Constitution simply gives no escape, even from a con-clusion that seems irrational by contemporary standards. Just as the two-thirds requirement may result in a tyrant remaining president, so too may the requirement for conviction of a specified crime cause bad results. But that would not justify ignoring either requirement.

---

18   Tribe and Matz, pp. 93–94.
19   Tribe, Laurence. "Trump must be impeached. Here's why." *Washington Post.* May 13, 2017.

Tribe and Matz bolster their textual arguments with a policy claim: that impeachment is a "forward," rather than "backward," remedy: it is not a punishment for past crimes, but a mechanism for preventing future misdeeds by public officials.[20] But the Framers required conviction based on past crime as a *prerequisite* for preventing future misbehavior. They could easily have devised constitutional criteria that were explicitly future-looking and preventive, but instead they chose to require conviction of designated past crimes as a safeguard against relying on unproved and unprovable predictions. All criminal law is based, at least in part, on preventing future harms. As Blackstone wrote, criminal "punishments are chiefly intended for the prevention of future crimes."[21] But we insist on conviction for past crimes as a prerequisite for invoking preventive incarceration.[22] We insist on the protection because as Niels Bohr quipped (or was it Yogi Berra?): "Prediction is very difficult, especially about the future." On a more fundamental level, the current criteria for impeachment are not directed at *potential* tyrants, but at *past* criminals. That may be a flaw, but it may not be remedied by ignoring the text of the Constitution.

Consider the following situation: a president is indicted for treason—either before or after he leaves office. A witness has a video of him planning and confessing to taking up arms against the United States. There is no second witness. It would be absurd to acquit him, especially since a video is far more reliable than a second witness. Convicting him on the basis of the available evidence would serve the purpose of the constitutional protections. At the time of the Constitution, there were no recording devices. If there had been, the Framers would have surely allowed conviction on the basis of one witness and a recorded out-of-court confession. Yet there is not a reasonable constitutional scholar who would permit this guilty traitor to be convicted, because the plain words of the Constitution—two witnesses or a confession in open court—have not been satisfied. A too-clever lawyer might argue that playing the confession in open court is the functional equivalent of a confession in open court, but that would be result-oriented sophistry. A confession in open court is the functional equivalent of a guilty plea, whereas

---

20   Tribe and Matz, p. 95

21   *Blackstone's Commentaries: Of the Nature of Crimes; and Their Punishment*, Vol. 5, Ch. 1 (1803).

22   Alan M. Dershowitz. *Pre-emption: A Knife That Cuts Both Ways.* 2007. W.W. Norton, New York, NY.

a defendant can plead not guilty even in the face of taped confession. The defendant in such a case cannot be convicted of the crime of treason. He must go free because the plain words—the dead words—of the Constitution demand it.[23] The only remedy for this "flaw" in the Constitution is by amendment. Whether Congress would be bound by the constitutional definition of treason in an impeachment proceeding is a complex question of first impression about which reasonable scholars could disagree.

Turning to the second provision—that senators must be under oath—the following questions arise: Why is a special oath required, since they are already under the general "oath of office"? What are they swearing to do when they sit as judges or jurors in a removal trial?

One obvious answer would seem to be that they are swearing to apply the constitutionally mandated criteria for impeachment and removal, and no other. Indeed, the special oath requires them to swear or affirm that "in all things pertaining to the trial . . . I will do impartial justice *according to the Constitution and the law*" (emphasis added). This does not sound like a political event, it sounds like a *legal* trial, governed by the rule of law. Just as judges and jurors swear to apply the law at criminal trials, senators must do the same if they are not to violate their oath. If they were to ignore the textual criteria for impeachment and removal—if they were to act on the Gerald Ford or Maxine Waters lawless "criteria"—they would be acting unconstitutionally and in violation of their oath. (For which, under *their* criteria, *they* could be impeached and removed if members of Congress were subject to such procedures.)

Turning to the third item—the requirement that the chief justice must preside in cases involving the trial of a president—it is arguable that his role may include assuring that there is compliance with the words of the Constitution, most especially with the constitutionally mandated criteria for impeachment and removal of a duly elected president of the United States. It would have

---

23   The two-witness rule for treason derives from the biblical two-witness rule: "At the mouth of two witnesses, or three witnesses, shall he that is to die be put to death; at the mouth of one witness he shall not be put to death." Deuteronomy 17:5. Of course, the rabbis figured out a way around the two-witness rule: "One who commits murder without witnesses is placed in a cell and [forcibly] fed with bread of adversity and water of affliction . . . until his stomach bursts." Sanhedrin 81. Our contemporary "rabbis"— judges—cannot so transparently circumvent the constitutional rule of two witnesses.

been easy for the Framers to have made an official of the Senate (one not in the line of presidential succession) the presiding judge.[24] If the trial were entirely political, as advocates of the broad view insist, then a political official would be the most appropriate presiding officer. The decision by the Framers to have the chief justice preside over the trial of a president may suggest that the decision was not intended to be entirely political. Indeed, it would be wrong for the chief justice to participate, much less preside over, an entirely political process. Judges are required to stay out of politics.

Supporters of the broad viewpoint to Hamilton's statement in *The Federalist Papers* argue that impeachment is proper for "offenses which proceed from the misconduct of public men, or, in other words, from the abuse or violation of some public trust. They are of a nature which may with peculiar propriety be denominated *political* (emphasis added), as they relate chiefly to injuries done immediately to the society itself."[25]

It is unclear, however, whether this statement, even if deemed authoritative, *broadens* or *narrows* the constitutional criteria for impeachment.

One interpretation is that the word "offenses" broadens impeachable acts beyond "high crimes and misdemeanors," because the word "offenses" is more inclusive than the constitutionally specified criteria. But another plausible interpretation is that "offenses" means "crimes," and that the mere commission of *ordinary* offenses or crimes—"low" crimes and misdemeanors—are not enough. To be impeachable, the offenses or crimes must also constitute "the abuse or violation of some public trust." It is such an abuse or violation, in addition to the explicit criteria, that makes the removal process "political." Put another way, conviction by the Senate of an enumerated crime is a *necessary* but not *sufficient* condition for removal. The added elements of violation of public trust and injury to society are required as well.

An episode from Hamilton's own life illustrates this distinction. He was accused of having an adulterous affair with a woman and paying money in response to a threat of extortion. He admitted the affair and the payment, but he vociferously denied paying the money from government funds, as some had accused him of doing. Had he done so, his high crime would have

---

24 Aaron Burr, as vice president, presided over the Senate impeachment trial of Justice Samuel Chase. The trial took place in 1804, after Burr killed Hamilton in a duel. This led to the following quip: "In most courts, the murderer was arraigned before the judge; in this court, the judge was arraigned before the murderer."

25 *The Federalist Papers*, No. 65 (A. Hamilton).

constituted "the abuse or violation of some public trust," but paying his own funds to cover up personal embarrassment may not cause "injuries" to the "Society itself." In other words, the crime or offense must have a "political," not just a legal, component. If that is so, then the Hamiltonian requirements narrow rather than broaden the criteria for removal by adding the additional requirements of abuse of public trust and injury to society to the enumerated criteria. Under that interpretation, the impeachment of President Bill Clinton was improper, as I and others argued back then.[26]

Hamilton's oft-quoted *Federalist Papers* essay does not purport to answer these and other questions, but rather to persuade the readers that they should not reject the Constitution based on its imperfections. He argued that it would have been wrong for the Framers to have left the trial of an impeached president to the Supreme Court because it would be unfair to have a president tried by judges for impeachment and then tried again by judges in a criminal proceeding. This would seem to presuppose that impeachment must be based on criminal conduct because, if it were not, there would be less concern about the double jeopardy implications in a subsequent criminal trial.

In any event, recourse to the "legislative history" or intended "original meaning" is inappropriate when the words are unambiguous. The plain meaning must prevail over all other interpretative mechanisms, since it was the word, not the intentions behind them, that were voted on and accepted. Tribe and Matz acknowledge that it would be difficult to determine, and certainly rely on, the original understanding of the Framers or others who participated in the creation of our Constitution:

> Few delegates at the Convention addressed impeachable conduct at all, as we don't know whether the views of those who did are representative of all thirty-nine men who signed the Constitution. Further, if we look beyond Convention Hall to gauge original meaning, the definition of impeachable conduct was barely discussed at most state ratifying conventions. That absence is telling. Given the diversity of state impeachment practice, it's likely that Americans around the country had divergent understandings of the Impeachment Clause that they ratified.[27]

---

26 Alan M. Dershowitz. *Sexual McCarthyism: Clinton, Starr, and the Emerging Constitutional Crisis.* 1998. Basic Books. New York, NY.

27 Tribe and Matz, p. 37.

This assessment would seem to bolster the conclusion that we are bound by the words ultimately adopted and ratified. These words include explicit, constitutionally mandated requirements for impeachment and removal. These requirements suggest that the following scenario may be possible. If the House of Representatives were to impeach a president on grounds that are not included in the constitutional criteria, the president's lawyers could file a motion in front of the chief justice to dismiss the "indictment" (impeachment is widely seen as analogous to indictment), on the ground that the Bill of Impeachment is insufficient as a matter of constitutional law, and that removal on such grounds would violate the oath required of senators. If such a motion were to be made, the chief justice might be obliged to decide it, and under principles of law that hark back to *Marbury v. Madison* and its progeny, the chief justice is bound to apply the Constitution to any act of the legislature. If the chief justice were to conclude that the Bill of Impeachment did not state a constitutional claim, he would be required to dismiss it.

This may sound far-fetched but, if so, the question then arises: What role is the chief justice supposed to play, if not the traditional role of a judge in a criminal, or even civil, trial? That role includes not only ruling on the admissibility of evidence and other procedural issues, but also making a legal determination as to whether the constitutional criteria have been met.

We will probably never know the answer because it is unlikely that the House of Representatives will impeach the president without charging him with criminal conduct. But if that were to occur, and if the president were to challenge that decision by way of a motion to the chief justice, there is no way of knowing how the chief justice would decide the matter—or whether Congress would abide by the ruling of the chief justice.

A variation on this scenario is the following: the Articles of Impeachment do charge a high crime, say obstruction of justice, for firing the director of the FBI, who was investigating the president. The president offers a constitutional defense to that crime: that Article II authorized the president to fire any person in the executive branch for any reason and separation of powers precludes the legislative branch from questioning any such executive action. Or the president argues that the admissible evidence of the charged crime is insufficient as a matter of law. Would the chief justice be obligated to rule on these dispositive motions? If the trial is entirely "political," as some urge, then the answer may well be no. (This raises the question of how a *trial*, which is a quintessential *legal* proceeding, could be entirely *political*.) If the trial is governed by the rule of law and the text of the Constitution, a different answer would seem to follow.

The argument made by those who insist that impeachment and removal are entirely political decisions, uncabined by legal constraints, sometimes takes the form of the following syllogism:

(A) A decision by the House to impeach a president or by the Senate to remove him is *non-reviewable* by the judicial branch, (B) therefore, these decisions are political in nature and not legal; (C) because they are political, not legal, the House and Senate are not bound by the text of the Constitution as to the criteria for impeaching and removing.

That argument begs the crucial question, and is entirely circular, as evidenced by the following counter-syllogism:

(A) The criteria for impeachment and removal are clearly set out in the text of the Constitution—just as is the requirement for a two-thirds vote by the Senate for removal; (B) therefore, if the House and Senate try to impeach or remove for an offense not specified in the text (or if the Senate decides to remove by a simple majority), they would be violating the Constitution and their unconstitutional actions *would* be reviewable by the judiciary; (C) because they would be reviewable by the judiciary, impeachment and removal are not entirely political acts ungoverned by law.

Neither of these syllogisms answers the critical questions, which are necessarily matters of degree: Which provisions of law, if any, are applicable to impeachment and removal proceedings? If some are applicable, may they be enforced in a presidential removal trial by the presiding chief justice? Are any aspects of a removal trial judicially reviewable?

The fallacy implicit in the first syllogism is the assumption that if a congressional action is not judicially reviewable, it necessarily follows that it is not governed by law and is, therefore, entirely political. That is certainly not how the Framers of the Constitution, who did not explicitly include judicial review of congressional actions as part of our system of checks and balances, saw it. They believed that Congress was obligated by the oath of individual members to comply with the Constitution, regardless of whether its actions were or were not reviewable by the courts. Congress is bound not to enact legislation that violates the Constitution and, if it does, the president is bound not to sign it. That would be the case even if there were no Supreme Court or judicial review.

It took *Marbury v. Madison* and its progeny to make many, but not all, actions of the other branches subject to judicial review. But this did not eliminate the obligation of the other branches to comply with the Constitution, regardless of whether their actions are or are not judicially reviewable.[28] But, because we have a Supreme Court and judicial review, some members of the legislative and executive branches have erroneously concluded that they are free to ignore the constraints of the Constitution. How often have we heard the following: "If it's unconstitutional, let the courts strike it down"? That is a clear abdication of the responsibility of *all* government officials *always* to comply with all provisions of the Constitution.

So it does not follow from the fact (if it is a fact) that impeachment and removal may not be judicially reviewable, that these government actions are completely political and not governed by the rule of law and the text of the Constitution.

Conceptually, the issue of whether impeachment and removal are subject to judicial review is separate from the issue of whether they are entirely political acts unbound by constitutional constraints. In practice, however, Congress would be free to act inconsistently with the Constitution if its actions were final and not subject to judicial review. That is essentially what was done by the Congress that impeached and nearly removed Andrew Johnson for actions that were not within the constitutionally mandated criteria (the vote was one short of the required two-thirds). But just because its decisions to impeach and remove (had there been a two-thirds vote) would have been final because they were not judicially reviewable, it would not make them right as a matter of constitutional law. It would make them lawless and unconstitutional actions that were not subject to judicial review (if the courts were to decide that they lacked the power to review).

I'm reminded of the quip by the late Justice Robert Jackson about the Supreme Court: "We are not final because we are infallible, but infallible only because we are final."[29] A Congress that impeached and removed a president in violation of the language of the Constitution would be "right"

---

28   Arthur J. Goldberg and Alan M. Dershowitz, "Declaring the Death Penalty Unconstitutional," 83 *Harvard Law Review*, 1773, 1807 (1970).

29   *Brown v. Allen*, 344 U.S. 443, 537 (1953).

only in the sense that it would be final (if there were no judicial review). But it would not be right—or constitutional—in any other sense.

Nor is it completely clear that a wrong decision to impeach and remove a president based on criteria other than those enumerated in the Constitution would necessarily be final. The decision to remove is not self-enforcing. The impeached and removed president would have to accept the legitimacy of such a decision and agree to leave office. What would happen if the president announced that he did not accept as final the unconstitutional decision of the Senate to remove him, because they had failed to charge and convict him of one of the crimes enumerated in the Constitution?

This would generate a constitutional crisis between the legislative and executive branches that would have to be resolved by the judicial branch. But what if Congress insisted that it, rather than the Supreme Court, was the final arbiter of impeachment and removal?

There is no precedent for the Supreme Court reviewing an impeachment and removal, and there is at least one precedent for the high court declining to do so in the case of a removed judge.[30] But there is also no precedent for a president being impeached and being removed and challenging his removal in court on the ground that he did not commit a crime specified in the Constitution as a prerequisite for removal.

If the chief justice issued a thoughtful constitutional opinion ruling that the Articles of Impeachment failed to charge a crime, as required by the Constitution, and, if the Senate voted to override that "judicial" finding, the president might well try to appeal the Senate's override of the chief justice's ruling to the entire Supreme Court. That would present the issue squarely as to whether the Supreme Court—as distinguished from the chief justice—has any judicial oversight role to play in the impeachment and removal process.

At least two justices—Byron White and David Souter—have suggested that there may be some room for judicial review even in the face of Article I, §3, which gives the Senate "the sole power to try all impeachments." This is what Justice White said:

> Finally, as applied to the special case of the President, the majority argument merely points out that, were the Senate to convict the President without any kind of trial, a Constitutional crisis might well result. It hardly follows that the Court ought to refrain from

---

upholding the Constitution in all impeachment cases. Nor does it follow that, in cases of presidential impeachment, the Justices ought to abandon their constitutional responsibilities because the Senate has precipitated a crisis.[31]

White's view was echoed by Justice Souter:

If the Senate were to act in a manner seriously threatening the integrity of its results . . . judicial interference might well be appropriate.[32]

There is no way of knowing how the Court would respond to a legitimate presidential challenge, especially if the president refused to leave office on the ground that his impeachment and removal were unconstitutional. A Supreme Court that inserted itself into the *Bush v. Gore* election in order to avoid a constitutional crisis might well decide to review a House decision to impeach and a Senate decision to remove a president who is not accused and convicted of a specified constitutional crime.

The Constitution does not provide clear answers to these questions, though *Marbury v. Madison* and its progeny suggest that the Supreme Court is the final arbiter of the constitutionality of the actions of all branches of government.

In the end, of course, the people are the final arbiters of all governmental actions. The people have the power to vote out legislators and presidents (and, in some states, judges). They have the power to amend the Constitution (though only through constitutionally mandated procedures). The people must accept the legitimacy of the actions of the various branches of government if democracy is to prevail over civil discord.

Were a president to announce that he refused to accept the actions of the Senate in voting for his removal, on the ground that he had not been convicted of an enumerated criterion for impeachment and removal, and that he would not leave office unless the Supreme Court affirmed his removal, the people might well agree with him. But if the high court then affirmed his removal and he refused to leave office, the people would probably not support him.

---

31   *Id.* at 244

32   *Id.* at 253. In standard jury instructions, jurors are told they are the "sole judges of facts" and yet they are subject to review by judges.

I raise these issues not only because they are fascinating and testing hypotheticals—I am, after all, a retired law professor who spent half a century constructing such hypotheticals—but also because *this* president (and perhaps others) might well refuse to leave office if Congress voted to impeach and remove him based on "offenses" that were not among those enumerated in the Constitution. He might even refuse to leave if the Supreme Court refused to review the actions of Congress, or affirmed them on technical grounds. Finally, there is even a risk that if the Supreme Court explicitly ruled that Congress had the power to impeach and remove a president for offenses that were not enumerated in the Constitution, this president might say that he will abide only by *his* own interpretation of the Constitution, which requires that he be convicted of an enumerated crime.

The Constitution is fragile and imperfect, as is democracy itself. Both require the legitimacy of the governed. Recall that presidential candidate Al Gore acceded to the Supreme Court's highly controversial ruling stopping the recount and giving the presidency to George W. Bush. Had he refused to accept that ruling, as some urged him to do, there would have been a major crisis. That is why *Congress* must comply with the text of the Constitution— especially with the enumerated criteria for impeaching and removing a president, regardless of whether its decisions are or are not subject to judicial review. It is also why the Supreme Court should remain the final arbiter in the event of a reasonably challenged removal.

On the basis of the constitutional text and the facts we currently have in the public record, the case against impeaching and removing President Trump is quite strong.

In the essays and interviews that follow this introduction, I lay out arguments against charging President Trump with, or impeaching him for, obstruction of justice based on actions he took or may take that are authorized under Article II of the Constitution, which sets out the powers of the president as the head of the executive branch of our government. These include the power to fire members of the executive branch, such as the director of the FBI, for any or no reason. They also include the power to pardon anyone for any or no reason. He may not, of course, solicit or receive a bribe for taking any such action. The very act of soliciting or accepting the bribe— for any reason—would be a crime. Nor could he lie to prosecutors, tell witnesses to lie, pay hush money to potential witnesses, or destroy evidence—all of which President Nixon was accused of. (President Clinton, as well, was charged with lying under oath.) But a president who does none of *these* things cannot, in my view, be charged with a crime for merely exercising his Article II powers to fire or pardon, *regardless* of his motive for doing so. Nor can his motives or state of mind in taking constitutionally authorized actions be questioned as part of a criminal or impeachment investigation. These restrictions do not place the president *above* the law, because they are required *by* the law, for the same reasons members of Congress and the judiciary cannot generally be charged or questioned for their legislative or judicial actions.[33] This is a controversial position, and I have been much criticized for taking it. But many commentators, who initially disagreed with this argument, are now assuming its validity and arguing that President Trump should be investigated for other misdeeds. My arguments in support of the position are set out in the essays that follow.

Even more controversial, but in my view equally correct, is my position that under our constitutional structure, the president, as head of our "unitary executive" branch, may direct the attorney general and the director of the FBI as to *who* and *what* to investigate and/or charge with crimes, as well as who not to investigate and charge with crimes. I do not personally approve of the president having such powers and I would favor a constitutional amendment limiting or even eliminating them. But I believe that the Constitution, as written and interpreted for generations, gives the president those powers and precludes him from being charged for exercising them—even for exercising them wrongly or in a self-serving manner. There is a difference between what we believe the law *should* be, and what the law *is*, especially when it comes to charging a president with a crime or impeachable offense.

I wrote about this problem during the impeachment of President Clinton:

> The time has come to recognize that the Framers of our Constitution made a serious mistake by creating the single office of attorney general to serve two conflicting functions. We must bring ourselves into the twenty-first century by breaking these two functions into two discrete offices, the way the rest of the democratic world has done. We can begin without tinkering with the Constitution, by simply having Congress create an Independent Office of Public Prosecution within the Justice Department. The director of that office would be a civil servant appointed for a fixed term by the president with the

---

33   See US Constitution, Article 1, §6.

consent of the Senate. By tradition, that person would be outside of politics and an eminent lawyer of great renown and acceptability to both parties. He or she would not be answerable to the attorney general on issues of prosecutorial policy or on specific cases, and would be removable only for good cause.

It is not certain whether the Constitution would have to be amended to accomplish this change. Article II grants to the president the responsibility to "take care that the laws be faithfully executed," but that responsibility may be delegated—as it has been—to the attorney general.

If Congress were to pass, and the president sign, a law creating a permanent, nonpartisan office of Director of Public Prosecutions, I believe it would be held constitutional.

If this legislative solution did not pass constitutional muster or did not work for other reasons, it might be necessary to amend the Constitution so as to create an independent prosecutorial office. The Constitution should never be amended except as a last resort, after all other reasonable legislative and administrative solutions have been tried. But the problems of our current Justice Department and its conflicting roles are so serious, and so likely to get even worse, that we must begin to consider new methods for dealing with them.[34]

But until the law is changed, a president should not be charged or impeached for exercising his current constitutional authority to direct the Justice Department or FBI who to investigate and who not to investigate.

What if President Trump were to be impeached for colluding with Russia during the presidential campaign? If there were proof of such collusion—and to date I have seen none—that would be a serious political *sin*. An American should not collude with a foreign power, especially a hostile foreign power, in an effort to enhance his candidacy. But once again, there is a dispositive difference between a political sin and a high crime and misdemeanor. There is no such crime of collusion in the context of an election. Collusion may entail other crimes, such as election law violations or accessory to crimes such as hacking. But collusion itself is simply not a crime. Consider the most extreme hypothetical: assume, absurdly, that candidate Trump called Vladimir Putin and said the following: "Hey, Vlad. Do I have a deal for you!"

---

34 Dershowitz, *Sexual McCarthyism*.

I want to be elected president, and you want to get rid of the Magnitsky sanctions, which I don't like anyway. You should help me get elected by giving me dirt you already have on Hillary Clinton because, if I'm elected, there's a better chance to get rid of the sanctions, which I disapprove of." Of course, no such conversation occurred and no such deal was made. But if it had been, one can search the federal criminal statutes for a crime that would cover this political sin. Politicians often seek contributions and support from individuals who expect to benefit from the election of their candidate. There are, of course, limitations on what a foreign government can contribute to a campaign, but these limitations are vague and subject to constitutional scrutiny, especially in the context of information rather than cash. Perhaps some election laws could be stretched to fit this conduct, but such stretching would raise serious constitutional issues. Obviously if one varies the facts a little bit, there would be a crime. For example, if a candidate asked Putin to get dirt on his opponent by hacking emails, that would be a crime. But merely passing along dirt that has already been obtained would not be. That is true even if the dirt had been obtained illegally through hacking. The person doing the hacking would be guilty of the crime, but the campaign would not be guilty for using the fruits of the hacking, any more than the *New York Times* and the *Washington Post* would be guilty of publishing the stolen Pentagon Papers or the materials stolen by Chelsea Manning and Edward Snowden. So, based on what we now know, it would seem clear that President Trump could not be charged criminally with colluding with Russia, even if there were evidence he did so.

But what if he were impeached for the political sin of colluding with a hostile foreign power? Such impeachment would raise the issue dramatically of whether Congress could go beyond the criteria for impeachment and removal. I think the answer is no, but there are those who disagree. This would be a good test case because, plainly, collusion with Russia *would be* a breach of the public trust and fulfill Hamilton's criteria for impeachment (if Hamilton intended those criteria to be a substitute for, rather than an addition to, the enumerated criteria). Or take a more extreme example. Assume Putin decides to "retake" Alaska, the way he "retook" Crimea. Assume further that a president allows him to do it, because he believed that Russia has a legitimate claim to "its" original territory.[35] That would be terrible, but would it be impeachable? Not under the text of the Constitution. (It would,

---

35   Thanks to Paul Finkelman for suggesting this example.

of course, be different if he did it because he was paid or extorted.) Such a dramatic event might appropriately result in a constitutional amendment broadening the criteria for impeachment, but it would not justify ignoring or defying the words of our current Constitution.

The Framers of the Constitution did not provide an impeachment remedy for an incompetent, nasty, even tyrannical president—unless he committed a designated crime. Perhaps they should have, but Congress is not authorized to "correct" constitutional errors or omissions through unconstitutional actions in impeaching and removing a president who has not committed a designated crime. Perhaps the Framers should have required a majority vote rather than a two-thirds vote to assure that a tyrannical president is removed. But the remedy lies in amending the Constitution, not violating it. The appropriate response to executive tyranny is not legislative tyranny.

As I write these words, more information seems to be emerging from both sides regarding improprieties during the campaign. I doubt we have heard the last of the allegations from either side. The bottom line is that the 2016 presidential campaign was deeply troubling for many reasons. That is why, from day one, I proposed that instead of appointing a special counsel to investigate *crimes*, Congress should have appointed a nonpartisan commission of experts to investigate the entirety of the 2016 election, including allegations of Russian interference, the impact of Comey's ill-advised public statements, the bias of some FBI agents, and other possible improprieties that do not rise to the level of indictable or impeachable crimes. I continue to urge the appointment of such a commission, since many in the public are losing faith in the Mueller investigation and in the hyper-partisan congressional committee investigations. The public has the right to know everything that happened during the 2016 presidential campaign in order to prevent recurrence in future campaigns. A nonpartisan commission is a far better way to learn the whole truth than any of the investigations currently being conducted.

In making the case against impeaching President Trump, I do not mean to whitewash anyone's conduct. I simply want to make sure that whatever actions are contemplated or taken are consistent with the United States Constitution, the rule of law, and civil liberties. Unlike the *political* case against impeaching President Trump that James Comey is making—voting him out is more democratic than impeaching him—my case against impeaching President Trump is *constitutional*. There is simply no evidence in the public record that he has committed any of the crimes enumerated in the Constitution as a prerequisite for impeachment and removal.

I am not making the case for President Trump's reelection. Every citizen must make that political decision for him- or herself. I would be making the same case against impeachment had Hillary Clinton won and it was the Republicans who were urging her impeachment or prosecution for acts that did not constitute crimes. As I elaborate in the next section, for me, the test has always been "the shoe on the other foot." (This is a colloquial variant on John Rawls's "veil of ignorance" test.[36]) What criteria would you advocate if the shoe were on the other foot—if Hillary Clinton or Bernie Sanders had been elected and were being investigated? I insist that the criteria be the same.

Of course, partisans always argue that the shoe doesn't fit: partisan Democrats insist that Trump's conduct is more impeachable than Clinton's, and partisan Republicans think that Clinton's is more impeachable than Trump's. That's not the point. The point is to agree on neutral criteria that would be equally applicable to all presidents.

I agree with James Comey that voting is more democratic than impeaching, but even if I didn't—even if I thought that impeachment would better serve the interests of democracy—I would oppose President Trump's impeachment unless the criteria explicitly enumerated in the Constitution were proved beyond a reasonable doubt, following an impeachment and trial at which all relevant substantive and procedural protections were accorded the president. No one is above the law, but neither is anyone—including the president—beneath the law.

If a controversial president is denied constitutional protections, then any citizen can be denied constitutional protections. That's why this constitutional issue is so important to all Americans.

---

36   In his thoughtful book, *Impeachment: A Citizen's Guide* (2017), Cass Sunstein also urges his readers to imagine themselves behind a Rawlsian veil of ignorance, knowing nothing of the president's identity or policies but only of the actions for which he or she is to be impeached.

The essays and interview transcripts that follow are derived from the many pieces I have written in national media, including for the *New York Times*, *Wall Street Journal*, *Boston Globe*, *The Hill*, *Newsmax*, *Gatestone*, *Fox News*, and others, as well as interviews on *Meet the Press with Chuck Todd*, *This Week with George Stephanopoulos*, and *Tucker Carlson Tonight*. In these columns and media appearances, I try to make the constitutional case against the impeachment and prosecution of President Donald J. Trump. I present them here, revised and modified, in hopes of provoking honest debate and contributing to the democratic process. Let the debate continue—civilly and on the merits, without personal attacks.

Opening Statements:
The Age of Hyper-Partisan Politics

It is an unfortunate reality that partisanship has become the driver of our political narrative. Democrats and Republicans borrow from the same playbook when taking to the field for a game of blame. However, at no level is government a game, regardless of how often it appears as a contest between two foes. I argue at the outset for a consistency of neutral principles as the essence for a moral and just system that applies equally to Democrats and Republicans. There should be no place for the constant bickering or the current trend to criminalize political differences.

People ask whether I have turned to the right for defending President Trump's constitutional rights. The answer lies in that consistency of principles: where there is no right or left, but simply my fifty years of staying true to the rule of law and mandates of the Constitution. In the following three essays and transcript, I explore the danger of making accusations and calls for criminalization when one's feet remain firmly ensconced only in one's own shoes.

The Partisan Shoe Is on the Other Foot[1]

Had Hillary Clinton been elected president, Republican partisans would be doing and saying about President Clinton what Democrat partisans are now saying about President Trump.

There would be shouts of "Lock her up!" as there were even before the election. There would be efforts to reopen the email investigation, as President Trump is now tweeting. There would be demands to appoint a special counsel. There would be claims that foreign contributions to the Clinton foundation and other entities were "emoluments."

If there were a DC grand jury investigating Clinton, there would be efforts by the prosecution to move it to a less overwhelmingly Democratic venue, like Virginia. There would be arguments that Bill Clinton obstructed justice by initiating a conversation with then–Attorney General Lynch in her airplane and that Lynch tried to influence the FBI director to refer to the email investigation as a "matter."

If President Hillary Clinton had fired FBI director James Comey—as she might well have done—there would have been allegations of a cover-up. There would be calls for her impeachment and prosecution.

My partisan Democrat friends would be appalled at these efforts to undo the election of their candidate. They would be railing against expanding the criminal law to target a political opponent. They would be dismissing the emoluments argument as the stretch that it is.

They would be complaining about the tactical advantage the prosecutor would obtain by moving the case from DC to Virginia. They would be insisting that President Clinton had every right to fire the director of the FBI and that exercising such a right cannot be an obstruction of justice.

In other words, Democratic partisans would be making exactly the same arguments in relation to a President Clinton that I am now making in relation to President Trump.

I would be joining them in making these arguments, because they are the right arguments for any civil libertarian to make regardless of which foot the shoe is on. But for partisans on both sides, everything depends on which foot the shoe is on. They remind me of my immigrant grandmother. When I would excitedly announce that the Brooklyn Dodgers had won a ballgame, she would ask rhetorically, "Yeah, but is it good or bad for the Jews?"

For her, everything was measured by its influence on the Jews. Similarly, today, partisans measure everything by whether it's good or bad for the Democrats or Republicans—for Clinton or Trump.

Now that it is President Trump who is being targeted, my partisan Democratic friends are vociferously rejecting these neutral civil liberties arguments, because they do not now serve their partisan political interests. Nor do they seem embarrassed by their apparent hypocrisy and double standards. Hypocrisy is a small price to pay for partisan political victories.

For me, the primary test for whether an argument is principled or partisan is "the shoe on the other foot" test. I employed this test in my book *Supreme Injustice*, in which I criticized the Supreme Court justices who voted to stop the recount in *Bush v. Gore*, thus handing the election to President Bush.

I examined the past opinions of the majority justices and showed that if the shoe had been on the other foot—if it were Bush who was seeking the recount—the justices who voted to stop it would have almost certainly voted the other way. These Republican partisan justices failed the "shoe on the other foot" test. My partisan Democratic friends applauded the "shoe on the other foot" test when it favored the Democrats. Now, these partisans are failing the very same test.

The time has come for all Americans who believe in enduring principles of morality and justice to insist on consistency. Ralph Waldo Emerson was wrong when he demeaned "foolish consistency" as "the hobgoblin of little minds, adored by little statesmen and philosophers and divines."

Consistency of principles is neither foolish nor small-minded. It is the essence of any moral system. Principled consistency may be difficult to achieve, especially in our current hyper-partisan atmosphere. But if we are ever to end the partisan bickering and name-calling that is coarsening dialogue and making reasoned compromise impossible, we must insist on a single standard of legality and morality that applies equally to Democrats and Republicans. We are far from that in the current shouting match in which each side calls the other "criminal," "racist," or worse.

We must declare an armistice in this divisive war of words and agree to do unto your political opponents what you would have your political opponents do unto you. That golden rule of consistency should be as applicable to political debate as it is to personal morality.

When Politics Is Criminalized[2]

We are surrounded on all sides by news of criminal investigations into politicians. Robert Mueller, the Special Counsel, has obtained an indictment relating to his investigation into possible collusion between the Trump campaign and the Russian government. Congressional committees are also investigating Russian meddling in the 2016 election. House Republicans have announced plans to look into the Obama administration's handling of Hillary Clinton's emails and its decision to give a Russian-controlled company, Uranium One, control of some American uranium reserves. Now the Justice Department is considering whether to appoint a special counsel in the uranium deal.

Government corruption should be prosecuted, Congress has a role to play in overseeing the executive branch, and our intelligence agencies are right to raise concerns about foreign interference in our elections. But there is something worrisome about the current frenzy of criminal investigations. To me they point to a frightening trend that afflicts both Democrats and Republicans: the criminalization of political differences.

The Framers of our Constitution did not seek to make it easy to convict Americans of crimes. They bestowed upon criminal defendants a bundle of rights to provide safeguards against overzealous prosecutors or legislators, including prohibitions against compelled self-incrimination, unreasonable searches, double jeopardy, and the passage of laws declaring people guilty of acts that were not criminal when committed.

Our legal system also came to require proof beyond a reasonable doubt, a unanimous jury, and clear statutes that differentiate between criminal and noncriminal conduct. No wonder Benjamin Franklin described our system as preferring that "a hundred guilty persons should escape than that one innocent person should suffer."

To be sure, these barriers to over-criminalization were sometimes more theoretical than practical when it came to political crimes. John Adams presided over an administration that imprisoned political opponents under the Alien and Sedition Acts. Thomas Jefferson went after his political opponents, especially Aaron Burr, with a vengeance, personally directing Burr's unsuccessful prosecution for treason.

Over time, though, the country's judicial standards and rigorous protections for the accused made the jailing of political enemies difficult, maintaining a crucial bulwark against autocracy. But that bulwark has eroded, largely because of a new approach: the use of politically neutral but overly malleable laws on obstruction of justice, corruption, and conspiracy that can be used to prosecute the ethically questionable, but not necessarily criminal, activities of political rivals.

Both sides deploy this tactic. We have seen it used against Republicans, including the former representative Tom DeLay, whose conviction on corruption charges was overturned after he was forced from office, and the former senator Ted Stevens, whose conviction on failing to report gifts was later voided—after he had lost his reelection bid. The Republican National Committee waged a media war to get Senator Robert Menendez, Democrat of New Jersey, to resign if a jury were to convict him on corruption charges so that the Republican governor of New Jersey could replace him before he leaves office early next year. (The case ended in mistrial when a jury could not reach a verdict, and the prosecutors then dropped the case.)

I raise this alarm as a loyal liberal who has supported every Democratic candidate for president since I campaigned for Adlai Stevenson in 1952. Yet because of my strong opposition to open-ended criminal laws, some critics on the left have accused me of becoming "President Trump's attack dog." Nothing could be further from the truth. I worked to prevent the election of Donald Trump, and since his swearing-in, I have been critical of many of his actions, including his travel ban, his rescission of protections for "Dreamers," his telling the Russians about intelligence gathering, and his failure to single out white nationalists for their provocations in Charlottesville.

But elastic criminal laws should not be stretched to cover Mr. Trump's exercise of his constitutionally authorized power. When the president asked the director of the FBI to drop its investigation into Michael Flynn, the former national security advisor, or fired James Comey from the FBI, or provided classified information to the Russians, he was acting within his constitutional powers. Those actions may deserve opprobrium, but they should not be deemed criminal. The proper place to litigate the wisdom of such actions should be at the ballot box, not in the jury box.

Even if it were to turn out that the Trump campaign collaborated, colluded, or cooperated with Russian agents, that alone would not be a crime, unless the campaign asked them or helped them to commit criminal acts such as hacking.

Today, the target for politically tinged investigations is Donald Trump and his campaign. Last year (and again today), it was Hillary Clinton—as it was her husband before her. Next up are Bernie Sanders and his wife, who are being investigated at the behest of a Republican Party official in Vermont.

An overly flexible, easily expanded criminal statute is a loaded weapon capable of being fired by zealous prosecutors at almost any target. It's time to store the weapon until it is really needed—and not the next time someone wants to wound his political enemies.

When Criminal Law Is Weaponized for Political Gain[3]

US Attorney General Jeff Sessions's appearance before the House Judiciary Committee in October 2017 well illustrates the growing problem of misusing the criminal law to settle political differences that I alluded to in the previous essay.

While the hearing was intended to uncover issues relating to Russia's attempt to interfere in our presidential elections, the tone and overall focus of the hearing quickly shifted to mutual recriminations when both Republicans and Democrats grilled the attorney general about alleged crimes committed by their rivals.

Republicans on the committee pressed Sessions about a host of accusations against Hillary Clinton. They kept returning to the same question: Why had a special counsel not yet been appointed to investigate her?

When Sessions answered that there would need to be a "factual basis" to appoint a special counsel to investigate Clinton, several of the Republican committee members scoffed. Republican Congressman Jim Jordan asked, "What's it gonna take to get a special counsel?" Meanwhile, his colleague, Representative Trent Franks, pressed on with accusations that Clinton had committed a crime by colluding with the Russians on the Uranium One deal: "What do you think the Justice Department can do to correct . . . what appears to be an injustice?"

Democrats on the committee took a similar tack, flinging around accusations of criminal conduct on the part of President Donald Trump.

Democratic Representative Ted Deutch aggressively questioned the attorney general about the president's firing of former FBI director James Comey, asking whether "it would be reasonable for the members of this committee to conclude that the president, by first interfering in one investigation and then interfering in an investigation into himself, committed obstruction of justice?"

These partisan attempts to criminalize policy differences are not new.

As I've previously noted, from the time President Thomas Jefferson instructed his attorney general to prosecute his former vice president Aaron Burr, politicians have sought to weaponize the criminal justice system to target their opponents. In recent years Ted Stevens, Tom DeLay, Rick Perry, Bob Menendez, and other elected and appointed officials—of both parties—have been accused of crimes. None of these public officials has been finally convicted, but as former Secretary of Labor Ray Donovan put it after he was acquitted of questionable charges: "Which office do I go to get my reputation back?"

But it's only gotten worse these past few years.

The 2016 presidential election was one of the most polarizing in our history. For Trump supporters, everything Hillary Clinton did was deceitful, wrong, and criminal. And for those who supported Hillary Clinton, Trump's behavior was abhorrent, inexcusable, and criminal. This hardening of positions, and deep-seated aversion to the other, manifested itself in increasingly tenuous demands to criminalize political differences.

Indeed, "Lock 'em up" has become the battle cry of both Democrats and Republicans when they do not like the policies propounded by their opponents. Boorish calls for indictment have replaced calibrated criticism of opposing views, and there have been far too few calibrated calls—on both sides of the aisle—for de-escalation of the mutual demands for criminal prosecution and/or impeachment.

Recall the political conventions in the summer of 2016, where this type of coarse rhetoric galvanized the crowds.

At the GOP convention in Cleveland, Roger Stone famously got up on the stage and called for action against Hillary Clinton: "We demand the prosecution of Bill and Hillary Clinton for their crimes."

During his convention speech, Chris Christie goaded the crowd into chanting "guilty" and "lock her up," while Florida attorney general Pam Bondi said from the convention platform: "'Lock her up!' I love that." Scott Walker echoed the same sentiment in his speech: "If she [Clinton] were any more inside, she'd be in prison."

And finally, a state representative from New Hampshire took the coercive rhetoric to its "logical" conclusion, calling for Clinton's execution. "This whole thing disgusts me . . . Hillary Clinton should be put in the firing line and shot for treason."

President Trump further stoked the fire, seeking to have his former political rival investigated and/or prosecuted. In his tweets he has called for

Clinton to be indicted and for a special counsel to be appointed to investigate her "crimes."

Here are some of Trump's tweets:

"So why aren't the Committees and investigators, and of course our beleaguered A.G., looking into Crooked Hillary crimes & Russia relations?" —July 24, 2017

"The Uranium to Russia deal, the 33,000 plus Emails, the Comey fix and so much more . . . There is so much GUILT by Democrats/ Clinton, and now the facts are pouring out. DO SOMETHING!" —Oct. 29, 2017

"Everybody is asking why the Justice Department (and FBI) isn't looking into all of the dishonesty going on with the Crooked Hillary & the Dems . . . People are angry. At some point the Justice Department, and the FBI, must do what is right and proper. The American public deserves it!" —Nov. 3, 2017

Democrats have played tit for tat, making mirror-image arguments. They were calling for criminal investigation, indictment, and impeachment of President Trump even before his inauguration. The fury against Trump has meant there has been little nuance in analyzing the actions of the current administration.

For many anti-Trump extremists, everything Trump has done is wrong, and since it is wrong, it must necessarily be criminal.

Democrats have accused the president—and members of his administration—of "treason," "obstruction of justice," and "collusion." For example, Senator Tim Kaine—Hillary Clinton's former running mate—said: "We're now beyond obstruction of justice in terms of what's being investigated . . . this is moving into perjury, false statements, and even into potentially treason."

Moreover, two different Articles of Impeachment have now been filed against the president.

The first cites Trump's alleged "obstruction of justice" for having fired James Comey—a constitutionally protected action within the president's authority—while the second accuses the president of being a "danger" to our democracy.

There is a dangerous fallacy inherent in attempts by both sides to turn alleged political sins into prosecutable crimes.

Under our Constitution, for a political act—or any act—to be a federal crime, it must violate a criminal statute, not some general prohibition against wrongdoing.

In the early days of the new Republic, the Supreme Court ruled that there are no federal "common law" crimes. Only statutory crimes may be prosecuted under federal law. There could be common law torts, under which the courts could expand and contract the law to meet changing needs. But when it comes to federal crimes, only Congress could enact them with unambiguous statutory language.

All such crimes require two distinct elements: a specifically prohibited *actus rea*, a criminal act; and a *mens rea*, a criminal intent that accompanies the act. Without these, there can be no constitutionally valid crime regardless of how heinous the conduct may be. This means that criminal prosecution must be a neutral sanction of last resort, not an initial weapon used to target political rivals.

Crimes may not be made up as we go along; they must be expressly prohibited by preexisting criminal statutes.

Here's how I made this point in recent interviews: "Today it's Clinton; tomorrow it's Trump; the next day it's [Bernie] Sanders; after that, it's you."

It was Lavrentiy Beria, the former head of the notorious Soviet KGB, who told Joseph Stalin: "Show me the man, and I'll find you the crime." We never want to become a country in which political leaders of either party can point to their political enemies and have prosecutors "find" the crime.

Consider the aforementioned criminal trial of Senator Bob Menendez (D-NJ) for vague crimes alleging political corruption. After weeks of testimony and days of deliberation, the case resulted in a hung jury. According to the press reports, jurors voted 10-2 for acquittal. Not content to await the outcome of the hotly contested trial, the RNC declared him guilty before the trial began and urged him to announce that he would immediately resign when he was convicted by a jury, which they took as a foregone conclusion.

The RNC set up a "war room" to "disseminate any potentially embarrassing details" that emerged at the trial. What actually emerged was the embarrassing reality that what Menendez was accused of having done—accepting plane rides and other favors from an old friend—is as common among Republicans as it is among Democrats.

The RNC doesn't care about raising the level of ethics in the Senate, as they claim. All they care about is raising the number of Republicans in the Senate. If Menendez had resigned immediately, the vacancy would have been filled by the outgoing New Jersey GOP governor, Chris Christie. The rush to get Senator Menendez to resign if convicted by a jury, rather than wait until the appellate process would be completed, was because there was a November gubernatorial election in New Jersey that Democrats were expected to win and did.

Could there be any clearer example both of the criminalization of political differences and of the hypocrisy of the RNC in the complaining—as I have done—about Democrats trying to criminalize their differences with President Trump and members of his administration? The difference is that I have railed against the criminalization of politics by both sides.

Both sides have violated this important principle. Democrats and Republicans alike have failed what I previously have called the "shoe on the other foot test." Neither would be making the argument they are putting forward against their political enemies if it were their political friends who were in the crosshairs. Both sides respond by arguing that the other side is worse. The RNC insists that Menendez is really guilty of corruption but Trump is innocent of obstruction of justice. Democrats insist that Trump is guilty of obstruction but Menendez is innocent of corruption.

The truth is that both sides advocate the stretching of already elastic crimes—such as corruption and obstruction—to fit their targeted political opponents.

Civil libertarians must resist this tactic because elastic criminal laws, capable of being stretched to fit nearly anyone, endanger the liberty of all Americans. A statute, once expanded to fit a criminal enemy, can be used by one's foes against political friends.

All Americans are at risk of over-criminalization. That's why civil libertarians, even those who despise Trump (or Clinton or Menendez) should stand in opposition to current efforts to criminalize President Trump's exercise of his constitutional authority. But authentic civil libertarians, who advocate neutral policies without regard to which political parties are helped or hurt, are becoming increasingly rare in our hyper-partisan age. "Whose side are you on?" has become the question. And the answer of "I am on the side of civil liberties for all" is regarded as wimpy, a cop-out, or worse.

Partisans regard it as a form of political treason—giving aid and comfort to the enemy in a time of political warfare.

I know because I have been accused of disloyalty by many of my Democratic friends because I have criticized efforts to accuse President Trump of crimes based on the exercise of his constitutional powers.

The criminal sanction should be reserved for unambiguous acts coupled with clear criminal intent based on clearly written and narrowly drafted statutes. All Americans would be better off if political differences were resolved at the ballot box, rather than in the courts of law.

If existing statutes are insufficient to prevent new evils, they should be amended, and future acts prosecuted under the newly enacted statutes. But vague accordion-like statutes—such as "obstruction of justice," "corruption," and "conspiracy"—should not be expanded to cover the political sins of one's enemies. Nor should never-used laws—such as the Logan Act—be resurrected to selectively target political enemies.

It is not too late to declare a cease-fire on the mutually destructive criminalization of political difference. Congress should appoint a nonpartisan commission of experts to investigate Russia's efforts to influence elections. This should be a bipartisan concern of all Americans. Evidence should be gathered and public hearings held. The purpose of such hearings would be to inform the American citizenry of what has taken place in the past, what we can expect in the future, and what can be done to prevent Russian intrusion into our political system. Congressional hearings do not accomplish this, as evidenced by the partisan bickering we saw when Attorney General Jeff Sessions testified. Partisan politicians are not interested in objective truth emerging from such hearings. They just want to win for their party. This does not help the American public. Nor will the investigation by the Special Council accomplish the goals of informing the citizens of our country and preventing future intrusions by Russia into our elections.

This is because prosecutors operate behind the closed doors of grand jury rooms and it is illegal to leak grand jury evidence.

Mueller's investigation—which is deploying prosecutorial tools long criticized by civil libertarians—should be put on hold until and unless a bipartisan commission completes its investigation and determines—if it does—that serious crimes were committed during the last election. That is how democracies are supposed to function and information ought to be gathered: in public, with sunshine as the best disinfectant against the contamination of partisanship.

Under the existing constitutional framework, the president has the power to fire officials of the executive branch, including the attorney general and the director of the FBI. He also has the power to pardon any defendant, either before or after trial.

He should not be prosecuted for exercising his authority—an entirely lawful act—regardless of his motive.

Presidents typically have mixed motives for their political actions: self-preservation, partisan benefits, doing what they regard as the right thing. To allow prosecutions to be based on psychoanalyzing motives poses dangers to our system of separation of powers.

The first President Bush exercised his constitutional authority based on questionable motives when he pardoned Caspar Weinberger on the eve of his criminal trial for lying to Congress regarding the infamous Iran-Contra affair.

Bush also pardoned five other defendants, thereby ending a multiyear investigation by Special Prosecutor Lawrence E. Walsh, who expressed outrage at the president's interference with his investigation—an investigation that might well have ended with a finding of guilt pointing directly at the president.

President Bush paid a heavy political price for his highly questionable but entirely lawful actions in pardoning defendants who might well have incriminated him. I do not recall any demands that he be prosecuted or impeached during that less partisan era.

Until and unless the Constitution is amended to deprive the president of these powers when the investigations and prosecutions he stops are directed at him or members of his administration, the problem will persist, because it is inherent in our structure of government. But we should not try to solve this problem by expanding existing criminal statutes to target lawful political actions.

Article II may provide a partial solution. It empowers Congress to enact legislation vesting the appointment of "inferior office" in "the courts of law." Congress could therefore create an office of director of public prosecution to be appointed by the courts. It is unlikely in the current partisan environment that such legislation would be enacted.

In the meantime, we must do everything we can under our current laws to depoliticize criminal prosecutions. The liberty of Americans is endangered when political considerations influence—sometimes determine—who is to be criminally investigated and prosecuted. That's why I—a liberal Democrat who voted for Hillary Clinton—will continue to vehemently oppose expansions of the criminal law to target President Trump for his alleged political sins.

I Haven't Changed. They Have.[4]

From an appearance on Tucker Carlson Tonight *in May 2018.*

TUCKER CARLSON, HOST: Professor Dershowitz joins us tonight. Professor, thanks for coming on.

I was struck by this story, your account of this because you've taken unpopular—really unpopular positions, some that I disagree with over the years and you haven't had this problem. What's the difference?

DERSHOWITZ: Well, it's Trump. Trump changes everything. Just yesterday, on Martha's Vineyard, there was a dinner party, to which my wife and I were not invited, but apparently, I was the subject of the entire conversation. People asking, what's happened to Dershowitz? Why has he turned to the right?

And I wish I had been there because I would have pointed my finger at my liberal friends and said, "It's all your fault." If you had worked as hard for the election of Hillary Clinton as I did and if she had been elected and they were trying to impeach or charge her, I'd be saying exactly the same things in defense of her rights, as I did in the defense of the rights of Bill Clinton and also in the defense of the rights of Richard Nixon going back to the 1970s.

I haven't changed. They have.

CARLSON: So, just as a reference point, you were involved in the defense for a little while anyway of O. J. Simpson, who I think was credibly accused of murdering two people with a knife.

When you went to Martha's Vineyard during those years, 1995/1996, did people attack you at dinner parties for that?

DERSHOWITZ: A little bit. But not as much as this. It's never been like this.

And this time, it includes some of my relatives. As I said, the only thing that hurts me is that up until now, people who are my relatives would tell me, oh, people come over to you and say you are related to Alan Dershowitz, wow; now, they say, you are related to Alan Dershowitz, how can you justify what he has been saying about Donald Trump?

So, it affects my relatives. And that hurts me. I have thick skin. I have been doing this for years. I have developed the thickest skin imaginable.

By the way, a lot of the tweets that I get, hundreds of tweets and messages, a lot of them not only focus on what I have been saying about the constitutional rights of Donald Trump, but they relate it to me being pro-Israel and Jewish and making an anti-Semitic thing out of it as well.

And so, there is not only some—too much—anti-Semitism on the right, there is quite a bit of it on the anti-Trump left as well. I'm feeling it.

CARLSON: Yes. I have noticed that. So, I mean, you've been at this for—I don't know, wouldn't even want to guess—half a century, an awfully long time, at the kind of forefront of the civil libertarian left. Has that group shrunk? Is it not just Trump, but maybe the left is less interested in traditional civil liberties than it used to be?

DERSHOWITZ: Shrunk? There are no civil libertarians left on the left. Certainly not the American Civil Liberties Union. They were the ones who said that the raid on Cohen's office, taking his lawyer/client files was a good thing.

Not even suggesting what I suggested and what was ultimately adopted by the judge to have a judicial monitor going through all of these emails. The ACLU is dead in the water when it comes to defending the civil liberties of people who they don't agree with. And that's just awful.

There are still some civil libertarians left. But you can count them on one hand. Everybody has to pass the "shoe on the other foot" test. If the shoe were on the other foot, would you be taking the same position you are taking today? I passed that test. There are some others who passed that test. But too many, both on the right and on the left, don't pass the test.

CARLSON: I agree.

DERSHOWITZ: If Hillary Clinton had been elected, a lot of the people who were supporting me and defending me on the right would be attacking me for criticizing the prosecution or the impeachment of Hillary Clinton.

We need neutral principles. We need standards of constitutionality that are apolitical and I refuse to allow partisan politics to preempt my views on the Constitution, which have stayed the same for fifty years.

CARLSON: Amen! When the FBI broke into the Gmail account of that creepy governor Eliot Spitzer, I defended that creepy governor Eliot Spitzer.

DERSHOWITZ: He is my friend.

CARLSON: I know!

DERSHOWITZ: He was my research assistant. I like Eliot.

CARLSON: But it was totally wrong what they did to him. And it's important to say that. Professor, thank you. Great to see you.

DERSHOWITZ: Likewise.

Trump: Accusations and Realities

The blame game continues and the double standard rules as Democrats, who were happy with FBI director James Comey's decision not to prosecute Hillary Clinton, remain keen on pursuing a case against Donald Trump based on evidence, or lack thereof, now available. "Corrupt motive" is alleged for President Trump's firing of Comey. I argue in these essays and transcripts that what constitutes this vague and open-ended term often depends on the political bias of the accuser and can be a double-edged sword used against both Democrats and Republicans by politically motivated prosecutors and legislators. As demands to prosecute President Trump for corruption persist, I point out the dangers of how expandable such a term can be, whereas, in fact, recent court rulings narrow the open-ended term, and lead us to conclude that President Trump's actions do not fit the definition of corruption under federal statutes.

A president is not above the law; however, under our constitutional system of checks and balances, the president cannot be charged with a crime if his or her actions were constitutionally authorized. We must not compromise our constitutional principles, and yet, partisan zeal prefers to ignore these fundamentals. I offer examples of past presidents exercising constitutional authority despite allegations or charges of obstruction of justice, and I take to task my colleague Larry Tribe's response to my argument, pointing out our differences with respect to the Constitution and efforts to criminalize political conduct.

In light of the fact that President Trump was constitutionally authorized to fire FBI director James Comey, and Deputy Attorney General Rod Rosenstein authored the memo justifying the firing, I ask whether Rosenstein should be recused from supervising Special Counsel Robert Mueller's investigation of possible obstruction of justice growing out of the Russia investigation.

Finally, I discuss several categories of cases relating to President Trump that are being investigated, including constitutional acts such as granting pardons, private acts that preceded his presidency, emoluments, and whether there was collusion.

A Partisan Rush to Prosecute Trump⁵

When I taught law at Harvard, I always gave a final exam that included what is called an "issue spotter." I presented a complex hypothetical case, often based on a real one, and asked the students to stretch their imaginations to come up with every conceivable crime that might be charged and every conceivable defense that might be offered. That was the first part of the question, and most students excelled at spotting the relevant issues. In the second part of the question, I asked them to use their judgment in deciding which, if any, of these crimes could realistically be charged and which defenses could realistically be offered. It was this part of the question that separated the very good lawyers, which included the vast majority of the students, from the truly exceptional ones. To be a great lawyer requires the exercise of judgment, subtlety, nuance, and an ability to predict what the courts will do.

I am reminded of these exams when I read op-eds and listen to TV appearances, some by my former excellent students, that apply only the first part of the test to the current legal situations confronting the Trump administration. These smart lawyers try to come up with every conceivable statute that an imaginative lawyer could identify, ranging from the Logan Act (which hasn't been used in 215 years), to treason (which is narrowly defined in the Constitution), to obstruction of justice, to witness tampering, to violations of campaign financing laws (which are so vague and open-ended that half of America's politicians would be in jail if they were broadly applied).

I have to admit that these lawyers show great imagination—imagination they rightly condemn when Republicans play the same game, accusing Hillary Clinton of espionage and other open-ended crimes. But they show scant judgment or nuance in distinguishing what might be possible based on the broadest interpretation of the language and what is realistic based on court precedents, prosecutorial discretion, equal application, and simple justice. It is not that these lawyers aren't brilliant. They are. It's not their intellect I am questioning. It is the double standard they seem to be applying to Donald Trump and Hillary Clinton, in particular, and to the opposing party and their party, in general. The hyper-partisanship I've already lamented as criminalizing our politics is one factor that must never enter into prosecutorial judgment, regardless how strong and even legitimate the negative feelings are about a political opponent.

It is tempting, because it is so easy, to comb the statute books in an effort to identify every conceivable crime that might be applicable to any given situation. As Harvey Silverglate wrote in his superb book, *Three Felonies a Day*, prosecutors play the following game: One names a well-known and controversial person, and the others search through the statute books to figure out which three felonies they committed on a given day. That is what prosecutors do when they are playing games. It's not supposed to be what they do when they destroy a person's life by indicting them.

Former FBI director James Comey understood the role of a prosecutor when he concluded that "there is evidence of potential violations of the statutes regarding the handling of classified information" by Clinton. But after engaging in the first part of the criminal law exam exercise, he turned to the second part, involving judgment, and concluded that "our judgment is that no reasonable prosecutor would bring such a case." Silverglate shows that our criminal statute books are overloaded with crimes that can be expanded to fit any politician or businessman or any controversial figure.

Comey's conclusion generated outcries of protest from Republican partisans who had played the same game that Democratic partisans are now playing when they demanded that if there is evidence of potential violations of the statutes, then a prosecution must be brought. But these zealots were wrong and Comey was right. (He was not right in making public his evaluation of the evidence and his finding that Clinton was "extremely careless [in her] handling of very sensitive, highly classified information." But that is a different matter.)

Democratic partisans, who were happy with Comey's conclusion not to prosecute Clinton, should be applying the same standards to Trump. No reasonable prosecutor would bring a charge of treason, tampering with witnesses, obstruction of justice, or violating campaign laws, based on the evidence that is now available. (It is possible that evidence may emerge of such crimes. But based on what we now know, that is highly unlikely.)

So, let's not treat the criminal justice system as a law school exam in which students are asked to catalog every possible violation of our accordion-like laws. But if we insist on doing so, let's at least include the second part of the exam question: showing judgment and nuance in deciding whether to bring a case even if there is "evidence of potential violations of the statutes." The rule of law cannot survive a double standard. What is good for the goose must be good for the gander, and what we applauded with regard to Hillary Clinton we must not condemn with regard to Donald Trump.

Why Donald Trump Can't Be Charged with Obstruction[6]

Let me further explain the conclusion of the previous essay:

The United States Constitution, unlike those of other Western democracies, provides for separation of powers as well as a system of checks and balances between the branches of government. This means that the three branches of government—the judicial, the executive, and the legislative—are equal and independent of each other, and that no branch may intrude on the power of the other. As part of this system of separation of powers, the members of each branch are given limited immunity from prosecution for performing their constitutionally authorized duties.

Thus, a senator or congressman may not be prosecuted for certain criminal acts that he or she commits while attending or travelling to or from Congress. Nor can a judge be prosecuted for judicial actions while on the bench. Although these immunities are limited, they do protect members of Congress and judges from prosecution for actions for which ordinary citizens can be prosecuted. These limited immunities do not place government official *above* the law because they are authorized *by* the law as part of our system of checks and balances.

In light of this reality, it should surprise no one that the president—who is the head of the executive branch of government—is also immune from prosecution for performing his constitutionally authorized duties. It follows, therefore, that a president may never be charged with obstruction of justice for firing the head of the FBI, pardoning potential witnesses against him, or directing law enforcement officials who to prosecute and who not to prosecute. The Constitution explicitly authorizes the president to pardon anyone. It also authorizes the president to see that the laws are faithfully executed. Actions made in the course of carrying out these functions are constitutionally protected.

Presidents Richard Nixon and Bill Clinton were both charged with obstruction of justice in Articles of Impeachment. But these charges were not for exercising their constitutional authority. Nixon was charged with instructing a witness to lie, paying hush money, and destroying evidence. President Clinton was charged for allegedly asking witnesses to lie. None of these acts are authorized by the Constitution or are part of a president's constitutionally protected activities.

Therein lays the constitutional distinction. A president can be charged with obstruction of justice for criminal acts that are not part of his constitutionally authorized powers—acts such as subornation of perjury, bribery, destroying evidence, and paying hush money. These are independent crimes that also constitute obstruction of justice. A president may not, however, be charged, for firing an executive official, telling law enforcement who to prosecute, or pardoning someone.

But what if his motive in engaging in these constitutional acts is corrupt? The same question could, of course, be asked about the motives of members of Congress or judges. The answer is that if an act is explicitly authorized by the Constitution, the doctrine of separation of powers precludes inquiry into the motives of government actors. To rule otherwise would interfere with our delicate system of separation of powers and checks and balances. President Bush's motives were likely corrupt: he pardoned potential witnesses against him in order to protect himself from prosecution, impeachment, and/or political criticism. Yet the Special Prosecutor had no authority to base charges on his assessment of the president's motives. Every government official always has mixed motives underlying his or her actions. These motives include self-aggrandizement, improving reelection prospects, getting a good advance for a book, or helping his or her party, as well as patriotism.

Limited immunity, by its very nature, means that public officials cannot have their motives serve as a basis for prosecution if their constitutionally authorized acts are protected by our system of separation of powers. This may mean that certain public officials will avoid being charged for actions for which ordinary citizens could be charged. That is the price we pay for our system of separation of powers.

For some political partisans, this price is too high. They believe that ending a presidency of Donald Trump is worth compromising constitutional principles. Partisans on the other side would have done the same had Hillary Clinton been elected president amid their shouts of "lock her up." I have been criticized by some of my friends on the left for placing constitutional principles above partisan consideration. I proudly plead guilty to that charge.

"Corrupt Motive" Is Not a Proper Criterion for Prosecuting a President[7]

Many of those who insist that President Trump has obstructed justice point to his allegedly "corrupt motive" in firing former FBI director James Comey after telling him that he "hoped" he would end his investigation of Lieutenant General Michael Flynn. They concede—as Comey himself did—that the president has the constitutional authority to fire the director and to order him to end (or start) any investigation, just as he has the authority to pardon anyone being investigated. But they argue that these constitutionally authorized innocent acts become criminal if the president was "corruptly motivated."

This is a dangerous argument that no civil libertarian should be pressing.

"Corrupt motive" is an extraordinarily vague and open-ended term that can be expanded or contracted at the whim of zealous or politically motivated prosecutors. It is bad enough when this accordion-like term is used in the context of economic corruption, but it is far worse—and more dangerous to liberty—when used in the context of political disagreements. In commercial cases where corrupt intent may be an element, the act itself is generally not constitutionally protected. It often involves a gray-area financial transaction. But in political cases—especially those not involving money—the act itself is constitutionally protected, and the motive, which is often mixed, is placed on trial. It becomes the sole criterion for turning a constitutionally authorized political act into a felony.

What constitutes a corrupt motive will often depend on the political bias of the accuser. For some Democrats, the motives of all Republicans are suspect. The same is true for some Republicans. Again, partisanship rears its ugly head. Corrupt motive is in the eye of the beholder, and the beholder's eyes are often more open to charges of corrupt motives on the part of their political enemies than their political allies.

I know because I am currently being accused of being corruptly motivated in making my argument against charging President Trump with obstruction of justice. My emails are filled with such charges. The following email is typical:

"I want to know how much the Trump administration is funneling to you under the table, of course, to keep your support of him off the record? And if it's not money, what sort payoff is it? Favors, promises, bribes . . . what?? Why all the secrecy when indirectly advising his legal team via cable networks' panel discussions? I think your games, shenanigans and defense of this very disturbing man give the legal profession a black eye. Shame on you! Why not come out and openly defend Trump which you are obviously doing through innuendo?"

Others emails I have received include the following: "PLEASE BE TRUTHFUL. YOU ARE NOT A LIBERAL BUT RATHER A ZIONIST REPUBLICAN AUTHORITARIAN BIGOT" as well as "SELLING YOUR OPINION/SERVICES TO THE HIGHEST BIDDER!"

My motives have also been questioned by some of my academic and political colleagues. Am I being paid? Am I auditioning to be Trump's lawyer? Do I want to be appointed to a judgeship? Am I really a secret Republican? Did I really vote for Clinton? Do I expect favors in return for my arguments?

The point is that many of those who disagree with my arguments refuse to believe that I am making them out of principle. They assume a corrupt motive.

The same is true in the larger political context. Each side believes the other is corrupt to the core. They question each other's motives. That is why using the concept of "corrupt motive" to criminalize constitutionally authorized political actions is a dangerous double-edged sword that can be used against both Democrats and Republicans by politically motivated prosecutors.

Before the recent efforts to expand the obstruction statute to cover President Trump, many civil libertarians, political liberals, defense attorneys, and even judges were rightly critical of the expansive use of "corrupt motive" in the context of both commercial and political cases. But now that they see an opportunity to use this overbroad concept to "get" President Trump, many of these same people have become enthusiastic supporters of expanding the open-ended law even further in a shortsighted effort to criminalize the constitutionally protected actions of a president they dislike.

Anglo-American law is based on precedent. What happens today can be used tomorrow. So, beware of creating precedents that lie around like loaded weapons in the hands of overzealous or politically motivated prosecutors.

The Ruling Shows I'm Right on Trump and Corruption[8]

The recent reversal of Sheldon Silver's corruption conviction by the US Court of Appeals for the Second Circuit confirms the point I've been making for months about President Trump: his actions, as controversial as they may be, do not fit the definition of "corruption," as that vague word is used in federal statutes.

My critics have argued for an extraordinarily broad definition of corruption capable of being expanded to fit nearly everything Trump has done—from firing FBI director James Comey, to asking him to consider dropping the investigation of Lieutenant General Michael Flynn, to his son's meeting with Russian surrogates.

This is the way the *New York Times* put it in its story about the court's narrowing the meaning of corruption in the context of federal criminal law: "There was a time when political corruption might have been described—as a former Supreme Court justice once said of pornography—as something you knew when you saw it." In other words, it was in the eye of the beholder rather than in a precise statutory definition.

That dangerous time—dangerous because it substituted the rule of individual prosecutors for the rule of law—came to a gradual end over the past several years as the Supreme Court repeatedly cabined the definition of corruption under federal statutes that relate to the provision of "honest services" (another broad category). It ruled that not all political actions that smell or look like corruption can be prosecuted criminally without Congress specifically making such conduct criminal by precisely worded legislation.

This salutary approach to defining overbroad words like "corruption" was applauded by many civil libertarians and liberals, and especially by criminal defense attorneys who had seen up close how expandable terms like corruption could be and were being abused by ambitious prosecutors determined to add notches to their belts by convicting dishonest politicians.

Now many of these same civil libertarians, liberals, and even defense attorneys have forgotten how dangerous those bad old days were and are demanding that President Trump and his family members should be prosecuted for corruption under the most expansive definition of corruption, despite recent court rulings narrowing that open-ended term.

"Just this one time, please. Just let us get Trump." That is what the fair-weather liberals, civil libertarians, and criminal defense lawyers seem to be saying. "Then, we will return to our principles."

But that's not the way the law works. There are no exceptions—no "just this one time." It's worth repeating my conclusion to the previous essay: the law operates on precedent. Today's exception may become tomorrow's rule. And even if it doesn't, it creates a precedent for more exceptions, which may be applied to our side of the political aisle, as Republicans tried to do with Hillary Clinton.

H. L. Mencken understood why it is so important to defend the rights of those you disagree with and not make exceptions for your political enemies: "The trouble about fighting for human freedom is that you have to spend much of your life defending sons of bitches; for oppressive laws are always aimed at them originally, and oppression must be stopped at the beginning if it is to be stopped at all."

It is, of course, true that by narrowing the criminal law definition of corruption, some dishonest politicians will fall through the cracks. As one former prosecutor put it: "Prosecutors were concerned from the start that [the Supreme Court's decisions narrowing the definition of corruption] would allow a lot of reprehensible behavior to go unpunished . . ."

Another put it this way: politicians "will learn the language of corruption. It will still be a bribe, but it will fall outside of anything that is *technically illegal*" (emphasis added). But there is no such animal as "technically illegal." Under the rule of law, actions and intentions are either legal or illegal. If they are not specifically prohibited by an existing criminal law, they are *legal*—not *technically* legal, but simply legal.

For prosecutors who believe that the recent court decisions "may be the beginning of a parade of horribles," as one former prosecutor put it, there is a democratic remedy: enact legislation that specifically covers the conduct you deem reprehensible and apply it to future cases. That's the way the rule of law is supposed to operate in a democratic society.

So, let's have one law for all politicians and citizens. Let's not stretch existing law to fit Donald Trump, Hillary Clinton, or anyone else. The courts have rightly interpreted corruption narrowly. If prosecutors—including the Special Counsel investigating the Trump administration—want to broaden that term, let them take their case to Congress, not to a grand jury.

No One Is Above the Law[9]

O ur Constitution provides that the members of each branch of government be protected from legal consequences for performing their constitutionally mandated functions. Thus, Article I of the Constitution explicitly immunizes from arrest all members of Congress "during their Attendance at the Session of their respective Houses, and in going to and returning from the same." This immunity, though limited, protects legislators from arrest for actions for which ordinary citizens could be prosecuted. This limited immunity does not put them "above" the law, since it is the law itself that provides the immunity.

Judges, too, are immunized from not only from criminal prosecution, but also from civil liability for actions taken within their judicial authority. This is how the Supreme Court put it in *Stump v. Sparkman* (in which a young woman sued the circuit judge who had tricked her into being involuntarily sterilized by misinforming her that it was an appendectomy!): "The governing principle of law is well established and is not questioned by the parties. As early as 1872, the court recognized that it was 'a general principle of the highest importance to the proper administration of justice that a judicial officer, in exercising the authority vested in him, [should] be free to act upon his own convictions, without apprehension of personal consequences to himself.'"

Prosecutors, too, have limited immunity for actions undertaken within their prosecutorial authority. It should come as no surprise, therefore, that the president—as head of the executive branch—cannot be prosecuted for acts that he or she is authorized to take pursuant to Article II of the Constitution. Article II of the Constitution explicitly allocated to the president the authority to "take care that the Laws be faithfully executed."

This grant of power authorizes the president to decide who should be investigated and prosecuted and who should not. Presidents including John

Adams, Thomas Jefferson, Abraham Lincoln, Franklin Roosevelt, John Kennedy, and Barack Obama have exercised this authority by instructing the Justice Department to investigate and prosecute individuals or groups— and not to investigate or prosecute others. Some have exercised that authority wisely, others not. But none have committed the crime of obstruction of justice by trying to influence prosecutorial decisions.

I've noted how President George H. W. Bush stopped an investigation in its tracks—an investigation that could have pointed directly to criminal action by him during the Iran-Contra scandal—when he pardoned Casper Weinberger and five other crucial witnesses who could have pointed the finger at him. The Special Prosecutor, Lawrence Walsh, was furious at this decision, claiming that it was intended to, and did, stop the investigation. Yet no one suggested that President Bush be charged with obstruction of justice, because in pardoning those witnesses he was exercising his constitutional authority under Article II.

I've also noted that President Andrew Johnson was impeached for firing Secretary of War Edwin Stanton in violation of a statute passed by Congress. He was acquitted by the Senate, and the Supreme Court subsequently declared the statute unconstitutional as impinging on the president's power to fire members of the executive branch.

Even former director of the FBI James Comey said that the president had the authority to fire him, for any reason or no reason. Now President Trump's political opponents are seeking to have the Special Counsel psychoanalyze the president to determine whether his motives were pure, mixed, or corrupt. Nearly all presidential actions are motivated by mixed intentions, ranging from self-aggrandizement, to political benefit, to partisan advantage, to patriotism. If a president or a senator or a judge acts within his or her constitutional authority, their motives should not be probed by prosecutors even if they suspect unsavory ones.

If a president's actions, on the other hand, are unlawful—as President Nixon's clearly were when he told subordinates to lie to the FBI and paid hush money—good intentions (they are hard to imagine in Nixon's case) would not be a defense. For purposes of the criminal law, presidents must be judged by the lawfulness or unlawfulness of their acts, not by the motivations that underlay them.

My argument, unlike that of President Trump's lawyer, is not that a president can never be charged with obstruction of justice. It is that he cannot be charged with that crime if his only actions were constitutionally authorized.

This distinction is central to our system of separation of powers and checks and balances.

The phrase "no one is above the law" has become weaponized by those who believe that President Trump is claiming to be above the law. But this misunderstands his position and that of his lawyers, who are arguing that his controversial actions are authorized by the law. They may be correct or incorrect, but it is not accurate to characterize their position as asserting that the president is "above the law."

Does Donald Trump Have

Congressional Immunity?[10]

[Professor Laurence Tribe responded to the previous essay, arguing that a president can be prosecuted or impeached for obstruction if he has corrupt motives. I replied.]

———————

My colleague Larry Tribe's response is unfortunately not responsive to my arguments. He erects several straw men, which he proceeds to knock down, but he fails to respond to my most compelling arguments.

Two striking examples: Larry correctly points out that congressional immunity is based explicitly on the text of the Constitution, but he fails to deal with my other primary example—judicial immunity. There is no mention of judicial immunity in the Constitution, and yet the Supreme Court has ruled that the separation of powers and checks and balances requires that judges be immune for conduct that is part of their constitutionally authorized powers. If he is to argue that the inclusion of congressional immunity in the Constitution precludes immunity for members of other branches, he must respond to my argument about judicial immunity. That he fails to do so reveals the weakness in his constitutional analysis.

Second, I provide three specific examples of presidential acts that he ignores: President George H. W. Bush was neither charged nor impeached for pardoning Casper Weinberger and other potential witnesses against him—acts that the Special Prosecutor believed were clearly motivated by a desire to protect himself. Nor does he deal with the fact that Presidents Nixon and Clinton were not impeached for merely exercising their constitutional authority. Congressional committees went out of their way to specify criminal acts beyond those authorized by Article II. Larry must deal with these examples. While doing so, he may also want to consider the failed impeachment of former president Andrew Johnson for firing a cabinet member in violation of the Tenure of Office Act passed by Congress. The Supreme

Court ultimately held that act unconstitutional as violative of separation of powers.

The cases Larry cites do not deal directly with the issue of whether a president can be charged with criminal conduct for merely exercising his constitutional powers. His inclusion of impeachment is yet another straw man, since my article does not suggest that a president could not be impeached for improperly pardoning or firing an executive official. That remains an open question. The text of the Constitution suggests that impeachment must be based on "treason, bribery, or other high crimes or misdemeanors." Congress may have the power to broaden these categories, but not ignore them.

Larry includes among alleged criminal acts by President Trump telling the director of the FBI to go easy on General Flynn. But he fails to respond to my more general point that our Constitution authorizes the president to direct his attorney general whom to prosecute and whom not to prosecute. Thomas Jefferson did that, as did Abraham Lincoln, FDR, and Barack Obama.

Larry's most dangerous argument—and several of his arguments endanger our liberties—is that "placing presidential pride over the nation's sovereignty is a grave abuse of presidential power by anyone's definition." All presidents are motivated in part by "pride" and other personal considerations. If questionable motives could turn an Article II exercise of presidential power into crimes, there would be no limits to the criminalization of political differences.

Finally, Larry characterizes my arguments as "familiar," as if that were a bad thing. He is, of course, correct about them being familiar since I have been making them for nearly fifty years. I opposed the naming of Richard Nixon as an unindicted co-conspirator. I railed against the impeachment and prosecution of former president Clinton (as did Larry). And I strongly opposed efforts to criminalize Hillary Clinton's carelessness. Yes, my arguments are familiar because I have been consistent in making them for half a century. They are not about Donald Trump. They are about the institution of the presidency and our constitutional system of separation of powers and checks and balances.

This exchange demonstrates that Larry Tribe and I respectfully disagree about fundamental issues regarding our Constitution and efforts to criminalize political conduct. I think the general public can learn from our clash of ideas. Accordingly, I renew the challenge to my friend and colleague to engage in a public debate now, while these important issues are at the fore-front of public controversy. CNN has offered an international platform for this debate. I have accepted CNN's invitation. I urge Larry to do so as well, so that we can respond to each other's arguments in the court of public opinion. And let the citizens decide. That's how democracy works best.

Rod Rosenstein Should Not Be Fired,
but Should He Be Recused?[11]

Deputy Attorney General Rod Rosenstein should not be fired. He is a distinguished public servant with a bipartisan reputation for fairness. But there is a real question whether he should be recused from participating in any investigation by the Special Counsel of alleged obstruction of justice by the president.

Five facts are indisputable. First, Rosenstein is currently supervising Robert Mueller, who he appointed to be Special Counsel to investigate the Russia matter and all ancillary issues. Second, these ancillary issues include any possible obstruction of justice growing out of the Russia investigation. Third, President Trump's firing of former FBI director James Comey may be an important building block in any possible obstruction case against the president. Fourth, Rosenstein played a central role in that firing, having written the memorandum justifying the president's action. Fifth, Rosenstein would be an important—perhaps the most important—witness in any investigation of the reasons behind the firing.

The question is whether a lawyer should both supervise an investigation and be an important witness in that very investigation. Attorney General Jeff Sessions recused himself because he might have been a witness or subject of the Russia investigation. Rosenstein might be a more central witness in any obstruction of justice investigation by the prosecutor who he is supervising.

One possible reason for why Rosenstein should not recuse himself would be if Mueller were not investigating alleged obstruction of justice by the president based on his firing of Comey. Perhaps Mueller realizes that charging a president with obstruction of justice for performing a constitutionally authorized act such as firing the director of the FBI would raise grave constitutional issues. Perhaps, therefore, that is not part of his current investigation.

If it is not, then Rosenstein has no clear conflict of interest. But the available evidence suggests that Mueller is looking into the Comey firing.

Although Rosenstein's remaining on the case does not violate the so-called "advocate-witness" rule that prohibits a lawyer being both an advocate and a witness at the same trial, it raises concerns about potential conflicts of interest. The advocate-witness prohibition is designed to prevent confusion over roles by the jury at trial. It does not deal with the broader issues of conflict of interest and the appearance of conflict.

In the Rosenstein matter, the supervising prosecutor has a potential stake in whether the line prosecutor will call him as a witness or will cross-examine him if he were to be called as a defense witness. Even more worrisome is the possibility—unlikely as it seems—that the supervising attorney may become a subject or target of the investigation. He could be named as a co-conspirator if Mueller believed that he knowingly provided a cover to hide the president's real intentions in firing Comey.

The more likely problem grows out of the possibility that President Trump's lawyer would try to shift the responsibility for the firing of Comey from the president to the author of the memo justifying the firing, namely, Rosenstein. "Advice of counsel" is a recognized defense, especially where state of mind—alleged corrupt intent—is at issue.

If President Trump's lawyer were to make this argument to the Special Counsel and his supervisor, could Rosenstein fairly consider and assess it? Would he have a conflict if he had to evaluate his own role in the firing? In an ordinary criminal case, recusal is not required based on speculation possibilities. But this is no ordinary case. When it is the president, or those around him, who are being investigated, everyone involved in the investigation and charging decisions must be "Caesar's wife," beyond any suspicion or even appearance of conflicting interests.

Does Rosenstein's continuing involvement in the Russia probe and possible obstruction of justice pass that daunting test? That is the relevant question, and more attention should be paid to that ethical issue than to the political question of whether or not he should be fired.

On Criminality and Presidential Advice[12]

From an April 2018 appearance on Meet the Press *with Chuck Todd and Bob Bauer, former White House counsel for Barack Obama.*

DERSHOWITZ: There are three categories of cases that are being investigated.

The first and most important are constitutionally authorized acts by the president, which include pardoning, firing, directing the prosecution. If he were ever to be charged or impeached for any of those acts, that would be a real constitutional conflict. And we'd have arguments on both sides constitutionally.

The second category is purely private acts that preceded his presidency, the allegations by women that may require him to testify under oath.

CHUCK TODD, MODERATOR: Right.

DERSHOWITZ: His business relations. He'd have no defense for that except factual, or he could argue that it was beyond the scope of the investigation. And then there's the third category, a hybrid category, including emoluments, whether there was collusion. Those are the three categories.

I do think that anything relating to pardon, he would have a strong constitutional defense. I think he's most vulnerable when it comes to women, if he testifies under oath, and gets into a she said/he said, which puts him in Clinton-land, and the basis on which Clinton was impeached.

TODD: Mr. Bauer, what do you say on the pardon issue?

BOB BAUER: I don't think there's any question, and I have to respectfully disagree with Professor Dershowitz. If the president uses the pardon power for corrupt purpose, then he is exposed to criminal liability for that. If his lawyer, with his authority, on his behalf, offered a pardon as a means of tainting or corrupting testimony in a criminal proceeding, then I don't see any basis for saying the president does not have to answer for that in the criminal justice system.

TODD: But if the president believes that this investigation is trumped up, that Mr. Mueller's investigation's out of control, then why wouldn't he offer pardons?

BAUER: Well, he may believe that, but he may also believe it's out of control because he fears for himself, because he's concerned about his own exposure. And it's precisely that element of self-protectiveness that I think threatens the legality of that offer of the pardons. It brings that into question.

TODD: Professor—go ahead.

DERSHOWITZ: There's a problem with that. And that is President Bush, the first, did exactly that. He pardoned Caspar Weinberger and five people on the eve of the trial, in order to end the investigation. His Special Counsel, at that time, Lawrence Walsh, accused him of doing that and said he had succeeded in ending the investigation. And yet, nobody, nobody, suggested obstruction of justice at that point.

Thomas Jefferson gave pardons to people in order to help the prosecution of his political enemy, Aaron Burr.

All throughout history, we see presidents offering and granting pardons. Once you start getting into the area of inquiring as to what the motive of a pardon was, you're really getting into constitutionally difficult areas. Of course, if the president were to take a bribe and give a pardon—

TODD: Right.

DERSHOWITZ: —the taking of the bribe itself would be the crime. The granting of the pardon would not be a crime. I do not believe that engaging in a constitutionally authorized act can ever be the basis of a criminal charge.

TODD: All right. Let me, I want to move the conversation here a little bit. And Bob, let me start with you. The fact that Flynn decided to cooperate and plead guilty and not accept the dangling of a pardon, did it—or does that—tell you something? And does Paul Manafort's decision not to cooperate tell you something with this pardon? Is there—what do you read into it?

BAUER: I don't know that I read a whole lot into it. I mean, it may be that Mr. Flynn just wasn't confident that the offer of the pardon was something he could count on. Who knows—who's to say why he would have done that?

But if I could, again, disagree with Professor Dershowitz. The Iran-Contra matter did involve, potentially, questions of high policy. But I don't see that here at all.

What's at issue here is whether or not a presidential campaign coordinated with a foreign power to affect the outcome of an election. And that is a core criminal concern. It's been part of our statutory framework since 1966, repeatedly strengthened by the Congress. And I don't see that that bears any analogy at all to Iran-Contra.

DERSHOWITZ: Well, except that the pardon was offered to stop a criminal investigation by a special prosecutor. Under your theory, that would be obstruction of justice. And yet it never occurred to anybody.

It doesn't matter what the subject matter was. If you obstruct justice for any subject matter, you're guilty.

The issue is whether granting a pardon in order to stop an investigation can be the basis for a criminal or—prosecution. And I think the answer to that, presidentially, is no. And it's no justification to say that matter—

TODD: Right. But—

DERSHOWITZ: —that involved matters of high policy.

TODD: But by the way—

DERSHOWITZ: And this involved matters of the Soviet Union, relationship with the Soviet Union. That's not a good argument.

TODD: You guys are two very bright legal minds. But there is no legal standard for impeachment.

DERSHOWITZ: Well, there is.

TODD: And so—I mean—

DERSHOWITZ: There is—there is a legal standard.

TODD: Per se, is there?

DERSHOWITZ: Yes.

TODD: So, it doesn't matter what you interpret as obstruction of justice, what Bob interprets as obstruction of justice. The end of the day, it's about what the members—what, what one hundred members of the United States Senate think.

DERSHOWITZ: I don't agree with that. The Constitution provides specifically you can only be impeached for bribery, treason, or other high crimes and misdemeanors.

They also put the chief justice in charge of the trial. And if I were ever, or any of the lawyers for Trump, if he got impeached for something that was not specified in the Constitution, the first motion that should be made is to the chief justice to dismiss it on legal grounds.

This is not purely a political decision. Otherwise, the chief justice, who's not political, would not be put in charge of the trial of a person who's been impeached.

So, I think it overstates it to say it's completely political, unbound by the words of the Constitution itself.

TODD: Mr. Bauer?

BAUER: Can I just bring this back to the criminal justice system? But you're absolutely correct. I mean, Congress certainly could act on an obstruction that didn't quite fit the criminal elements in the law.

TODD: Right.

BAUER: But still was enough for impeachment.

But let's be clear again what we're talking about. We're talking about the potential that a presidential campaign in the United States aided a foreign government in influencing the outcome of the federal election. That is a crime. It is a crime.

It is not correct, as Professor Dershowitz has said from time to time, that collaboration with a foreign government to help in an American presidential candidate's election is not criminal. It is.

TODD: Professor?

DERSHOWITZ: What's the statute? What's the statute—

BAUER: The federal election camp—

DERSHOWITZ: I searched the statute books over and over again. The word "collusion" appears once in the federal criminal code. It only applies—

BAUER: If—

DERSHOWITZ: —to when businesses collude with each other in violation of the antitrust laws.

Collusion between a candidate and a foreign government is a political sin. It would be a terrible thing to do. But in and of itself, it wouldn't be a crime.

Of course, it could involve criminal activities, if you accepted campaign contributions and did things of that kind.

TODD: Let—I want—

DERSHOWITZ: But the collusion itself would not be a crime. If it occurred, and I've seen no evidence that it has occurred in this case.

TODD: Very quickly, Professor Dershowitz, the president wants to talk to Mueller, at least he said so. What parameters would you advise him to accept?

DERSHOWITZ: Any he can get. I mean—

TODD: You—would you advise him to do it?

DERSHOWITZ: First of all, Mueller has the ultimate authority to call him in front of a grand jury without his lawyer, and no limitations on time. So, he has to come to a compromise.

I would surely suggest that he never testify in any of the cases involving women, that he not make the mistake that Bill Clinton made, advised by Bob Bennett, that he testify about his sex life.

But as far as the Special Counsel is concerned, he doesn't control that. The Special Counsel controls that. So any compromise that could be made, sitting with his lawyer, it doesn't matter whether it's under oath or not, because either is a crime.

TODD: Right.

DERSHOWITZ: But constraints on time, constraints on subject matter, anything he can get would be a plus because the Special Prosecutor has the power to call him in front of the grand jury.

TODD: Very quickly? I mean—

BAUER: Very quickly, I would simply say—since Donald Trump may have known that the Kremlin sent emissaries to his campaign in June of 2016 to talk about support for his campaign, he might take the advice that he gave Bill Clinton in 1999—take the Fifth.

TODD: Very interesting.

DERSHOWITZ: Bad advice. Bad advice.

TODD: Professor Dershowitz, very quickly, any chance you'll lead the president's legal team or join it in any capacity whatsoever if he asks?

DERSHOWITZ: No. I want to remain independent. I want to say what I say. I want to say what I said about Hillary Clinton.

TODD: Has he asked you? Has he asked you to join the team?

DERSHOWITZ: I—you know that no lawyer could ever comment about whether—

TODD: Ah.

DERSHOWITZ: —he's ever been asked.

TODD: Fair enough.

DERSHOWITZ: But let me say, I would have said the same thing if Hillary Clinton had been elected president and they were saying, "lock her up."

TODD: Gotcha.

DERSHOWITZ: I'm taking exactly the same position now—

TODD: I know.

DERSHOWITZ: —that I've made for fifty years as a civil libertarian.

TODD: Professor Dershowitz—Professor Dershowitz, I appreciate your coming on during this holiday week.

DERSHOWITZ: Thank you.

Mueller and the Need for a
Nonpartisan Commission

The drafters of our Fifth Amendment intended grand juries to serve as protection against overaggressive prosecutors. Instead, grand juries today empower prosecutors against criminal defendants. I explore why Special Counsel Robert Mueller impaneled a second grand jury in the District of Columbia when one already exists in Virginia. What advantage would a prosecutor have? I then turn attention to retired Lieutenant General Michael Flynn, and ask why he would have lied to the FBI, and why Mueller only charged him with lying, when in fact there was nothing criminal about Flynn's request to Russian ambassador Sergey Kislyak to delay or oppose a UN Security Council vote on an anti-Israel resolution that the outgoing Obama administration refused to veto.

Concern whether the Trump team was seeking to fire Mueller was widespread. And at the time, I wrote that the action taken by the team to challenge Mueller and his investigation on the legal grounds was a more viable and practical tactic. On the other hand, I ask civil libertarians who are unwilling to give President Trump the benefit of law and civil liberties to consider the issue of legitimately criticizing Mueller rather than seeing any skepticism regarding his history as a desire to help Trump.

President Trump is criticized for demanding loyalty from Attorney General Jeff Sessions, yet I point out that every previous president has expected the same. The blame should not solely go to the president, but should be shared by our system that merges the role of attorney general as both political advisor to the president and head law enforcement officer and chief prosecutor of the United States. I indicate that these conflicting loyalties and obligations are the very reason our country appoints special counsel and independent prosecutors. I have long proposed that the Justice Department be broken up into two separate agencies, with separate heads:

one a loyal political advisor to the president and a member of the cabinet, the other completely independent and not a member of the cabinet.

⌐In the same vein, I argue that the appointment of a special counsel to investigate Russian meddling in the 2016 presidential election was misguided and, instead, Congress should have created a nonpartisan commission of objective experts to conduct the investigation. I point out that the public has lost faith in the leadership of the Justice Department and the FBI and does not trust congressional investigative committees⌐ A remedy to regain public trust is to let Congress appoint a nonpartisan commission to conduct a transparent investigation, and let the Special Counsel suspend his investigation until the nonpartisan commission issues its report.

Why Did Mueller Impanel
a Second Grand Jury in DC?[13]

The decision by Robert Mueller to impanel a grand jury in the District of Columbia raises some intriguing questions, which are unlikely to be answered by the secretive Special Counsel.

The first and most obvious is why a second grand jury was needed at all. There is already a grand jury in Virginia, which is investigating aspects of the so-called Russian connection. That grand jury is fully capable of doing anything the new grand jury can do. It can issue subpoenas for additional documents, summon additional witnesses, and consider additional aspects of the case or cases being investigated by Mueller.

So, if grand juries really were independent decision-makers of the kind contemplated by the Bill of Rights—if they truly served as a protection for defendants against overaggressive prosecutors—then it would make no sense for a special counsel to bifurcate its work into two separate grand juries. A prosecutor would want one grand jury to hear all the evidence before deciding to indict. But all experienced lawyers know that today's grand juries are merely twenty-three chairs, with twenty-three puppets, who do whatever their puppet master, the prosecutor, wants them to do. As the former chief judge of New York famously put it, a prosecutor can get a grand jury to indict a ham sandwich.

The drafters of our Fifth Amendment, which guarantees a defendant the right to grand jury consideration of his or her case before he or she can be brought to trial in a federal court, would be turning over in their graves if they knew how this shield against overzealous prosecutors has been turned into a sword for the use of prosecutors against criminal defendants. I don't know a single criminal defense lawyer who wouldn't vote to abolish grand juries if they had that option.

The decision to impanel a second grand jury may have little to do, therefore, with the work of the grand jury, which could have just as easily been conducted a few miles away in a northern Virginia courtroom. It may, however, have everything to do with the petit jury—the twelve citizens who will try any defendant—that may eventually be selected if any defendant is ultimately indicted.

Defendants are brought to trial in the venue where they are indicted. Had the Virginia grand jury remained the only grand jury investigating the Russian connection, then any cases indicted by that grand jury would have been tried in Virginia. But now that a second grand jury has been impaneled in DC, any defendant indicted by that grand jury would be tried in front of a DC petit jury composed of citizens of the District.

Does this change of venue provide any tactical litigation advantage to the Special Counsel? Any honest lawyer, with experience as a prosecutor or defense attorney, would say yes. Why? Because this District of Columbia jury pool is different than the Virginia jury pool.

The District of Columbia jury pool will be overwhelmingly Democratic, by a ratio of close to 10 to 1. The Virginia pool is likely to be more diverse in its political affiliations, though probably still more Democratic than Republican. There is no guarantee, of course, that a Democratic juror would vote to convict an indicted member of the Trump administration, or that a Republican juror would vote to acquit. But in selecting jurors from among the pool, most prosecutors would favor Democrats and most defense attorneys would favor Republicans, all other things being equal. For that reason, most prosecutors would prefer to have such a trial in DC than in Virginia.

Then there is the third-rail issue of race, which prosecutors and defense attorneys do not like to talk about but which plays a significant role in jury selection, as the Supreme Court has recognized. A predominantly white jury can be a different institution than a predominantly black jury. Again, there is no one-to-one association; predominantly black juries convict black defendants and acquit white defendants all the time, and predominantly white juries acquit black defendants and convict white defendants as well. But to say that race doesn't matter at all blinks away reality—or at least that's what most experienced prosecutors and defense attorneys will tell you, when speaking off the record.

Prosecutors, who have wide discretion in choosing where a case will be tried, often consider the racial composition of the jury pool, along with other factors, in deciding the venue of a trial. That is simply a fact of life that few will dispute.

But when I made this factual point following Mueller's decision to impanel the District of Columbia grand jury, Congresswoman Maxine Waters (D-CA) called me a racist. This is what she said:

What he [Dershowitz] is saying is "all of those black people are there and they don't like Trump and so he's not going to get a fair trial and so they should take it out of that jurisdiction. It shouldn't be there to begin with." I don't like that, and I'm surprised that Alan Dershowitz is talking like that. We will not stand for it. We will push back against that because that is absolutely racist.

I responded as follows:

If I had said that race didn't matter, she'd have called me a racist. She throws around the term so loosely and so inappropriately, and it weakens her credibility just by calling everybody a racist by calling me a racist, when she calls real racists racists, nobody is going to believe her. . . . Race matters and Maxine Waters ought to know that. . . . Being black doesn't give you a license to call people racist any more than being Jewish gives you a license to call people anti-Semitic. So, she ought to understand that every criminal defense lawyer knows that race matters, ethnicity matters, political affiliation matters . . . she targeted me for no good reason; she ought to be ashamed of herself.

The man who taught me the most about the role of race in jury selection was my friend and colleague Johnnie Cochran, who would clearly have agreed with my point. Would Waters call Cochran a racist? I doubt it. When Cochran died in 2005, Maxine Waters introduced a bill in the House of Representatives proposing that Congress "honor Johnnie Cochran, Jr., for his service to the nation, his pioneering work as a lawyer, author, TV commentator, and philanthropist, and his personal integrity and professional excellence."

Following my dispute with Waters, I then participated in a radio debate with former Judge Nancy Gertner, an old friend. I asked her whether she thought that I was a racist, confident that she would say, "No." Instead, she said: "I refuse to answer on the grounds that it may tend to incriminate me."

If I were generous, I would believe she meant that if she answered the question honestly—that of course, I'm not a racist for having made a correct statement—she would have incriminated herself among her partisan friends. But listeners interpreted her equivocal statement to mean that I am a racist for saying to the media what I have heard her say many times: that the racial composition of a trial jury always matters.

In an opinion piece for *Cognoscenti*, Gertner later wrote that since a Trump-related trial would not involve race, the racial composition of the jury wouldn't matter because when it comes "to espionage and the selling of the presidency we are all Americans." It would follow from this argument that an all-white jury in Mississippi, composed of "all Americans," would be as fair to a black man charged with espionage as would a more diverse jury. Nonsense!

The National Association of Criminal Defense Lawyers—a group in which Gertner has been active—conducts seminars on "difficult topics," such as race in jury selection. Does she regard this as racist?

Joel Cohen—a prominent former prosecutor and current defense lawyer—offered a critique of some of my arguments, while acknowledging that what I have said is accurate:

"[A]ny prosecutor, holding a glass of wine in his hand—in vino veritas—who might seek indictments arising out of the current investigation, would acknowledge that he would prefer a trial jury made up of black Democrats, rather than white and perhaps Republicans. And where the indicting grand jury sits is where the trial will ultimately take place."

Cohen notes that prosecutors "often try to challenge black jurors potentially seated for a prosecution of a black defendant, believing a black juror would favor a black defendant (or a Jewish juror a Jewish defendant; a Russian juror—you get it)." He notes that while in 1986 the Supreme Court denounced this practice by prosecutors, this "old-school wisdom" still persists.

Reasonable people can disagree about whether Mueller took this "wisdom" into account in making this decision, and it is a fair subject for debate without name-calling. Cohen did this when he acknowledged that, while he disagrees with some of my arguments, I'm "not a racist. Period!" He aptly notes that the issues are nuanced, and that I am analyzing and appraising them as such: "[Dershowitz] is a commentator, and one willing (and inclined) to stick his neck out over controversial issues. And here, he is indeed speaking reality." Gertner could have said something similar.

Gertner's argument that I'm "irresponsible" because Mueller cannot respond is wrong. Grand jury secrecy does not prevent Mueller from explaining why he needed a second grand jury. I have heard Gertner criticize judges and prosecutors who could not respond.

If Hillary Clinton had been elected president and she were being investigated in Washington, and the prosecutor sought a second grand jury in Virginia, many of my Democratic friends would complain that moving the case from the overwhelmingly Democratic District of Columbia to more diverse Virginia would give the prosecutor an advantage. The double standard of people criticizing me for making an argument they would have made had the shoe been on the other foot should be obvious to everyone.

Flynn Plea Reveals Weakness,
Not Strength, of Mueller Probe[14]

The charge to which retired Lieutenant General Michael Flynn has pleaded guilty may tell us a great deal about the Robert Mueller investigation.

The first question is why did Flynn lie? People who lie to the FBI generally do so because, if they told the truth, they would be admitting to a crime. But the two conversations that Flynn falsely denied having were not criminal. He may have believed they were criminal, but if he did, he was wrong.

Consider his request to Sergey Kislyak, the Russian ambassador to the US, to delay or oppose a UN Security Council vote on an anti-Israel resolution that the outgoing Obama administration refused to veto. Not only was that request not criminal, it was the right thing to do.

President Obama's unilateral decision to change decades-long American policy by not vetoing a perniciously one-sided anti-Israel resolution was opposed by Congress and by most Americans. It was not good for America, for Israel, or for peace. It was done out of Obama's personal pique against Israeli Prime Minister Benjamin Netanyahu rather than on principle.

Many Americans of both parties, including me, urged the lame-duck Obama not to tie the hands of the president-elect by allowing the passage of a resolution that would make it more difficult to achieve a negotiated peace in the Mideast.

As the president-elect, Donald Trump was constitutionally and politically entitled to try to protect his ability to broker a fair peace between the Israelis and Palestinians by urging all members of the Security Council to vote against or delay the enactment of the resolution. The fact that such efforts to do the right thing did not succeed does not diminish the correctness of the effort. I wish it had succeeded. We would be in a better place today.

Some left-wing pundits, who know better, are trotting out the Logan Act, which, if it were the law, would prohibit private citizens (including presidents-elect) from negotiating with foreign governments. But this anachronistic law hasn't been used for more than two hundred years. Under the principle of desuetude—a legal doctrine that prohibits the selective resurrection of a statute that has not been used for many decades—it is dead-letter. [Moreover, the Logan Act is unconstitutional insofar as it prohibits the exercise of free speech.]

If it were good law, former Presidents Reagan and Carter would have been prosecuted: Reagan for negotiating with Iran's ayatollahs when he was president-elect, to delay releasing the American hostages until he was sworn in; Carter for advising Palestinian leader Yasser Arafat to reject former President Clinton's peace offer in 2000–2001.

Moreover, Jesse Jackson, Jane Fonda, Dennis Rodman, and others who have negotiated with North Korea and other rogue regimes would have gone to prison.

So, there was nothing criminal about Flynn's request of Kislyak, even if he were instructed to do so by higher-ups in the Trump transition team. The same is true of his discussions regarding sanctions. The president-elect is entitled to have different policies about sanctions and to have his transition team discuss them with Russian officials.

This is the way the *New York Times* has put it: "Mr. Flynn's discussions with Sergey I. Kislyak, the Russian ambassador, were part of a coordinated effort by Mr. Trump's aides to create foreign policy before they were in power, documents released as part of Mr. Flynn's plea agreement show. Their efforts undermined the existing policy of President Barack Obama and flouted a warning from a senior Obama administration official to stop meddling in foreign affairs before the inauguration."

If that characterization is accurate, it demonstrates conclusively that the Flynn conversations were political and not criminal. Flouting a warning from the Obama administration to stop meddling may be a political sin (though some would call it a political virtue), but it most assuredly is not a crime.

So why did Flynn lie about these conversations, and were his lies even material to Mueller's criminal investigation if they were not about crimes?

The second question is why did Mueller charge Flynn only with lying? The last thing a prosecutor ever wants to do is to charge a key witness with lying.

A witness such as Flynn who has admitted he lied—whether or not to cover up a crime—is a tainted witness who is unlikely to be believed by jurors who know he's made a deal to protect himself and his son. They will suspect that he is not only "singing for his supper," but that he may be "composing" as well—that is, telling the prosecutor what he wants to hear, even if it is exaggerated or flat-out false.

A "bought" witness knows that the "better" his testimony, the sweeter the deal he will get. That's why prosecutors postpone the sentencing until after the witness has testified, because experience has taught them that you can't "buy" a witness; you can only "rent" them for as long as you have the Sword of Damocles hanging over them.

So, despite the banner headlines calling the Flynn guilty plea a "thunderclap," I think it may be a show of weakness on the part of the Special Counsel rather than a sign of strength. So far, he has had to charge potential witnesses with crimes that bear little or no relationship to any possible crimes committed by current White House incumbents. Mueller would have much preferred to indict Flynn for conspiracy or some other crime directly involving other people, but he apparently lacks the evidence to do so.

I do not believe he will indict anyone under the Logan Act. If he were to do so, that would be unethical and irresponsible. Nor do I think he will charge President Trump with any crimes growing out of the president's exercise of his constitutional authority to fire the director of the FBI or to ask him not to prosecute Flynn.

The investigation will probably not end quickly, but it may end with not a thunderclap, but several whimpers.

Trump Doesn't Need to Fire Mueller—
Here's Why[15]

The Trump team is probably not going to seek to fire Special Counsel Robert Mueller. To do so would be to provoke Trump's crucial supporters in Congress. Instead, they seem to be seeking to discredit him and his investigation.

This is apparently designed to achieve two possible results: the first is to put pressure on the Special Counsel to lean over backward in order to avoid any accusation of bias against Trump and his team. Mueller cares deeply about his reputation for integrity and will want to emerge from this process with that reputation intact. Accordingly, he may err—consciously or unconsciously—in favor of Trump in close cases so that the public will regard him as unbiased and fair-minded.

This is a classic tactic used by lawyers, athletic coaches, businesspeople, and others in how they deal with decision-makers. The great Red Auerbach, former coach of the Boston Celtics, once told me that when he screams loudly at officials, he generally gets the next close call in his favor. I have heard the same from baseball managers regarding balls and strikes.

This is a somewhat risky strategy in the context of law, because attacking the decision-maker could also backfire. Whoever thinks about using this tactic should understand the particular decision-maker against whom it is directed. Mueller seems like an appropriate target because of his concern for his reputation for fairness.

Even if this tactic were not to work, the attack on Mueller gives the Trump team some legal weaponry in the event of an indictment or a recommendation for impeachment. If a significant portion of the country believes that the Special Counsel was unfair, this could help in legal proceedings before judges or jurors.

So, attacking Mueller may appear to be a win-win tactic for the team—certainly a lot better than firing Mueller. Fortunately for the Trump team,

Mueller has played into their hands by his sloppiness in conducting the investigation. He has been incautious with his choice of personnel—too many of them seem biased against Trump, not only by their backgrounds, but by their tweets and messages. As I have said, when you go after a president, you must be Caesar's wife—above suspicion or reproach. Mueller seems to be failing the Caesar's wife test. Moreover, the manner by which he acquired emails and other documents from the Trump transition team may raise some legal questions. The same may be true if he used the questionable dossier against Trump as a basis for securing warrants.

All in all, the Trump team is in a better position continuing to challenge Mueller than trying to get rid of him as the Special Counsel.

This is not a game, of course. Lives and liberty are at stake, but games-manship has always been part of our legal system, for better or worse.

Mueller can improve his situation in several ways. First, he should appoint an ethics expert to advise him—a former judge who is beyond reproach. Names like George Mitchell, Louie Freeh, and Justice David Souter come to mind. That advisor could assure him in going forward there will be no more embarrassing revelations of messages or emails that create the appearance, if not the reality, of bias. He must also be more careful in how he obtains evidence. The last thing he should do is give ammunition to defense attorneys to challenge his evidence-gathering methods.

In setting out this analysis, I am not taking sides. I am simply sharing my fifty years of experience as a criminal defense lawyer who has seen the criminal justice system up close, warts and all. As James Madison wrote in *The Federalist Papers*, No. 51, "Perhaps everyone will agree that if we were all angels, no state would be necessary, and if angels were the governors, they would require neither internal nor external constraints to ensure that they governed justly." Neither the Trump team nor the Mueller team are angels. They are human beings with human limitations. But an investigation of a president must be as close to angelic as any human endeavor can be. Otherwise the public will not have confidence in the results.

Desire to "Get Trump"
Risks Death of Civil Liberties[16]

Just as the first casualty of war is truth, so too, the first casualty of hyper-partisan politics is civil liberties. I've regretfully asserted in previous essays that many traditional civil libertarians have allowed their strong anti-Trump sentiments to erase their long-standing commitment to neutral civil liberties. They are so desperate to get President Trump that they are prepared to compromise the most basic due process rights. They forget the lesson of history that such compromises made against one's enemies are often used as precedents against one's friends.

In the play and movie *A Man For All Seasons*, Robert Bolt put the following words in the mouth of Sir Thomas More in response to Roper asking if he would give the devil the benefit of the law: "When the last law was down, and the devil turned round on you, where would you hide, Roper, the laws all being flat? This country's planted thick with laws from coast to coast—man's laws, not God's—and if you cut them down, and you're just the man to do it, do you really think you could stand upright in the winds that would blow then? Yes, I'd give the devil benefit of law, for my own safety's sake."

Today, fair-weather civil libertarians are unwilling to give President Trump, who they regard as the devil, the "benefit of law" and civil liberties. Consider the issue of criticizing Special Counsel Robert Mueller. Any criticism or even skepticism regarding Mueller's history is seen as motivated by a desire to help Trump.

Mueller was an assistant US attorney in Boston, the head of its criminal division, then head of the criminal division at the main Justice Department, and then FBI director during the most scandalous miscarriage of justice in the FBI's modern history. Four people were framed by the FBI in order to protect murderous gangsters working as FBI informers. An FBI agent, who is now in prison, was tipping off crime boss Whitey Bulger as to who might testify against him so that those individuals could be killed.

Those tips later enabled Bulger to escape and remain on the lam for sixteen years. What responsibility, if any, did Mueller—who was in key positions of authority and capable of preventing these horrible miscarriages— have in this sordid incident? No less a legal figure than Judge Mark Wolf, a former prosecutor who conducted extensive hearings about this entire mess, made the following findings:

> The files relating to the Wheeler murder, and the FBI's handling of them, exemplify recurring irregularities with regard to the preparation, maintenance, and production in this case of documents damaging to [Stephen] Flemmi and Bulger. First, there appears to be a pattern of false statements placed in Flemmi's informant file to divert attention from his possible crimes and/or FBI misconduct . . .
>
> Second, contrary to the FBI's usual policy and practice, all but one of the reports containing . . . allegations against Bulger and Flemmi were not indexed and placed in an investigative file referencing their names. Thus, those documents were not discoverable by a standard search of the FBI's indices . . . Third, when documents damaging to the FBI were found by the Bureau, they were in some instances not produced to the defendants or the court at the time required by the court's orders . . .

Judge Wolf also referenced what Mueller may or may not have known of two murders Bulger committed while acting as an FBI informer, writing:

> The source also claimed to have information that Bulger and Pat Nee had murdered Halloran and Bucky Barrett. The source subsequently said that there was an eyewitness to the Halloran shooting who might come forward, and elaborated, "There is a person named John, who claims he talked to Whitey and Nee as they sat in the car waiting for Halloran on Northern Avenue. He sits in a bar and talks about it. He saw the whole operation."

He continued, "The source added that the person providing the information to the source 'will be willing to talk to you soon.' On Feb. 3, 1988, Weld directed Keeney to have the information that he had received sent to the United States attorney in Boston, Frank McNamara, and to the strike force chief, Jeremiah O'Sullivan. Weld added, 'Both O'Sullivan and Bob Mueller are well aware of the history, and the information sounds good.'" Mueller at this time was assistant US attorney in Boston.

It is widely believed among Boston law enforcement observers that the FBI was not really looking for Bulger during the years that Mueller was its director and that the FBI was fearful about what Bulger would disclose about his relationship with agents over the years. It took a US Marshals officer to find Bulger, who was hiding in plain view in California.

Much of this and other details surrounding the scandal have been reported by Fox News and in other media accounts. Recently, Nancy Gertner, a former federal judge and civil libertarian, rushed to Mueller's defense in a *New York Times* opinion column, declaring "without equivocation" that Mueller had "no involvement" in the massive miscarriage of justice. Her evidence is the lack of evidence in the files.

Yet, no civil libertarian should place such great trust in government files, especially in light of Judge Wolf's findings. They should join my call for an objective investigation by the Justice Department's inspector general before they assure the public "without equivocation" that Mueller had absolutely "no involvement."

Moreover, new information has been uncovered suggesting that both Mueller and his deputy may have had a role in keeping the innocent defendants in prison. And Gertner herself, when she was a judge, characterized the position taken by the FBI as "chilling." Mueller was director of the FBI at that time.

But the "get Trump at any cost" partisans have rejected my call for an investigation out of fear that it may turn up information that might tarnish the image of the Special Counsel who is investigating Trump. Instead they criticize those of us who point out that Mueller was "at the center" of the Justice Department and FBI when this miscarriage of justice occurred.

All civil libertarians should want the truth about this sordid episode— and Mueller's possible role—regardless of its impact, if any, on the Trump investigation. Mueller, too, should welcome an objective investigation, which might eliminate any question about his role in this travesty. Yet, as I have written previously, for too many former civil libertarians, the hope of getting Trump trumps civil liberties.

It is ironic to see many right-wingers criticizing overreach by law enforcement, while many left-wingers now defend such overreaching. Hypocrisy and selective outrage abound, as neutral principles take a back seat. Conservatives used to say "a conservative is a liberal who has been mugged." I would respond that "a liberal is a conservative who is being audited or whose kid was busted for pot."

Today, a civil libertarian is a conservative whose candidate is being investigated, while a "law and order" type is a liberal who wants to see Trump charged or impeached. I am a liberal who voted against Trump but who insists that his civil liberties must be respected, for all of our sakes.

Does the President Have the Right to Expect Loyalty from His Attorney General?[17]

R ecent news reports describe the president chastising Attorney General Jeff Sessions for disloyalty. Critics insist that the president has the right to demand loyalty of every other member of his cabinet but not of the attorney general. The attorney general is different, these critics insist, because he is the chief law enforcement officer of the United States. The *Atlantic*'s David A. Graham, for example, criticized Trump's demand for unconditional "loyalty," saying that, "for Trump, there is only one loyalty: to the president himself. When his aides and staffers make the mistake of following any other principle—rule of law, standard ethics policies, US alliances—that might conflict with the principle of loyalty to Trump, the president becomes enraged."

Well, the issue is far more complex, especially when it comes to the office of attorney general. The complexity results from a fundamental mistake the Framers of our Constitution and legal system made at the founding of our nation. Most democracies divide the role of our attorney general into two distinct offices: the first, often called the minister of justice, is an advisor to the chief executive. His or her role is to be loyal to the president or prime minister. He or she serves at their will and is part of the governing executive. The president is absolutely entitled to demand complete loyalty from his minister of justice.

Then there is a second office, sometimes called director of public prosecution, chief prosecutor, or attorney general. That office, and the person who holds it, is supposed to be completely independent of the executive. Indeed, it is supposed to serve as a check on the executive. No chief executive is entitled to expect loyalty from the chief prosecutor, especially if that prosecutor is investigating him or his colleagues. The chief executive is entitled not to loyalty, but to independence, integrity, and fairness.

We are one of the few Western democracies that mistakenly merged these roles into one. Our attorney general is supposed to advise the president politically, as Sessions has done with regard to immigration reform and other matters. But at the same time, the attorney general is supposed to be the head law enforcement officer of the United States—the chief prosecutor. This conflation of roles inevitably creates a schizophrenic attorney general with conflicting loyalties and obligations. It is because of this inherent schizophrenia that our country has had to suffer the appointment of special counsel, independent prosecutors, and the like. I say "suffer" because even the strongest advocates of these artificial positions concede that they operate outside of the usual prosecutorial role. We wouldn't need them if we adopted the English or the Israeli approach, which totally separates the role of political advisor from the very different role of chief prosecutor. So, don't blame Trump alone for demanding loyalty from his attorney general. Every president expects that. John Kennedy appointed his brother; Ronald Reagan appointed his personal lawyer; Jimmy Carter appointed his close friend; and other presidents have appointed political loyalists precisely in order to be assured of complete loyalty.

The system should be changed. The Justice Department should be broken up into two completely separate agencies, with two separate heads: the minister of justice would be a loyal political advisor to the president and a member of his cabinet, while the director of public prosecution would be completely independent and not a member of the cabinet. This separation will not be easy to achieve. But it may be possible, without a constitutional amendment, if Congress and the courts have the will to do it.

The Supreme Court has held that the appointment of an independent prosecutor does not violate the constitutional separation of powers or infringe on the executive authority of the president. Under that controversial precedent, Congress may be empowered—though it is far from certain—to establish a permanent independent prosecutorial authority outside of the current Justice Department structure. The president would almost certainly still have to make the appointment of the permanent prosecutor, but it could be for a term of years that transcends any presidential incumbency. This was the idea behind the appointment and removal of the director of the FBI. Obviously, that did not prevent President Trump from firing Director Comey, but he did have to pay a heavy political price for that decision. The same would be true if a president fired the permanent prosecutor in a situation where he was investigating the president or his associates.

Under our constitutional structure there is no perfect cure for the mistake made by our founders in merging the two incompatible goals of the current attorney general: that of political advisor to the president and that of independent chief prosecutor. But we can perhaps improve the situation.

The Nunes FISA Memo Deserves More Investigation. Time for a Nonpartisan Commission[18]

T he memo made public by House Republicans on Friday, February 2, 2018, accusing the FBI and Justice Department of abusing their surveillance powers in investigating a former Trump campaign advisor constitutes probable cause for further investigation.

The memo purports to describe what is in the Foreign Intelligence Surveillance Act (FISA) application that resulted in wiretap warrants being issued against Republican operatives. It is, of course, a secondhand, hearsay account of what is actually in the application.

Democratic members of Congress have been quick to point out that they see matters differently and that the Republican memo leaves out salient information.

So, let the Democrats present their version, which will also be second-hand and hearsay. It will help to level the playing field, but it will not provide the American public with a firsthand look at what was presented to the FISA court. Subject to real needs of national security, the American public should see a redacted version of the actual FISA application so that we can judge for ourselves whether it unfairly omitted important facts, including the source of the so-called Steele Dossier, which made allegations of misconduct against the Trump campaign, and the credibility of its author, a former British spy.

The Republican memo standing alone raises some serious questions about the process by which the warrants were obtained from the FISA court. The Democratic memo, if it is forthcoming, may purport to answer some of those questions. But it will never be able to answer them definitely without an objective assessment of the actual FISA application itself.

This episode strengthens the view—expressed by me from day one of the investigation of Russian meddling in the 2016 presidential election—that the entire enterprise of appointing a special counsel was misguided. Instead, Congress should have created a nonpartisan commission of objective experts to investigate the entire issue of Russian involvement in the election and other claims made by either party about any unfairness surrounding it.

Nor are congressional committees an adequate substitute for a nonpartisan commission. Congressional committees by their very nature are highly partisan, as evidenced by the dueling accounts of the FISA application.

It's not too late for Congress to create such a commission, because the American public has lost faith in the objectivity of congressional committees. Many Americans, though certainly not all, have also lost faith in the investigation currently being conducted by Special Counsel Robert Mueller.

Mueller himself continues to be held in high regard by most Americans, but many of his underlings are widely regarded as partisan. In a presidential investigation, that is inexcusable.

Mueller did the right thing by reassigning FBI agent Peter Strzok after his anti-Trump communications with his girlfriend were revealed. But Strzok should have recused himself from the Clinton investigation based on his own knowledge of his bias against Trump.

The Republican memo just released should not be considered the last word on the issue. It is the opening salvo by Republicans. The Democrats are responding in kind. Both sides have partisan agendas. Now it is time for the American people to have their interests considered.

As Supreme Court Justice Louis Brandeis once put it: "Sunlight is the best disinfectant." The corollary is that overclassification keeps the infection spreading. Let the FISA application be declassified, with appropriate redactions, and let the public interest in the integrity of our law enforcement agencies be served.

Trump Is Right: The Special Counsel Should Never Have Been Appointed[19]

President Trump is right in saying that a special counsel should never have been appointed to investigate the so-called Russian connection. There was no evidence of any crime committed by the Trump administration. But there was plenty of evidence that Russian operatives had tried to interfere with the 2016 presidential election, and perhaps other elections, in the hope of destabilizing democracy. Yet appointing a special counsel to look for crimes, behind the closed doors of a grand jury, was precisely the wrong way to address this ongoing challenge to our democracy.

As I've said many times before, the right way would have been (and still is) to appoint a nonpartisan investigative commission, such as the one appointed following the terrorist attacks of 9/11, to conduct a broad and open investigation of the Russian involvement in our elections. This is what other democracies, such as Great Britain and Israel, do in response to systemic problems. The virtue of such a commission is precisely the nonpartisan credibility of its objective experts, who have no political stake in the outcome.

Such a commission could have informed the American public of what Russia did and how to prevent it from doing it again. It would not seek partisan benefit from its findings, the way congressional committees invariably do. Nor would it be searching for crimes in an effort to criminalize political sins, the way special counsels do to justify their existence and budget. Its only job would be to gather information and make recommendations.

The vice of a special counsel is that he is supposed to find crimes, and if he comes up empty-handed, after spending lots of taxpayer money, then he is deemed a failure. If he can't charge the designated target—in this case, the president—he must at least charge some of those close to the target, even if it is for crimes unrelated to the special counsel's core mandate. By indicting these low-hanging fruits, he shows that he is trying. Maybe those lesser defendants will flip and sing against higher-ups, but the problem is that the pressure to sing may cause certain defendants to "compose," meaning make up or enhance evidence in order to get a better deal for themselves.

In this case, the appointment of a special counsel has done more harm than good. It has politicized our justice system beyond repair. The FBI deputy director has been fired for leaking and lying. His testimony appears to be in conflict with that of the former FBI director as to whether the leaks were authorized. Messages by high-ranking FBI agents suggest strong bias against Trump. A tweet by the former CIA director reveals equally strong negative views of the president. Perhaps these revelations prove nothing more than that law enforcement and national security officials are human and hold political views like everyone else.

But these views are not supposed to influence their decisions. In our age of hyper-partisanship, the public has understandably lost confidence in the ability and willingness of our leaders to separate their political views from their law enforcement decisions. This is not all attributable to the appointment of the Special Counsel, but the criminalization of political differences on both sides of the aisle has certainly contributed to the atmosphere of distrust in our justice system.

The public has lost faith in the leadership of the Justice Department and the FBI. They don't trust congressional investigative committees. They don't know whom to believe when they hear conflicting accounts. There are leaks galore followed by denials of leaks. It's a total mess. And what do we have to show for it? Just a handful of low-level indictments based largely on alleged crimes that are either unrelated or only marginally related to Russia's attempt to influence our presidential election in 2016.

It's not too late to try to repair some of the damage done. Let Congress now appoint a nonpartisan commission to conduct a transparent investigation of Russia's efforts to influence our elections. Let the Special Counsel suspend his investigation until the nonpartisan commission issues its report. If the report identifies crimes and criminals, there will be time enough to indict and prosecute. Right now, we need the nonpartisan truth, because we aren't getting it from the Special Counsel.

Accountability, Civil Liberties,
and Michael Cohen

I believe that it is the special responsibility of decent conservatives and liberals alike to condemn and marginalize extremists and bigots from either side. This condemnation must be rightly directed to the offending party—such as toward the Nazi and KKK demonstrators in Charlottesville—as opposed to trying to evenhandedly condemn all parties as when President Trump condemned the same display of hatred, bigotry, and violence shown by demonstrators "on many sides."

Meanwhile, civil libertarians sit on the sidelines as President Trump and his allies have their Fourth and Sixth Amendment rights violated. Consider President Trump's lawyer, Michael Cohen, whose law office and hotel room were raided by FBI agents who may have seized material protected by lawyer-client privilege. I condemn the double standard of the American Civil Liberties Union that has turned from a neutral civil liberties organization to a left-wing, agenda-driven group that protects its contributors and constituents.

In the essays and transcript that follow, I explain that prosecutors and FBI agents create firewalls and taint teams to preclude privileged information from being used against the client in a criminal case. Instead, to protect privileged communications between lawyer and client, doctor and patient, priest and penitent, or husband and wife, I argue for judicial officers, trusted not to leak information, to accompany FBI agents on their raids. I am grateful that Judge Kimba Wood—who was my student back in the day—did appoint a former judge to serve as a taint monitor.

Finally, I point out what I call an epic battle for the soul and cooperation of Michael Cohen. On one side, prosecutors have an array of weapons at their disposal. On the other, the president has the power to pardon. What will ultimately happen can only be surmised at this point.

The President Has a Special Obligation to Condemn the Racist Right[20]

All decent Americans have an obligation to condemn the violent bigotry of the Nazi and KKK demonstrators in Charlottesville or wherever else they spew their poisonous and threatening rhetoric. But President Donald Trump has a special obligation to single out for condemnation, and distance himself from, individuals and groups that claim—even if falsely—to speak in his name, as the racist provocateurs in Charlottesville did.

David Duke, the notorious bigot, told reporters that white nationalists were working to "fulfill the promises of Donald Trump." Richard Spencer, the founder of the *Daily Stormer* (a not-so-coded homage to the Nazi publication *Der Stürmer*,) attributed the growth of the ultra-nationalist alt-right to the Trump presidency: "Obviously the alt-right has come very far in the past two years in terms of public exposure . . . is Donald Trump one of the major causes of that? Of course."

Trump initially responded as follows: "We must ALL be united and condemn all that hate stands for. There is no place for this kind of violence in America." But then, following the car ramming that killed a peaceful protester, President Trump made the following statement: "We condemn in the strongest possible terms this egregious display of hatred, bigotry, and violence on many sides—on many sides."

President Trump's inclusion of the words "violence on many sides"—which seemed improvised—suggested to some a moral equivalence between the Nazis and the KKK, on the one hand, and those protesting and resisting them, on the other hand. Trump denied that he was suggesting any such equivalence and subsequently made the following statement: "Racism is evil. And those who cause violence in its name are criminals and thugs, including KKK, Neo-Nazis, White Supremacists, and other hate groups, are repugnant to everything we hold dear as Americans. Those who spread violence in the name of bigotry strike at the very core of America."

But a day later, he seemed to double down on his attempt to be even-handed in his comments about the "many sides" of this conflict. He pointed to "very fine people on both sides," implying that Nazis and Klansmen could be "fine," because their protests were "very legal." Then he denounced "alt-left" groups that were "very, very violent." Once again, he blamed "both sides," and asked rhetorically, "what about the 'alt-left,' that as you say, came charging at the alt-right? Don't they have any semblance of guilt?"

David Duke immediately praised President Trump's condemnation of the "alt-left," thanking him "for your honesty & courage to tell the truth about #Charlottesville & condemn the leftist terrorists in BLM/Antifa."

Finally (though nothing this president ever tweets is final), President Trump praised the anti-racist "protestors in Boston who are speaking out against bigotry and hate."

It is against this background that the president's back-and-forth statements must be evaluated.

Even if it were true—and the evidence is to the contrary—that Black Lives Matter and Antifa were as blameworthy for Charlottesville as the Nazis and KKK, it would still be incumbent on President Trump to focus his condemnation especially on the violent racist right that claims to speak on his behalf. The hard-left—which does, in part, include some violent and bigoted elements—does not purport to speak on the president's behalf and does not claim to be trying to "fulfill the promises of Donald Trump." To the contrary, they oppose everything he stands for.

This situation poses a delicate dilemma for President Trump. He has denounced the ideology of the violent racists on the alt-right who claim to be acting in his name—not quickly or forcefully enough. And he has declared his opposition to "racism" and specifically to "those who cause violence in its name," who he has called "criminals" and "thugs." He specifically included within these categories the "KKK, Neo-Nazis, [and] White Supremacists," the very groups that purport to speak in his name.

Why is that not enough? Why should he not at the same time condemn the alt-left for its violence? These are reasonable questions that require nuanced answers. Let me try to provide some.

I have long believed that it is the special responsibility of decent conservatives to expose, condemn, and marginalize hard-right extremists and bigots. William Buckley showed the way when he refused to defend Patrick Buchanan against charges that what he had said amounted to anti-Semitism. Other decent conservatives followed Buckley's lead and marginalized anti-Semites and racists who expressed bigotry in the false name of conservatism.

I also believe that it is the special responsibility of decent liberals to do the same with regard to hard-left bigoted extremists. I must acknowledge, as a liberal, that we have not done as good a job as decent conservatives have done. Perhaps this is because hard-left extremists often march under banners of benevolence, whereas hard-right extremists tend not to hide their malevolence.

Consider, for example, Antifa, the radical hard-left group, some of whose members violently confronted the Nazis and Klansmen in Charlottesville. As reported by the *New York Times*, the organization comprises a "diverse collection of anarchists, communists, and socialists" with its "antecedents in Germany and Italy." According to the *Times*, "Its adherents express disdain for mainstream liberal politics" and support "direct action" by which they mean "using force and violence," rather than free speech and civil disobedience. Their leaders claim that violence is necessary because "it's full on war."

Nor is this merely rhetoric. On university campuses, particularly at Berkeley, "black-clad protestors, some of whom identified themselves as Antifa, smashed windows, threw gasoline bombs and broke into campus buildings, causing $100,000 in damage." They model themselves on the "Weathermen" of the 1970s, who were responsible for numerous acts of violence.

They claim to be using counterviolence in defense against the violence of Neo-Nazis and Klansmen, but that is not true. They also use violence to shut down speakers with whose worldviews they disagree; they include not only right-wing extremists, but also mainstream conservatives, moderate Zionists, and even some liberals. They reject dialogue in favor of intimidation, and force.

As a liberal, I will not give these hard-left violent bigots a pass. It is true that the Nazis and KKK are currently more dangerous in terms of physical violence than hard-left groups. (It is also true that the most violent groups by far are radical Islamic terrorists, who are not the targets of Antifa protests.) But the violence of the racist right (and radical jihadists) must not lead us to ignore the reality that Antifa and its radical allies pose real danger to the future of our nation, because of their increasing influence on university campuses where our future leaders are being educated. The recent events in Charlottesville and elsewhere have made them heroes among some mainstream liberals, who are willing to excuse their anti-liberal bigotry because they are on the barricades against fascism.

It's far too easy to self-righteously condemn your political enemies when they step (or leap) over the line to bigotry and violence. It's far more difficult to condemn those who share your wing, whether left or right, but who go too far. But that is what morality and decency require, as Buckley taught us.

So, President Trump must stop being evenhanded in his condemnations. He should focus his condemnation on extreme right-wing bigots who speak and act in his name and leave it to those of us on the left to focus our condemnation on left-wing extremists and bigots.

Enough with the Anti-Trump
McCarthyism!²¹

[Talia Lavin wrote an article accusing me of being a "Trump Jew" who should remember that as a Jew, I'm a "guest" in America. I responded.]

I don't know what is worse about Talia Lavin's article calling me a Trump Jew: is it her blatant McCarthyism or her insistence that Jews behave like "guests" in an alien country?

Let's begin with her mendacious McCarthyism: I am not a Trump Jew. I voted, campaigned, and contributed against Trump and for Hillary Clinton. I have criticized many of Trump's policies and statements. I am not his lawyer. I have never provided him with "legal advice."

I am doing what the ACLU is failing to do: defending the constitutional rights of all Americans, including this president's. I would be doing the same thing had Hillary Clinton been elected president and Republicans were trying to "lock her up."

When, as a student at Brooklyn College, I defended the right of communists to speak, McCarthyists called me a "Communist Jew." When I defended the right of Nazis to march in Skokie, McCarthyists called me a "Nazi Jew." When I defended unpopular criminal defendants, McCarthyists said I was a Jew who was complicit in murder. Associating an advocate of civil liberties with those whose liberties he advocates is the worst kind of McCarthyism.

What is even more disturbing is her *shanda fur di goyim* (shame in front of gentiles) mentality based on her father's belief that "you're just a guest in America."

In my book *Chutzpah,* written over twenty-five years ago, I lament the fact that many American Jews still regard themselves "as second-class citizens—as guests in another people's land. [They] obsess about what the 'real' Americans will think of [them] . . ." and "don't accept that we are entitled to first-class status in this diverse and heterogeneous democracy." Lavin seems to believe that Jews in America do not have first-class citizenship. In her America, Jews are not allowed to be supportive of a president or the party of which she (and I) disapprove. Lavin even goes so far to suggest their "herem— expulsion from the fold."

I will not allow Lavin to define what it means to be an American or a Jew. Although I have been a lifelong Democrat, I would never want to live in a country where Jews cannot be supportive of any political candidate or party they choose. That's what it means to have equal citizenship under the law, something Lavin seems to deny those Jews, who make her "experience a cringing sense of shame."

It is important that Israel remain a bipartisan issue, and this requires that Jews remain free to support any party or candidate of their choice without fear of offending our "hosts" or of being placed in "herem" by our fellow "guests."

Of course, there are Neo-Nazis in America today who would explicitly deny Jews the right to equal citizenship. Ironically, Lavin seems to be adopting language similar to that of *Der Stürmer* when she writes that "Trump has a tendency to surround himself with badly behaved Jews," making their Jewishness, no matter how significant or insignificant in their lives, their primary identifier.

As a first-class American and no one's "guest," I will act no differently from other Americans. I will continue to advocate what I believe, regardless of what *di goyim* or fearful Jewish "guests" like Lavin think.

Targeting Trump's Lawyer
Should Worry Us All[22]

I believe we would have been hearing more from civil libertarians—the American Civil Liberties Union, attorney groups, and privacy advocates—if the raid had been on Hillary Clinton's lawyer. I've described how many civil libertarians have remained silent about potential violations of President Trump's rights because they strongly disapprove of him and his policies. That is a serious mistake because these violations establish precedents that lie around like loaded guns capable of being aimed at other targets.

I have been widely attacked for defending the constitutional rights of a president I voted against. In our hyper-partisan age, everyone is expected to choose a side, either for or against Trump. But the essence of civil liberties is that they must be equally applicable to all. The silence of civil libertarians following the raid on Michael Cohen shows that we are losing that valuable neutrality.

What else does the raid tell us? It seems likely that Special Counsel Robert Mueller is bifurcating the investigation. He will keep control over matters relating to Russia, the campaign, and any possible obstruction, but he has handed over to the US attorney for the Southern District of New York any matters relating to Trump's personal and business affairs. Mueller will work hand in hand with the New York prosecutors, but they will be in charge of the other matters. If they manage to find prosecutable evidence against Trump's lawyer, they may try to squeeze him into cooperating against his client.

It is doubtful that Cohen would cooperate, even if he has anything on his client. But prosecutors often try to get lawyers to "sing" against their clients—to become "canaries"—in order to save their own feathers. Some flipped witnesses will tell prosecutors anything they want to hear in order to earn a "get out of jail free card." They know that the "better" their story, the more leniency they will earn. So, in addition to singing, they "compose" by making up incriminating details.

I have seen this on many occasions. Mueller has already apparently flipped several witnesses, but Cohen would be his biggest catch in the unlikely event he could be induced to turn against his client. So, stay tuned to this unfolding drama, but remember that prosecutorial tactics used today against President Trump may tomorrow be used against Democrats—and even against you.

For ACLU,
Getting Trump Trumps Civil Liberties[23]

The American Civil Liberties Union, on whose national board I used to serve with pride, raises vast sums of money claiming to defend the civil liberties of all Americans. Unfortunately, however, over the last several years it has turned from being a neutral civil liberties organization to a left-wing, agenda-driven group that protects its contributors and constituents while ignoring the civil liberties of Americans with whom it disagrees.

Sure, it occasionally defends a Nazi or a Klansman as an easy, pretend show of its willingness to protect the free speech of the most despicable racists. But it has been scandalously silent when it comes to the real current threats to civil liberties and free speech, especially on university campuses where the hard-left demands suspension of free speech and due process rights for those with whom it disagrees.

Now, since the election of President Trump, it has sunk to a new low, becoming a cheerleader for the violation of the civil liberties of those on the other side of the political spectrum. Consider the recent raid on the law office and hotel room of Donald Trump's lawyer, Michael Cohen. In that raid, it appears as if FBI agents may well have seized material protected by the lawyer-client privilege, including communications between President Trump and his attorney. On the day of the raid, I said that if a similar raid had been conducted on Hillary Clinton, had she been elected and a special prosecutor appointed to investigate her emails, the ACLU would have been up in arms. I condemned its doubled-standard silence.

When I said that, I couldn't possibly imagine that the ACLU would actually go out of its way to justify and defend the raid, even before all the facts were known. But that is exactly what it has done. David Cole, who identifies himself as the ACLU legal director, said the organization relies on the good faith of the Justice Department, the FBI, and the judge who issued the warrant to assure all Americans that this raid on a lawyer's office is a "sign that the rule of law is alive."

The ACLU acknowledges that material covered by the lawyer-client privilege will be shown to a "privilege team," sometimes called a "firewall" or "taint team." This team consists of FBI agents and government lawyers who will get to read communications between lawyers and clients that are privileged and not subject to any exceptions. They will then turn over to prosecutors only those communications that are not privileged, but these government agents will have read communications that are privileged. It is enough for the ACLU that these privileged communications will not be used in a criminal case against the client. But the ACLU does not discuss the violations of the Fourth and Sixth Amendments that occur as soon as government agents read communications that were supposed to be protected by those constitutional amendments.

Imagine that the search was of your lawyer's office, or your doctor's office, or your spouse's computer, or the rectory of your priest. Imagine that government agents got to read the most intimate, privileged communications between you, your lawyer, your doctor, your spouse, or your priest. Would it be enough that the government (and the ACLU) told you that the information wouldn't be used in a criminal case against you? Would you believe that your civil liberties had been violated as soon as government agents read this material? Would you trust government agents not to leak embarrassing information about your conversations, especially if you were a controversial public figure?

The ACLU does not address any of these questions because the person whose lawyer's office was searched was Donald Trump. Virtually every contributor to the ACLU voted against Trump, as I did. It is understandable in our hyper-partisan age that many Democrats, liberals, and leftists are so outraged at President Trump that they are willing to ignore violations of his civil liberties, even if these violations establish a precedent for future use against all Americans. It is inexcusable that the ACLU should ignore these potentially blatant violations of the right of privacy under the Fourth Amendment, the right to counsel and confidentiality under the Sixth Amendment. But for the ACLU, getting Trump trumps civil liberties.

It is precisely because the ACLU has abandoned its role as a neutral defender of civil liberties that I have had to speak up so loudly and repeatedly in opposition to the criminalization of political differences and to the violation of President Trump's civil liberties. I wish I didn't have to, but the hyper-partisan nature of American life—reflected by the ACLU's decision to justify potential intrusions into Trump's Fourth and Sixth Amendment rights—makes it necessary for someone to take over the traditional role of the ACLU. I hope others, both Democrats and Republicans, liberals and conservatives, will join me in protecting the civil liberties of all Americans.

The Final Nail in the ACLU's Coffin

The director of the American Civil Liberties Union (ACLU) has now acknowledged what should have been obvious to everybody over the past several years: that the ACLU is no longer a neutral defender of everyone's civil liberties, and it has morphed into a hyper-partisan, hard-left political advocacy group. The final nail in its coffin was the announcement that, for the first time in its history, the ACLU would become involved in partisan electoral politics, supporting candidates, referenda, and other agenda-driven political goals.

The headline in the June 8, 2018 edition of the *New Yorker* tells it all: "The ACLU is getting involved in elections—and reinventing itself for the Trump era." The article continues:

> In this midterm year, however, as progressive groups have mushroomed and grown more active, and as liberal billionaires such as Howard Schultz and Tom Steyer have begun to imagine themselves as political heroes and eye presidential runs, the ACLU, itself newly flush, has begun to move in step with the times. For the first time in its history, the ACLU is taking an active role in elections. The group has plans to spend more than twenty-five million dollars on races and ballot initiatives by Election Day in November.

Since its establishment nearly a hundred years ago, the ACLU has been, in the words of the *New Yorker*, "Fastidiously nonpartisan, so prudish about any alliance with any political power that its leadership, in the 1980s and '90s, declined even to give awards to likeminded legislators for fear that it might give the wrong impression." I know because I served on its national board in the early days of my own career. In those days, the board consisted of individuals who were deeply committed to core civil liberties, especially freedom of speech, opposition to prosecutorial overreach, and political equality. Its board members included Republicans and Democrats, conservatives and liberals, right-wingers and left-wingers—all of whom supported neutral civil liberties. The key test in those days was what I have come to call "the shoe on the other foot" test: would you vote the same way if the shoe were on the other foot—that is, if the party labels were switched?

Today, the ACLU wears only one shoe and it is on its left foot. Its color is blue. And the only dispute is whether it supports the progressive wing of the Democratic Party or its more centrist wing. There is little doubt that most board members today support the progressive wing, though some think that even that wing is not sufficiently left. There is no longer any room in the ACLU for true conservatives who are deeply committed to neutral civil liberties. The litmus test is support for hard-left policies.

To be sure, the ACLU will still occasionally take a high-profile case involving a Nazi or Klan member who has been denied freedom of speech, though there are now some on the board who would oppose supporting such right-wing extremists. But the core mission of the ACLU—and its financial priority—is now to promote its left-wing agenda in litigation, in public commentary, and in elections.

If you want to know the reason for this shift, just follow the money. ACLU contributors, including some of its most generous ones, are strong anti-Trump zealots who believe that the end (getting rid of Trump) justifies any means (including denying Trump and his associates core civil liberties and due process).

Anthony Romero, the current radical leftist who directs the ACLU, refers to those of us who favor the ACLU's traditional mission as "the old guard." The leading critic of the ACLU's newfound partisan mission is Romero's predecessor, Ira Glasser, who was the executive director of the ACLU from 1978 until 2001. Glasser believes that this transformation in the way the ACLU has operated since 1920 "has the capacity to destroy the organization as it has always existed." Glasser points out that some of the greatest violations of civil liberties throughout history have come from "progressive politicians, such as President Franklin D. Roosevelt, who interned 110,000 Japanese-American citizens." He worries, and I worry, that when the ACLU supports candidates' parties and partisan agendas, it will become less willing to criticize those whom it has supported when they violate civil liberties.

The presidency of Donald Trump has introduced a new dynamic. Trump himself has denied fundamental civil liberties by his immigration policies, his attitude, his actions regarding the press, and his calls for criminal investigations of his political enemies. The ACLU will criticize those actions, as it should. But the Trump presidency has also pushed the ACLU further to the left and into partisan politics. President Trump is so despised by contributors to the ACLU that they have increased their contributions—but also demanded that the ACLU be on the forefront of ending the Trump presidency, either through impeachment, criminal prosecution, or electoral defeat.

The move of the ACLU to the hard-left reflects an even more dangerous and more general trend in the United States: the right is moving further right, the left is moving further left, and the center is shrinking. The center left is losing its influence in organizations like the ACLU, and the center right is losing its influence in conservative organizations. America has always thrived at the center and has always suffered when extremes gain power. The ACLU's move from the neutral protector of civil liberties to a partisan advocate of hard-left politics is both a symptom and consequence of this change. If America is to remain strong, its major institutions must move closer to the center and reject the extremes of both sides. If the ACLU does not return to its core values, a new organization must be created to champion those values.

"Firewalls" and "Taint Teams" Do Not Protect Fourth and Sixth Amendment Rights—We Need a New Law to Protect Lawyer-Client Communications[24, 25]

Many TV pundits are telling viewers not to worry about the government's intrusion into possible lawyer/client privileged communications between President Trump and his lawyer, since prosecutors will not get to see or use any privileged material. This is because prosecutors and FBI agents create firewalls and taint teams to preclude privileged information from being used against the client in a criminal case. But that analysis completely misses the point and ignores the distinction between the Fifth Amendment on the one hand and the Fourth and Sixth Amendments on the other.

The Fifth Amendment is an exclusionary rule. By its terms, it prevents material obtained in violation of the privilege of self-incrimination from being used to incriminate a defendant—that is, to convict him of a crime. But the Fourth and Sixth Amendments provide far broader protections: they prohibit government officials from intruding on the privacy of lawyer/client confidential rights of citizens. In other words, if the government improperly seizes private or privileged material, the violation has already occurred, even if the government never uses the material from the person from whom it was seized.

Not surprisingly, therefore, firewalls and taint teams were developed in the context of the Fifth Amendment, not the Fourth or Sixth Amendments. Remember who composes the firewall and taint teams: other FBI agents, prosecutors, and government officials who have no right under the Fourth and Sixth Amendments even to see private or confidential materials, regardless of whether they are ever used against a defendant. The very fact that this material is seen or read by a government official constitutes a core violation. It would be the same if the government surreptitiously recorded a confession of a penitent to a priest, or a description of symptoms by a patient to a doctor, or a discussion of their sex life between a husband and wife. The government simply has no right to this material, whether it ever uses it against the penitent or the patient or the spouse in a criminal case.

So, let's not dismiss the potential violation of the rights of Michael Cohen and his client if it were to turn out that included among the materials seized by the government in the raid were private or confidential information or documents.

The recourses for intrusions on the Fourth and Sixth Amendments are multifold: the victim of the intrusion can sue for damages; he or she can exclude it from use by the government in criminal or civil cases; or the victim can demand the material back. But none of these remedies undo the harm to privacy and confidentiality done to the citizen by the government's intrusion into his private and confidential affairs.

An equally important harm is to important relationships that are protected by the law: between lawyer and client, priest and penitent, doctor and patient, husband and wife, etc. If an ordinary citizen, seeing that even the president's confidential communications with his lawyer can be seized and perused, he or she will be far less willing to engage in such communications. As a society, we value such communications; that is why our laws protect them, and that is why it should be extremely difficult for the government to intrude upon them except as a last recourse in extremely important cases.

From what we know, this case does not meet those stringent standards. Much of the material sought by the warrant could probably be obtained through other sources, such as bank, tax, and other records that are subject to subpoena. Moreover, the alleged crimes at issue—highly technical violations of banking and election laws—would not seem to warrant the extreme measure of a highly publicized search and seizure of records that may well include some that are subject to the lawyer/client privilege.

Someday soon, the government is going to have to justify its decision to conduct this raid. I challenge any reader who is not concerned about this raid to honestly answer the following question: If the raid had been conducted on Hillary Clinton's lawyer's office and home, would you be as unconcerned? The truth, now!

This episode dramatically demonstrates the need for new legislation to ensure that no FBI agents or US attorneys ever get to read privileged, personal communications. There is a better and safer way to deal with this issue than the current approach of using prosecutors and FBI agents to do the sifting.

A law should be enacted under which anytime the government is seeking to search an office or home that may contain confidential and privileged information, the search team must be accompanied by a judicial officer—a judge, a magistrate, or someone appointed to fulfill that function.

That judicial officer should be the only one ever to read material that is eventually deemed to be confidential. A judge can be trusted not to leak far better than FBI agents or prosecutors. If a judge were to leak, it would be easy to identify the source of the unlawful disclosure, since the single judge would be the only one to have access to the confidential material.

This procedure might be somewhat more cumbersome and expensive than the current "taint team" approach, but it would provide much better safeguards to the fundamental rights that we as Americans possess. The taint team could be retained in the context for which it was originally developed, which is to prevent potential violations of the Fifth Amendment by the use of immunized self-incriminating testimony. Taint teams should never be used in the context of the Fourth or Sixth Amendments because the privacy and confidentiality at stake there is very different than that at stake under the Fifth Amendment.

The Fifth Amendment merely prohibits the use of illegally obtained self-incriminatory information at the defendant's criminal trial. The Fourth Amendment prohibits unlawful intrusions into the privacy of any American, and the Sixth Amendment implicitly prohibits violations of the lawyer-client privilege. Such violations occur the moment private or confidential information is viewed by government agents, regardless whether it is ultimately used in a criminal trial.

When I proposed this new law on CNN, legal analyst Jeffrey Toobin responded that lawyers, doctors, penitents, and spouses are not above the law, and if there is probable cause to believe they may have committed a crime, it should be permissible to search their records without the direct supervision of a judge. But with due respect to my former student, that answer misses the point.

The focus of my proposed law is not on the privacy rights of guilty lawyers, doctors, priests, and spouses. Its focus is on the privacy and confidentiality rights of their innocent clients, patients, penitents, and spouses. The proposed law is intended to protect the rights of these innocent bystanders. The legitimate confidentiality right of innocent people must be given priority over any inconvenience that might be caused by requiring a judge to be the one to filter out protected communications.

My proposed law would not prevent the government from seizing incriminating evidence from guilty lawyers, doctors, priests, or spouses, so long as the evidence was not covered by a legitimate privilege. It would put prosecutors in the same position they are in today: They would not be able to use information that was ultimately deemed to be privileged. But it would protect the innocent clients, patients, penitents, and spouses from having their private and confidential information reviewed by FBI agents and prosecutors who might well leak the information or misuse it in other ways.

Congress should seriously consider enacting such a law—not to help Donald Trump, but to protect the constitutional rights of all Americans whose private and confidential communications are now reviewed by taint teams comprising FBI agents and prosecutors. All Americans should support this reasonable protection. (And there is precedent—Judge Kimba Wood appointed a former judge to serve as a "Taint" monitor.)

The Sword of Damocles[26]

From an April 2018 appearance on This Week *with George Stephanopoulos, including Mimi Rocah of Pace Law School and ABC Chief Legal Analyst Dan Abrams.*

GEORGE STEPHANOPOULOS: Welcome to all of you. Professor Dershowitz, let me begin with you. The president is clearly agitated by all of this pressure on Michael Cohen. He also called the raid on Cohen an attack on our country. After those raids, how serious is the threat to Cohen and Trump?

DERSHOWITZ: Oh, it's a very serious threat. This is an epic battle for the soul and cooperation of Michael Cohen. And prosecutors have enormous weapons at their disposal. They can threaten essentially with life imprisonment. They can threaten his parents. They can threaten his spouse. They have these enormous abilities to really put pressure and coerce a witness.

On the other hand, the president has a unique weapon that no other criminal defendant or suspect ever has: he has the pardon power. And go back to Christmas 1992 when President Bush exercised that pardon power and pardoned Caspar Weinberger, precluding him from pointing the finger at him.

GEORGE STEPHANOPOULOS: Put a lot on the table right there. We'll get to each of it in terms—I mean, I've got to go to you first because I saw you sort of squinting as Professor Dershowitz was talking about all those threats the prosecutors can make.

MIMI ROCAH, CRIMINAL JUSTICE FELLOW, PACE LAW SCHOOL: Yes. I have a response to that. You know, look, that's not what prosecutors do in my experience, having been one for sixteen-and-a-half years and having, you know, worked with many of them across different districts, including New York.

They do not threaten people's parents and children. I mean, I just—I don't know, it sounds good but I don't know where that accusation is coming from.

DERSHOWITZ: Do you want some examples?

ROCAH: But, if I could, what they do with cooperators is, especially a cooperator like Michael Cohen, they don't trust him to begin with. They don't just take what he says and write it down. They listen to what he says. They're skeptical. They test it against other evidence. They try to corroborate it. They don't just take at face value what a cooperator says.

STEPHANOPOULOS: So you don't get a deal until you're certain, or certain as you can be, that the potential cooperator is telling the truth.

ROCAH: Absolutely. Absolutely.

DERSHOWITZ: Absolutely not.

DAN ABRAMS: Let's be clear, though, about this issue of cooperating, right? He can't cooperate on attorney-client matters, right? The president could invoke the privilege and say, "He's not allowed to talk about private conversations that we had as attorney-client."

STEPHANOPOULOS: Separate from business matters.

ABRAMS: Correct, correct, correct. But my point is there are going to be—everyone is sort of presuming that Michael Cohen could just flip on everything. He could just turn the president in if he decided to do that. If he decides to cooperate, there are going to be a lot of questions as to what he is actually allowed to disclose, when was he the attorney, when was he not the attorney, et cetera.

And I think—I still think it's unlikely that he is going to flip on him. I think—one of the things that struck me, and this is kind of a media thing, is immediately after the raid, Michael Cohen made phone calls to various mainstream media people. And it struck me that, gosh, for a team that shows such disdain for the mainstream media, why call these sorts of big figures in the mainstream media if—you know, if that's the position . . .

STEPHANOPOULOS: Well, Michael Cohen has always had deep ties to the . . .

ABRAMS: Yes, he has.

STEPHANOPOULOS: There's no question about that.

DERSHOWITZ: . . . this stuff matters and it doesn't matter whether he likes the president or doesn't like the president. What matters is the Sword of Damocles hanging over his head. Michael Milken, they told him they were going to indict his brother unless he pleaded guilty. Jonathan Pollard, they told him they were going to indict his wife. I can go down case after case after case . . .

ROCAH: But that may be . . .

DERSHOWITZ: . . . where the prosecutors . . .

ROCAH: . . . involved in criminal activity.

DERSHOWITZ: Well, of course, that's the point. The point . . .

ROCAH: But to say that the government threatens people's relatives with the . . .

DERSHOWITZ: I didn't say no basis. I said they threaten relatives and then they create the basis. They wouldn't otherwise go after these people. But they hold these people hostage. That's what prosecutors do. Every defense attorney knows that. And to look in the camera and say that prosecutors don't threaten relatives is to mislead the American public. Sorry.

ROCAH: I disagree, obviously. But the other point is that, you know, cooperators—I just have to keep coming back to this. It's—they're not going to just take what he says at face value. They're going to test it. It's not going to be a case written down what Michael Cohen says.

STEPHANOPOULOS: They already have some documents.

ROCAH: Correct. They have lots of evidence. We know that because they got a search warrant. And the search warrant, you know, was based on probable cause to believe that . . .

ABRAMS: But against Michael Cohen. I mean, we keep lumping in Cohen and Trump.

STEPHANOPOULOS: That's actually where we should be (INAUDIBLE) right now. The point is that Michael Cohen is now under serious threat. He has had this raid. We've even had the judge in the Stormy Daniels case say that it's very possible, if not likely, he's going to get indicted. We've seen another attorney he worked with flip as well.

After a raid like this, the chances of indictment are quite high.

ABRAMS: Very high. Very high that he's going to be indicted. But we have to separate out the two. They got a warrant here not because there was information on Donald Trump that they wanted from Michael Cohen. They got the warrant because there was information on Michael Cohen potentially committing a crime.

DERSHOWITZ: And if you believe that I have a bridge . . .

ABRAMS: So, you're actually going to say that a judge signed off on a warrant . . .

DERSHOWITZ: Absolutely.

ABRAMS: . . . to get to . . .

DERSHOWITZ: You can get judges to sign off on warrants like Christmas presents.

ABRAMS: To get information on his client? So, they signed off on a warrant saying, we want information on his client, not on him?

DERSHOWITZ: There's no way in which they would go after Michael Cohen if they weren't interested in his client. They're interested in his client in two different ways. Number one . . .

ABRAMS: Because there's no way he could have committed a crime by himself.

DERSHOWITZ: He might have. But they wouldn't have even looked at what he was doing if he weren't the president's lawyer. They're going after him for two reasons: one, to try to flip him, and two, to try to find information that would show that there is an exception to the lawyer-client privilege under the crime fraud.

You know, if you're going to . . .

ABRAMS: Who's the "they," by the way?

DERSHOWITZ: The prosecutors.

ABRAMS: Well, which prosecutor?

DERSHOWITZ: The Southern District of New York.

ABRAMS: OK. So, it's not Mueller's team now.

DERSHOWITZ: They're working together. If they weren't working together, then Sessions would be back on the case because he only recused himself . . .

ABRAMS: In theory.

DERSHOWITZ: . . . from the Russia investigation. If these were separate investigations . . .

ABRAMS: So, there's no such thing as independent work on the part . . .

DERSHOWITZ: Not in this case.

ABRAMS: So, and in the District of Columbia, when they're investigating McCabe, that, too, is going to be hand in hand?

DERSHOWITZ: Absolutely. Of course, they're all working close together to try to target the president or people close to him. That's what's . . .

STEPHANOPOULOS: I wanted to get . . .

STEPHANOPOULOS: Hold on a second. What is the significance of moving it to the Southern District? Does that somehow protect the investigation if the president chooses to move against Rosenstein or Mueller?

ROCAH: I think it would have that effect of protecting it. But I don't think that's why it was done, necessarily. I mean, obviously, I'm not in

Mueller's head. I think it was done because Mueller did what any prosecutor and investigator should do, came across criminal activity about apparently Michael Cohen. And we know that from the search warrant.

And what's he supposed to do, sweep it under the rug? No. And it doesn't fall within the mandate of what he's looking at. So, he did the absolute appropriate thing, which is referred it to a US Attorney's office.

DERSHOWITZ: This is so naive. Mueller is looking for low-hanging fruit. He's looking for anything . . .

ROCAH: That's what's called investigating.

DERSHOWITZ: . . . he can find against anybody who is associated with the president so he can flip them . . .

STEPHANOPOULOS: But if it weren't there it wouldn't be a problem.

DERSHOWITZ: Of course. But it's there—you know, crime—broad federal criminal statutes, campaign contributions, bank records, you can find them against almost every very complex business person or political person. The question is how hard you look. And when you look hard, you have enough for a search warrant, which is fairly minimal. And then the pressure increases.

STEPHANOPOULOS: Let me bring up the issue that Alan brought up earlier, the issue of a pardon. Again, the significance of that, one of the things that people have speculated about, it moved to the Southern District, if, indeed, Michael Cohen is pardoned either preemptively or after the fact by President Trump, this could move over into state court.

ABRAMS: It could but, see, I think people are assuming that it would be pretty easy to prosecute in New York State court, for example, on the same set of facts. It wouldn't. First of all, in New York State there is a specific prohibition against trying someone for the same facts as they were indicted for in a federal court.

DERSHOWITZ: And they're trying to get rid of that now.

ABRAMS: They are trying to get rid of it, but it's still the law in New York State as of today. So, I think those who are counting on the state courts to kind of come in on the white horse and prosecute anyone that Trump pardons are betting on the wrong horse, so to speak.

It is not easy. And in New York, it's specifically prohibited.

STEPHANOPOULOS: So, a pardon could be real protection for Michael Cohen.

ROCAH: It could. And I think the president is trying to use that. I mean, he keeps tweeting about it. I think these tweets and these phone calls to Michael Cohen, you know, the president should not be doing that. This is a witness in a case who at least potentially has information about the president. And that is just not something you should be doing with a . . .

STEPHANOPOULOS: Any danger at all, these tweets, on that point, build up a possible obstruction case?

DERSHOWITZ: I don't think so. I don't think so. When you get the president of the United States, George H. W. Bush, pardoning, and the Special Prosecutor saying the following, in light of President Bush's own misconduct, we are greatly concerned about his decision to pardon others who lied to Congress and obstructed official investigations.

That, it seems to me, makes it clear you can't go after a president for exercising a pardon. Look, there's another vulnerability in a pardon. You pardon somebody, he doesn't have a Fifth Amendment. So as soon as you pardon him, he doesn't need immunity. You call him as a witness. And he has to testify or else he goes to jail. Then the president has to pardon him for contempt. And it becomes very, very different for a president.

STEPHANOPOULOS: We're just about out of time. Before we all go, let me get your best judgment right now. Do you think Michael Cohen flips?

DERSHOWITZ: I think it's very hard not to flip when they're threatening you with long, long imprisonment. But I don't think we know the answer to that question. I don't know enough about Michael Cohen.

ABRAMS: I don't think he flips.

ROCAH: I think he flips because I think he committed a lot of crimes, and he has got a lot of jail time that he's facing for that reason.

ABRAMS: I think he's going to be pardoned. I think he feels confident about that.

STEPHANOPOULOS: Pardon?

DERSHOWITZ: I don't think he's going to be pardoned.

The Epic Struggle for Michael Cohen's Soul and Testimony[27]

There is an epic battle for the soul, cooperation, and testimony of Donald Trump's lawyer, Michael Cohen, whose office was recently searched by federal authorities. Prosecutors are almost certainly trying to flip him—that is, turn him against his client and into a cooperating government witness. The president's lawyers certainly would prefer him to remain loyal to his client, either by testifying in his favor or invoking his Fifth Amendment privilege to remain silent.

Each side has powerful weapons. Prosecutors can threaten him with double-digit prison sentences, while President Trump has the constitutional power to pardon him, either before or after trial. This struggle illustrates one of the most disturbing disparities in our criminal justice system. Under current law, prosecutors can threaten Cohen with life imprisonment unless he cooperates with them. Prosecutors have been known to threaten parents, siblings, spouses, and even children unless the recalcitrant witness agrees to testify for the government.

I have seen such threats in many cases, including those of Michael Milken and Jonathan Pollard. In one case in which I was counsel, prosecutors threatened to go after my client's twenty-four-year-old son, who was about to graduate from Columbia Law School. In the current investigation, the Special Counsel threatened to prosecute the son of former national security advisor Michael Flynn, unless he cooperated.

Of course, prosecutors need some basis for threatening relatives, in the form of some possible wrongdoing on their part. But often it's minimal, as evidenced by the fact that they end the threat if the cooperation is obtained. Not surprisingly, these threats often work. Not only do they get flipped witnesses to "sing," they often get them to "compose," that is to embellish, elaborate, or even make up incriminating stories. These threatened witnesses know that the better the story, the sweeter the deal.

I am not suggesting that prosecutors or FBI agents deliberately suborn perjury (though some do), but rather that the Sword of Damocles hanging over the heads of flipped witnesses incentivizes them sometimes to compose. There are few limits to what a prosecutor or FBI agent can do to coerce a reluctant witness to give the government what it wants. There are cases in which government agents have threatened to send a reluctant witness to a prison where he will be raped by other inmates.

There are other cases in which the government pays enormous sums of money to get a witness to testify. There is at least one case in which the government offered the witness a contingent-fee bonus if his testimony resulted in a conviction. None of this is regarded by current law as tampering with a witness or obstruction of justice if done by law enforcement officials. Contrast that with what a defendant and his lawyer can and cannot do to a potential witness. They can't do anything without running afoul of the law. Unlike the president, ordinary defendants cannot pardon potential witnesses, nor can they replicate coercive tactics used by the prosecutors and FBI agents.

If a defendant who believes that a potential witness is about to lie simply asks the witness to tell the truth, the defendant can be charged with obstruction. If he merely advises the witness that he has the Fifth Amendment right not to testify, he can also be charged with obstruction of justice. If he offers the witness a single penny to testify truthfully in his behalf, he is tampering with a witness. The law says that a witness, in theory, belongs to neither side—every witness belongs only to "the truth"—but in practice, witnesses are owned lock, stock, and barrel by the prosecution. They can be bought, rented, coerced, threatened, and then thrown away like a rotten piece of fish.

Why does this disparity exist in the law today? For several reasons. First, prosecutors and former prosecutors who serve in legislatures get to write the laws, and former prosecutors who serve as judges get to interpret them, so the criminal justice system ends up heavily skewed in favor of prosecutors. Second, the system trusts prosecutors more than defense attorneys to serve the interest of truth. Third, many of these flipped witnesses are former associates of the target or subject, and they won't testify against their friends unless pressured or coerced to do so.

These may be understandable reasons, but the effect of the disparate rules is to give prosecutors enormous leverage over potential witnesses.

The ordinary citizen has no comparable leverage. Even the president's lever-age—the power to pardon—is limited. If President Trump were to pardon Cohen, the latter could be called as a witness, and Cohen would probably not be able to invoke his privilege against self-incrimination. Moreover, there are those who argue that a president could be charged with obstruction of justice if he pardoned a potential witness in order to get him to not testify against him.

I disagree. Again I will refer to President George H. W. Bush, who did precisely that: he pardoned Caspar Weinberger and five other defendants on the eve of their trials. Yet no one suggested charging President Bush with obstruction of justice. It is impossible to predict at this time whether Cohen will flip with so many variables. What, if anything, do they have on Cohen? What, if anything, does Cohen have on President Trump? How loyal is Cohen? Does he believe he will be pardoned if he refuses to cooperate? One conclusion is clear: prosecutors have the upper hand in this epic battle.

Federal Judge Rightly Rebukes Mueller for Questionable Tactics[28]

An experienced federal judge has confirmed what I have been arguing for months: namely, that the *modus operandi* of the Special Counsel is to charge associates of President Trump with any crime he can find in order to squeeze them into turning against Trump. This is what Judge T. S. Ellis, III said at a hearing on Friday, May 4, 2018:

"You don't really care about Mr. Manafort's bank fraud. . . . What you really care about is what information Mr. Manafort could give you that would reflect on Mr. Trump or lead to his prosecution or impeachment."

This tactic is as old as Adam turning against Eve. But as the judge correctly pointed out, it risks the possibility that the squeezed witness will not only sing, he will compose! Here is what Ellis said about that:

"This vernacular to 'sing' is what prosecutors use. What you got to be careful of is that they may not only sing, they may compose."

I have been using this "compose" metaphor for decades and I am gratified that a judge borrowed it to express an important civil liberties concern.

Every experienced criminal lawyer has seen this phenomenon at work. I have seen it used by prosecutors who threaten wives, parents, siblings, and in one case the innocent son of a potential witness who was about to graduate from law school. Most judges, many of whom were former prosecutors, have also seen it. But few have the courage to expose it publicly, as Judge Ellis has done.

Defenders of Mueller's tactic argue that the threatened witnesses and their relatives are generally guilty of some crime, or else they wouldn't be vulnerable to the prosecutor's threats. This may be true, but the crimes they are threatened to be charged with are often highly technical, elastic charges that are brought only as leverage. They are dropped as soon as the witness cooperates. This was precisely the point Judge Ellis was making with regard to Manafort. A similar point could be made with regard to Michael Flynn and perhaps to Michael Cohen. Indeed, Flynn pleaded guilty to a highly questionable charge precisely because his son was threatened with prosecution.

Civil libertarians have long criticized this tactic since the time it was used by Joseph McCarthy and his minions to pressure witnesses to testify against suspected communists. In recent decades it has been deployed against mobsters, terrorists, and corporate predators. But Judge Ellis has accused Mueller of using this questionable approach to develop a political case against the duly elected president of the United States.

For those who argue that everything is fair if the goal is to prevent a president from being above the law, Judge Ellis provided a compelling response:

"What we don't want in this country is that we don't want anyone with unfettered power . . . It's unlikely you're going to persuade me that the special counsel has unlimited powers to do anything he or she wants."

He was referring to the manner by which the Special Counsel was using his power to "tighten the screws" on Manafort by indicting him for an alleged crime that the judge believes has nothing to do "with what the Special Counsel is authorized to investigate."

Civil libertarians should be applauding Judge Ellis for seeking to cabin the "unfettered power" of the Special Counsel to do "anything he wants." But no. Because his ruling may help Trump, and because Trump has applauded it, the civil liberties and criminal defense communities have not been heard from.

Judge Ellis has not yet ruled on the propriety of the Special Counsel's actions, and it is unlikely he will dismiss the charges against Manafort. But Mueller is on notice that he may not have unfettered power to indict President Trump's associates for old crimes that are unrelated to the Russia investigation for the purpose of making them sing or compose against Trump. Equally important, the civil liberties community no longer has an excuse to ignore— or defend, as some have done—tactics that pose considerable dangers to civil liberties just because they are being used against President Trump.

The week of Ellis's rebuke was not a good one for Special Counsel Mueller. Nor was it particularly good for President Trump, as his new lawyer Rudy Giuliani presented a somewhat garbled narrative with regard to the payment made to Stormy Daniels. But it was an excellent week for the Constitution and for all Americans, because a federal judge made it clear that no one—not even the Special Counsel—is above the law and beyond scrutiny by our system of checks and balances.

Trump's Legal Defense and Moving Forward

In fifty years of practicing criminal law, I have never advised a client to speak to prosecutors unless the alternative is worse; doing so is fraught with inherent risks. Rather than accepting a negotiated appearance, I suggest that there could be grounds for a subpoena to be challenged by President Trump's lawyers if issued by Special Counsel Robert Mueller. In the essays and transcripts that follow, I discuss why a subpoena directed at questions about Trump's actions before he was in office might be more difficult to fight.

I suggest again that it was a mistake to appoint a special counsel, and instead, a nonpartisan, independent commission like for 9/11 should have been appointed to find out how the 2016 election went wrong. I question the investigation's objectivity since Mueller and former FBI director James Comey were so close. I raise again the point that Deputy Attorney General Rod Rosenstein should be recused because he is a witness in the Comey firing. I draw attention to cases that say it may be perfectly legal to have a foreign person involved in US elections as long as they don't make substantial campaign contributions.

Finally, I explore the question of whether Trump can pardon himself and refer to points from an article I had originally written in *The Hill* in July 2017, but reissued recently after President Trump tweeted that he has the authority to do so. My conclusion now, as almost a year ago, is the same: No one knows because no president has ever tried it, and I believe it is unlikely that we will ever know for sure whether a self-pardon is constitutionally permissible.

Trump's Better off Litigating Than Testifying[29]

In my experience, subjects of criminal investigations rarely help themselves by speaking to prosecutors or testifying before a grand jury. Far more often, they hurt themselves by falling into a perjury trap carefully set by prosecutors.

When prosecutors invite a subject to talk to them, they are not trying to help the subject. They are trying to bolster their case against him. Subjects can become targets and then defendants even if they tell the truth.

They can fill gaps or make statements that are contradicted by other witnesses who the prosecutors chose to believe. That is why, in my half-century of practicing criminal law, I have never advised a client to speak to prosecutors unless the alternative is worse.

In this case, the alternative may well be a grand jury subpoena, which is worse in that the subject must appear without his lawyer and without limitations of time and subject matter. But it is better in that it can be challenged legally. A negotiated appearance cannot.

There are several grounds on which President Trump's lawyers could challenge a subpoena. The broadest ground would be that a sitting president cannot be compelled to appear before a grand jury and answer questions. The courts are likely to reject so broad an argument, as they rejected President Clinton's claim that he could not be required to sit for a deposition.

A somewhat narrower objection would be to answering any questions that relate to the exercise of his presidential authority under Article II of the Constitution. Just as members of Congress and the judiciary cannot be questioned about the exercise of their constitutional powers, so, too, a president cannot be required to explain why he fired FBI director James Comey or national security advisor Michael Flynn.

I think that President Trump would have a good chance of prevailing on this issue.

Finally, he could challenge questions that go beyond the scope of the Special Counsel's mandate. Even if he prevailed on that challenge, it would only be a Pyrrhic victory, since the same questions could be put to him by a grand jury in the Southern District of New York.

All in all, I think the president is probably better off litigating than testifying, though he might end up doing both.

The Trump Defense[30]

From an interview on Meet the Press *with Chuck Todd, May 2018.*

———————

CHUCK TODD: Look. I think I believe, and I think you've said this before on the obstruction part of this, the obstruction case is only as strong as probably the actual conspiracy case itself. And I understand that. But did Mr. Giuliani actually strengthen, potentially, an obstruction case against the president by declaring that rationale as representing the president on television?

DERSHOWITZ: Well, we now have, obviously, two narratives. The president himself said, both on television and in a meeting with the Russians, that he was motivated at least in part to end the Russian probe. I'm sure he was also motivated in part by what Comey refused to tell him.

Motives are complex. Motives are multifaceted. That's why motives should never form the basis of a crime. That's why it's wrong to question what a president's motives are when the president acted within his constitutional authority. We don't want to turn motives—

TODD: Right.

DERSHOWITZ: —and analysis of the president's mind into criminal statutes. We have to look at what the president did, not what his motives are because motives are always complex, in both situations. The payment to Stormy Daniels—

TODD: Right.

DERSHOWITZ: —and the firing of Comey, we see complex motives at work. But this can be presented much more effectively as a defense than it's been presented thus far by the Trump team.

TODD: I want to ask you actually about that in particular. When it comes to the questions that Mueller wants to ask the president, you have, I think, believed that a sitting president couldn't be compelled to answer questions via subpoena about his actions while in office. But what if—

DERSHOWITZ: No, no, about the motives behind his actions.

TODD: Motives behind, right. I understand that.

DERSHOWITZ: Right, yes.

TODD: But if Mueller wants to question the president about his actions and about his motives before he's in office, for everything that took place in the campaign, isn't that a much tougher subpoena for Mr. Trump's attorneys to fight?

DERSHOWITZ: Yes. There are three categories. There's what happened before he was president. That, he can fight on Judge Ellis's grounds, that it has nothing to do with the mandate that was given to—

TODD: But that's a hard—

DERSHOWITZ: —the Special Counsel.

TODD: It's probably a high bar.

DERSHOWITZ: That's a hard—that's a high bar.

TODD: OK.

DERSHOWITZ: The second is actions he took while president that are authorized by the Constitution. I think he prevails on that. And then there are actions during the campaign and the transition period, which have kind of quasi-legal protection. So, there are three categories.

And if they were to fight the subpoena, I think they would have a partial victory. But in the end, they would probably have to answer some questions. And I'm sure that's what they're thinking about now. Because when you volunteer—

TODD: Right.

DERSHOWITZ: —at least maybe you can constrain the questions. When you're subpoenaed, a subpoena is broad. Your lawyer isn't present. This is a tough decision for the president's team to make.

You Won't Have Any Doubt
at the End of This[31]

From a May 2018 appearance on This Week *with George Stephanopoulos, again with Dan Abrams.*

———————

DAN ABRAMS: Yes, I mean look, what we know for certain as a result of this investigation is that the Russians did meddle in the election, thirteen Russians have been indicted by the Special Counsel.

At least six others have been indicted in the last year in connection with this investigation. So, this notion that sort of nothing is (inaudible), here we are a year later and we're still waiting, a lot has happened in the first year.

The question still remains as to what's next, meaning will they be able to indict and will they indict any senior members of the Trump campaign in connection with that? We don't know the answer to that.

But the notion that up to this point, it's been a witch hunt or a hoax just makes no sense.

STEPHANOPOULOS: One thing we also know, Professor Dershowitz, is another Special Counsel investigation, and you've criticized this having gone on for far longer than a year.

DERSHOWITZ: Well I think it was a mistake to appoint a Special Counsel. They should have appointed a nonpartisan, independent commission like 9/11 to find out how this election went wrong.

And it went wrong in so many different ways. This is one of the worst elections in modern history with Russian attempts to influence, other attempts by Gulf countries to influence the existence of FBI agents who were trying desperately to turn the election away from Trump.

We should have had a massive investigation and then we should change the laws to make it clear what you can do and what you can't do. I don't think this investigation has gotten us what we need to know, knowledge and information about how to prevent this in the future.

ABRAMS: (Inaudible) isn't passing that—oh, when—you know, we've got evidence that the FBI agents were trying to turn this against Trump, we don't have any evidence that FBI agents were trying to turn the election.

DERSHOWITZ: How about Strzok's tweets when he said we need a guarantee, we need an insurance policy, we have to investigate that.

STEPHANOPOULOS: (Inaudible) hold on, those were not tweets, those were private texts.

DERSHOWITZ: What's the difference? We've got them. They show a state of mind, and now we have—

ABRAMS: Did you read all of his texts? Did you read all of his texts? Actually, the total context is not saying oh my goodness, Donald Trump is the problem. Also, he talked about Hillary Clinton and problems with Hillary Clinton, et cetera.

The bottom line is, to sort of throw that in there with all the rest of what the—what the Special Counsel has found, to me, it just minimizes what we've really found with regard to Russian meddling.

DERSHOWITZ: And I think it should minimize it because what we found is not particularly significant. What we—

ABRAMS: You don't think it's significant?

DERSHOWITZ: No.

ABRAMS: Russian meddling is not significant?

DERSHOWITZ: No, I think it's very significant.

ABRAMS: Oh.

DERSHOWITZ: The meddling. I don't think the criminal charges are very significant because we, to this day, don't even know what the law still is. You know, the Supreme Court has said that foreign governments can intrude themselves into elections if they have an interest in the outcome of the election. What they can't do is contribute money. The law is very unclear. Now we have information of an FBI informant in the campaign.

That's wanting an investigation.

ABRAMS: Again, FBI informant in the campaign. Again, no evidence an FBI informant was—

DERSHOWITZ: No evidence?

ABRAMS: None. The—here's the evidence we have. The evidence we have is that an FBI informant spoke to members of the Trump campaign.

DERSHOWITZ: That's—

ABRAMS: That's not in the campaign.

DERSHOWITZ: That's good enough to get an investigation going. This was a—Dan, let me ask you a question. Was this a good election? Was this something we should be proud of? Or is this an election that warrants an investigation, a nonpartisan investigation on both sides to make sure that in the future, (A) we know what the rules are, and (B) we know how to stop countries from improperly intruding on elections.

That's what we need to know. We need to look forward, we need to stop this in the future and stop making up crimes and expanding the criminal law to fit people that we've targeted. That's dangerous to democracy.

ABRAMS: But look, Alan's been very consistent on this issue about the law over the years. And—and I—and I respect that. But the notion that the Special Counsel can't view this objectively, that Robert Mueller is some-how—what? Robert Mueller is so compromised? Which way?

DERSHOWITZ: I'm not suggesting—

ABRAMS: —long-term Republican, so why can't Robert Mueller be the one to assess whether there are any crimes here?

DERSHOWITZ: First of all, this long-term Republican—Comey was a long-term Republican, they're all long-term Republicans who hated Trump. So that doesn't help at all—

ABRAMS: —you know that Mueller hated Trump?

DERSHOWITZ: Well—you won't have any doubt about that at the end of this—

DERSHOWITZ: No, but maybe he and Comey are so close—their history is so close together that when you read Comey's book and you see what he has said, you really wonder about the objectivity of the investigation. Look, if there was evidence of crime, the US attorneys can investigate it, as the Southern District is doing. The main justice could investigate it.

There's one person that should be recused from this case and that's Rod Rosenstein, because he's a witness. He's the main witness. There was never a need for a Special Counsel—special counsels have targets, they're looking to try to find crimes against people. That doesn't serve the interest of America. America's interest is served by finding out the truth, the facts, changing the law, and making sure it never happens again.

STEPHANOPOULOS: It sounds like you're in league with President Trump on impeaching the credibility at this point of the Special Counsel. But in the meantime, the investigation is continuing, and one of the things we learned this weekend is that *New York Times* report on the cover of the

New York Times this morning that now Robert Mueller is investigating this meeting that Donald Trump Jr. and other aides had with emissaries of Gulf nations, wealthy Arab Gulf nations offering help to win the election.

The president's tweeted on that this morning. And so, all he says is that things are getting really ridiculous. Failing crooked *New York Times* has done a long and boring story indicating the world's most expensive witch hunt has found nothing on Russia and me so now they are looking at the rest of the world. Now, this story, Dan, is—is a bit complicated. I'll grant that. But what it does say is that Donald Jr. had a meeting with an emissary of the UAE and Saudi Arabia who was offering some help, perhaps working with an Israeli firm on social media.

ABRAMS: I read the article twice. And then again. And still am not certain after reading it three times whether there is any potential criminal activity.

DERSHOWITZ: Isn't that a problem? Isn't that a problem that we don't even know what the law is today? As to whether—

ABRAMS: Well, look. Here's—no, it's actually—

ABRAMS: —it's actually not that we don't know what the law is, it's that we don't know what the facts are.

DERSHOWITZ: No, it's that we don't know what the law is.

ABRAMS: Well, at least for me. As far as I know—

STEPHANOPOULOS: Let Dan finish—

ABRAMS: The basic law as I understand is that a foreign national can't provide anything of value, which has been interpreted to mean typically substantial assistance in connection with an election.

DERSHOWITZ: OK.

ABRAMS: Period.

DERSHOWITZ: Let's take the following scenario. You have countries in the world who hate the Democrats because of the fact that they made a deal with Iranians that they think endangers their security. Therefore, they want to see a Republican elected. Is that a crime? You don't know the answer to that, I don't know the answer to that because the Supreme Court and the legislature—

ABRAMS: —wait, I do know the answer to that.

DERSHOWITZ: What is it?

ABRAMS: If they gave money, that would be a crime.

DERSHOWITZ: That would be one.

ABRAMS: If they gave—if they gave any campaign assistance that has a value, that would be a crime.

DERSHOWITZ: No, that's not true. The United States Supreme Court has said case after case where you can give things a value if they are protected by the First Amendment, if they are informational, if they are a concert, for example. There are cases all over the place and they go both ways—

ABRAMS: But Alan—

DERSHOWITZ: The law is not clear.

ABRAMS: But Alan, the law in every area has gray areas, right? That's why cases make it to the Supreme Court, because appellate courts end up interpreting things in different ways and then it makes its way up to the Supreme Court where the Supreme Court has to resolve exactly what it means.

To suggest oh, this area of the law is so much vaguer than any—it's not.

DERSHOWITZ: No, no, no, it is. Let me tell you, we don't know what—first of all, you talk about the Israeli person, we've had foreign people involved in American elections in the very beginning (inaudible).

That's perfectly legal to have a foreign person involved as long as they don't make substantial campaign contributions. There's a volunteer exception, there's another exception that says that if you're doing it for your own purpose—

ABRAMS: You're—you're—you're intentionally making this more complicated than it needs to be. Bottom—

DERSHOWITZ: Boy, it's complicated enough.

ABRAMS: It is, but you know what, they're going to figure out whether they're—under current law, the same way they do in every other area of the law, was a—was a law violated?

It's just not that hard, and to sort of throw your arms and say oh, we just can't—we can't interpret this area of the law.

DERSHOWITZ: You and I can't agree—

ABRAMS: You're a law professor, law professors point to specific difficult questions. That's what you've done for a living.

DERSHOWITZ: —never see the basis for criminal prosecution. And unless you know with absolute clarity where the line is and you make—

—decision to be or not to be a felon, it should not be crime, crime should not be matters of a degree.

Can Trump Pardon Himself?
The Answer Is: No One Actually Knows[32]

President Trump has tweeted that he has the authority to pardon himself. His lawyer, Rudy Giuliani, has said that this is probably correct. In response to this assertion of presidential power, academics, pundits, and talking heads are weighing in.

So let me weigh in as well. The answer is crystal clear: No one knows, and we will probably never obtain a definitive answer to this fascinating hypothetical question.

The more important question is, why did President Trump feel the need to assert a power he will almost certainly never to try to exercise?

Here is what I wrote in *The Hill* in July 2017 about this very question:

No president has ever tried it. No court has ever ruled on it. The Framers of our Constitution never opined on it. History provides no guidance. There is a clean slate.

Yet pundits and academic know-it-alls will express certainty on both sides of this issue. That's what pundits and academics do. Rarely do they acknowledge they don't know, because as experts they are supposed to know. But this is one question whose answer they cannot know.

They will have opinions, as we all do. But many will deliberately confuse the "is" with the "ought." If they want the answer to be no, they will pretend the answer is no. If they want the answer to be yes, they will pretend it is yes. That's the way some pundits and academics advocate: by claiming to be describing what they are not so subtly prescribing.

This has been the case especially with regard to Trump. Too many academics have said that non-criminal conduct by Trump and his administration is a crime, when they wish it were a crime, so that

Trump can be removed from office. But wishful thinking is not a substitute for rigorous analysis, which has been sorely lacking among some of my fellow liberal academics.

So let's rigorously analyze the question of whether a president can pardon himself. The preliminary question is whether a sitting president can be indicted, tried, and convicted for an alleged crime committed before he assumed office or while serving in office. The answer to that question probably is no, as most authorities suggest.

That has been the Justice Department's view for some time now. It is also the view of most experts that once a president leaves office—by his term ending or by impeachment or resignation—he could be prosecuted. If that were the case, there would be no reason for the president to even consider pardoning himself now. He could wait until his last day in office.

Why the last day? Because if he can be prosecuted as soon as he leaves office, pardoning himself would protect him from that possibility, if the self-pardon were valid. Why would he not do it any earlier? Because he might well be impeached if he pardoned himself, and the pardon power does not extend to impeachment.

But he couldn't be impeached on his last day or after he leaves office. If he had doubts about the validity of a self-pardon, he could also make a deal—explicit or implicit—with the vice president to resign a day before his term was up in exchange for a pardon from the one-day president.

So timing would be everything. Will we ever know for sure whether a self-pardon is constitutionally permissible? Unlikely.

First, a president would have to pardon himself. The political cost of such an action would be very high. Second, a prosecutor would then have to try to prosecute the former president. Third, the former president would have to raise the pardon as a defense.

Finally, the courts would have to decide whether, under our system of separation of powers, the courts have jurisdiction to review a presidential self-pardon. This last contingency is interesting, because as Justice Oliver Wendell Holmes reminded us, the power to pardon is not a mere "private act of grace," but rather an important part of our "constitutional scheme," of checks and balances and separation of powers.

But the pardon power is not without limit. A president could almost certainly be prosecuted after leaving office for accepting a bribe to grant a pardon. Although he would be prosecuted for accepting the bribe, the granting of the pardon would be the quid pro quo, and thus an essential of the crime.

James Madison wrote in *The Federalist Papers* that no person "is allowed to be a judge in his own case." Would violation of this principle bestow jurisdiction on a court to invalidate a self-pardon? The answer to that question remains unclear.

I'm relatively certain these contingencies will never come to pass. So we will have to learn to live with the uncertainty of never knowing whether a president has the constitutional authority to pardon himself.

Trump Will Not Pardon Himself

or Testify in Sex Cases[33]

From an interview by Chuck Todd on Meet the Press, *June 5, 2018.*

———————

CHUCK TODD: Welcome back. On this question of whether the president—on the president pardoning himself, as you heard Giuliani say right there, politically, it could be a nonstarter. But what about legally? That question hasn't really been asked before, and many legal scholars say we don't know what that answer would be.

So we're going to continue our constitutional law class right here. Joining me now is one such legal scholar and a frequent defender of President Trump's current legal predicament. It's Alan Dershowitz.

He is a Professor Emeritus at Harvard Law School, author of the upcoming book, *The Case Against Impeaching Trump.*

Professor Dershowitz, if any day we need to make sure to use the professor title, it is on a day like this. Thank you for coming on, sir.

DERSHOWITZ: Well, thank you.

TODD: Let me start—

DERSHOWITZ: Sure.

TODD: Let me start with this, you wrote that we don't know whether or not the president can pardon himself.

DERSHOWITZ: That's right.

TODD: In a tweet storm last night, Senator Ted Cruz did cite a 1974 Justice Department memo that made a finding that said it wasn't true.

And it wrote, in part, in this—and I'm curious of your take on it. This is from August 5, 1974. Presidential or legislative pardon of the president under the fundamental rule that no one may be a judge in his own case, the president cannot pardon himself.

I do note the date, August 5, 1974, three days before Richard Nixon would resign the presidency. What do you make of that finding? A finding is not a ruling—a Supreme Court ruling. That, I understand, but what do you make of that rationale?

DERSHOWITZ: It's a logical argument against self-pardoning. Madison made the same point during the constitutional debates. On the other hand, the constitutional text itself says a president may issue pardons in any case, except in cases of impeachment. That suggests one of two things.

Either the president can pardon himself or, more likely, that the Framers contemplated that a president couldn't be prosecuted. And if he couldn't be prosecuted, there would be no need to pardon himself. He certainly couldn't be prosecuted while he was president.

Of course, Richard Nixon was pardoned when he left office. At the time he left office. So it would be [a] great law school exam question because no one knows the answer. And I have to tell you, anybody who tells you definitively—

TODD: Sure.

DERSHOWITZ: —that either it can be done or can't be done is pulling your leg. Nobody knows the answer to the question.

TODD: Well, right, you have to have—we'd have to have an instance for it to be tested into the courts, and I think we're all hoping we don't ever get to a situation like this.

DERSHOWITZ: It won't.

TODD: But do you—

DERSHOWITZ: It won't ever happen, yes.

TODD: Do you think it's so unclear that it's something that should be dealt with in the Constitution itself? That if we believe that's the case, then instead of worrying about a ruling or a finding, you pass a constitutional amendment that says the president's powers of pardon are unlimited unless it involves himself. His or herself.

DERSHOWITZ: I think that would be a big mistake. You don't amend the Constitution unless there are absolutely compelling reasons. I guarantee you no president will pardon himself or herself. There are much easier ways to do it.

If, for example, the president feared that he would be prosecuted after he left office or even if he was impeached, on the verge of being impeached, he could make a deal with his vice president that he would leave and retire earlier like Nixon did and then have the vice president pardon.

So I don't think you amend the Constitution based on an unlikely hypothetical.

And the other point that I think is very important to make is that, you know, we hear the cliché thrown around and weaponized now that the president believes he's above the law. I think that's a misunderstanding of what they have been arguing.

What they're arguing is that the law permits the president to be exempt and immunized from certain kinds of criminal or civil actions that other people can be subjected to.

We know already the Constitution does that for members of Congress. Members of Congress cannot be prosecuted, questioned, or sued for much of what they do on the floor or on the way to the Senate.

Judges can't be prosecuted or sued.

TODD: Right. Members of the military.

DERSHOWITZ: Prosecutors can't be—

TODD: Members of the military, individually, carrying out—

DERSHOWITZ: Well, some of the members of the military.

TODD: Yes.

DERSHOWITZ: Yes, it turns out none of them are above the law. What they're—they are subject to different rules under the law.

TODD: Right.

DERSHOWITZ: So I think we should be very careful when we throw around the term "above the law" rather than within the law.

TODD: Fair enough. Let's talk about, though, this idea of what power the president has inside the executive branch on the justice system and—because this is—

DERSHOWITZ: That's a great question, yes.

TODD: Mr. Giuliani and I had an interesting back-and-forth. So for instance, one of the things he said on Sunday to me that before he sat down with an interview, he wants to make Rosenstein and Mueller produce sort of the evidence that triggered the investigation in—specifically.

And I said to Mr. Giuliani, well, if you guys have this broad interpretation of the president's executive authority when it comes to investigations, then can't he just order the Justice Department to produce this information?

DERSHOWITZ: And there are—

TODD: Where are you on this?

DERSHOWITZ: There are two answers to the question if you look at the constitutional history.

Jefferson ran the Justice Department like it was his own little, you know, house. He told the prosecutors who to prosecute. He, in fact, gave immunity to witnesses by giving them pardons if they would testify against his archenemy, Burr.

Lincoln told prosecutors who to prosecute. Roosevelt did.

So, constitutionally, the president does have that authority. But traditionally, we want to see a separation between that one particular department, Justice, and the presidency.

TODD: Right.

DERSHOWITZ: You know, the president does have a right to demand loyalty of his cabinet members. And the attorney general serves two roles, and it's a constitutional flaw. One here is be loyal—

TODD: I was just going to say I think—

DERSHOWITZ: Yes.

TODD: I'm glad you used the word "flaw" because I was about to ask you, is this is a flaw?

DERSHOWITZ: It is a flaw.

TODD: Yes.

DERSHOWITZ: It is. He can demand loyalty from the man who is the attorney general. That is as who is his advisor on legal affairs but not the man who is the director of public prosecution. Most Western countries divide those roles.

TODD: Right.

DERSHOWITZ: In England, there is a director of public prosecution and a minister of justice. The minister of justice is loyal to the prime minister. Director of public prosecution, no. Israel, the same thing.

In the United States, we ask the attorney general to serve in this schizophrenic role. Loyal some days of the week, disloyal or not loyal other days of the week, loyal to the rule of law.

TODD: Right.

DERSHOWITZ: It's an impossible role. And almost every president has tried to appoint loyalists.

TODD: Right.

DERSHOWITZ: Starting, obviously, with John Kennedy appointing his brother. Ronald Reagan appointing his own personal lawyer.

TODD: Right.

DERSHOWITZ: President Obama appointing a loyalist. So the president wasn't wrong when he said I want loyalty from my attorney general.

TODD: Right.

DERSHOWITZ: It's the Constitution that's wrong for allowing that kind of a division to occur.

TODD: No, at best, I keep wondering if we should at least go to the Federal Reserve model when it comes to attorney general or the Justice Department.

DERSHOWITZ: Right.

TODD: So that there are five-year terms and different parties appoint different people and all sorts of issues there. But I want to move on to a couple of quick things before I lose you and we run out of time. Number one, the president has claimed the Special Counsel isn't constitutional.

DERSHOWITZ: He's wrong about that. He's wrong about that.

TODD: Yes.

DERSHOWITZ: There's nothing in the Constitution that would preclude it. Look, Steven Calabresi, who wrote the article, is a brilliant, brilliant analyst, and he makes an important point that the Special Counsel isn't confirmed by the Senate.

But I think in the end, the attorney general has the right to appoint a Special Counsel to make recommendations, essentially, to the attorney general. In the end, the attorney general is responsible for deciding who to prosecute, so I think the president is wrong about that.

TODD: All right. And a judge ruled today that President Trump can be deposed in a defamation lawsuit brought last year by a former *Apprentice* contestant. She accuses the president of unwanted sexual conduct.

Now, the president's lawyers are appealing that deposition. Marc Kasowitz is essentially saying, you know, that this is a critical constitutional issue.

Can the president—because this involves state courts. It doesn't involve federal courts. It's a little bit different. What do you think his chances are on appeal here?

DERSHOWITZ: Oh, I think zero or less. In fact, the fact that it's a state court makes it much more difficult for a federal court to intervene. It seems to me the Supreme Court has ruled unanimously in the case involving Bill Clinton that a president cannot refuse to sit for a subpoena.

Now, one expects this president will not make the same mistake that President Clinton did, led into a perjury trap by his lawyer, Robert Bennett, who allowed him to testify fully about his sex life, which ended up getting him impeached. I would think this president will figure out some way of not having to testify about his sex life.

TODD: And going back to Robert Mueller, if he subpoenas the president and says he wants to question him about his actions before he was president—

DERSHOWITZ: I think—

TODD: —is there any way the president can avoid that issue subpoena?

DERSHOWITZ: He can. He can but it would be a Pyrrhic victory because then the Southern District of New York would issue a similar subpoena and he would not be able to resist as Mr. Trump, businessman.

TODD: Interesting.

DERSHOWITZ: He is subject to the rule of law like anybody else is, so it would be a Pyrrhic victory.

TODD: All right, Alan Dershowitz, Professor Emeritus at Harvard.

DERSHOWITZ: Thank you.

TODD: You are churning out a lot of books here, sir.

DERSHOWITZ: Thank you.

TODD: I feel like I just promoted a pretty recent one. Now, you got a new one coming. We will see you soon. Thanks so much for—

DERSHOWITZ: And I got another one right after that. Thanks.

TODD: All right, fair enough. Thank you, Professor.

People Confuse My Advocacy[34]

From a June 12, 2018, interview on Outnumbered Overtime *with Harris Faulkner on Fox News.*

———————

FAULKNER: Is [Rudy Giuliani] right? Could [James Comey] find himself in trouble?

DERSHOWITZ: Rudy is a friend of mine and a great lawyer, but I disagree with criminalizing political differences in this context. I have been a longtime opponent of trying to criminalize political differences against Donald Trump and people in the Trump administration. And now that the shoe is on the other foot, I take the same position. Let's not turn disagreements into crimes. Even if he acted insubordinately, that's not a crime. And we have to start disarming both sides and stop weaponizing the criminal justice system and using it against political opponents. So, if is he criticized, that's fine—in the marketplace of ideas. But let's not turn criticism into criminalization on either side.

FAULKNER: All right. So that's Rudy Giuliani's take on it but, let's take a look and hear from Bob Goodlatte: "I think, and many others in Congress continue to think, that we need to have an independent special counsel separate and apart from the work that Mr. Mueller is doing."

So, Alan, what I hear Congressman Goodlatte saying there is, 'Let's have somebody take a look at this so can you see whether or not it's simply politics.'

DERSHOWITZ: Well, that's what the Inspector General is doing. But, you know, I don't think two wrongs make a right. I think it was wrong to appoint a special counsel to investigate Trump. I think it's equally wrong to appoint a special counsel to investigate Comey.

FAULKNER: Even though we know he has leaked information. We know some of the things that James Comey has done. And by the way, politically, he is not making either side of the aisle happy.

DERSHOWITZ: There's no question about that. But you don't turn political opposition into criminalization. Leaking something is not a crime unless it's leaking of grand jury material. Let's understand that there are criminal statutes and they should be defined narrowly and we shouldn't be weaponizing the criminal justice system against either side. I was critical of President Trump when he called for locking up Hillary Clinton and when he called for a special counsel to investigate Hillary Clinton. The president has said that he thinks special counsels are unconstitutional.

I don't agree with that but if he thinks they are unconstitutional as to him, they are surely unconstitutional as to Comey or anybody else as well. We have to have neutral principles. The same principles.

FAULKNER: All right.

DERSHOWITZ: People confuse my advocacy. I'm not there as advocate for President Trump.

I'm an advocate for civil liberties.

FAULKNER: We had text messages flowing between at least two employees that we know about who were having an affair. Was there bias inside the FBI? I mean, the Inspector General is looking at a whole lot here.

DERSHOWITZ: And he should be. Those are appropriate functions for the inspector general. Having an honest inspector general obviates the need for a special counsel.

FAULKNER: We know that he can't prosecute, so if there are signs of bias—

DERSHOWITZ: —he can't prosecute but he could recommend prosecution, but he has to show that there is an actual crime committed and that crime would be prosecuted whether it was done by a Democrat or Republican or an independent. We have to have one standard of justice for all and we have to use the criminal law only as a last resort when there is clear evidence that an existing statutory crime has been committed. I don't think that standard has been met for anybody involved so far in this whole disaster—the 2016 election.

Tweeting with POTUS

The following is my Twitter exchange with President Trump on June 7, 2018, regarding the Special Counsel:

@realDonaldTrump
Alan Dershowitz, Harvard Law Professor: "It all proves that we never needed a Special Counsel . . . .All of this could have been done by the Justice Dept. Don't need a multi-million dollar group of people with a target on someone's back. Not the way Justice should operate." So true!
9:05 AM

***

@AlanDersh, replying to @realDonaldTrump
If @realDonaldTrump agrees with me, he should withdraw his request for a special counsel to investigate Clinton. Neutral principles. 10:47 AM
@realDonaldTrump
Alan Dershowitz, Harvard Law Professor: "It all proves that we never needed a Special Counsel . . . .All of this could have been done by the Justice Dept. Don't need a multi-million dollar group of people with a target on someone's back. Not the way Justice should operate." So true!

***

@AlanDersh
I appreciate @realDonaldTrump agreeing with my position on special counsel. To be consistent, he should withdraw his demand for a special counsel to investigate Clinton. If he thinks special counsel is unconstitutional, it is as unconstitutional for her as for him.
10:48 AM

Conclusion

Part I

Critics of my views on impeachment and prosecution of a sitting president—in particular, President Trump—point to the fact that I stand alone in many of my conclusions. My belief that a president can be impeached and removed only if he has committed a designated high crime and misdemeanor is widely rejected by other academics.[37] My conclusion that a president cannot be

---

37 See, e.g., "Senate Trials and Factional Disputes: Impeachment as a Madisonian Device," 49 *Duke Law Journal* 1, 37 (October 1999)."[T]he impeachment standard was clearly intended to extend beyond criminal acts to include some noncriminal acts."; Akhil Amar, "On Impeaching Presidents," 28 *Hofstra Law Review*, 291, 295 (Winter 1999) ("A statute-book offense is not necessary for impeachment."); Noah Feldman and Jacob Weisberg, "What Are Impeachable Offenses?"*New York Review of Books*, Sept. 28, 2017 ("Crimes and misdemeanors are thus 'high' when they relate to the president's exercise of the distinctive duties of his office. They may be crimes in the sense that they are found in the statute books—but high crimes and misdemeanors may go beyond the US Code. High crimes and misdemeanors are presidential actions that contradict, undermine, and derogate democracy and the rule of law."); Laurence Tribe and Joshua Matz, *To End a Presidency*, "[I]mpeachment and criminal punishment are distinct. Some lawyers, however, continue to insist that an official can be impeached *only* if the official has committed a crime. Although this restrictive position enjoyed a measure of support in the early 1800s, it has long since been widely and convincingly rejected."; Cass Sunstein, *Impeachment, A Citizen's Guide* (2007) ("No crime is necessary. If the president is acting in an 'atrocious' way that harms most of the states, he is committing a 'misdemeanor', even if no violation of the law is involved."); Erwin Chemerinsky, "Is It Time to Start Talking Impeachment?" *Los Angeles Daily News*, May 24, 2017 ("Criminal activity always has been regarded as sufficient to meet this standard. But it also has been understood to include serious abuses of power, even if not illegal"). Even Joseph Story wrote as early as 1833 in his *Commentaries on the Constitution*, "[N]o one has as yet been bold enough to assert, that the power of impeachment is limited to offences positively defined in the statute book of the Union, as impeachable high crimes and misdemeanors." *Commentaries on the Constitution*, Sec. 795. A minority of academics takes the view that the president can be removed for unenumerated crimes, such as for crimes against humanity, see Allan Lichtman, note *supra*. Richard Painter,

convicted of a crime for merely exercising his constitutional authority to fire, pardon, or end an investigation is an outlier in the academic community. My conclusion that collusion with a foreign power during an election is not currently a crime under the federal criminal code surprises many people.[38]

It is gratifying that some of these views, which were rejected out of hand when I first proposed them, have now become part of the debate and accepted by at least some of my erstwhile critics. Some of my own views have been modified as well by listening and learning from my reasoned critics. But many have remained the same despite compelling counterarguments. Some of these issues are uncharted, and so we all write on empty slates. My own views are very much influenced by my deep commitment to civil liberties, the rights of the accused, and my own history as a criminal defense lawyer. They are also affected by my coming of age during McCarthyism and, while in college, defending the civil liberties of communists, who I despised and who would deny civil liberties to noncommunists.

Over my half century of participating in national and international debates, I have never been one to follow the crowd, or to place partisan politics over constitutional analysis. I have tried to be consistent in my views, regardless of who was in power and who might benefit from my analysis. I try to call them as I see them—to always pass the "shoe on the other foot" test. I challenge my opponents to submit their views to that test as well.

I welcome criticism of my views on their merits and demerits, but I am appalled at the personal *ad hominem* attacks that have often substituted for

---

who is hoping to win a Senate seat on his impeachment platform, suggested that Trump could be impeached for violating the First Amendment by threatening and intimidating the press, for violating the emoluments clause by receiving payments from foreign governments, and "for treason and betrayal" because of alleged collusion with the Russian government. Ambassador Norm Eisen also shared this view with Painter; see Norman L. Eisen and Richard W. Painter, "Did Donald, Jr. Break the Law?" *New York Times*, July 11, 2017. In connection with the investigation of Trump's fixer Michael Cohen, scholars and pundits alike have come up with new crimes which could lead to Trump's imminent downfall, such as bank and wire fraud, as well as campaign finance violations. I am sure by the time this book goes to press, these pundits will have come up with new crimes *du jour* on which Trump could be indicted. As I argue in essays in this book, if the shoe was on the other foot and Hillary Clinton were investigated, the ACLU and other liberal organizations would bemoan how vague these federal crimes are, and how much leverage they give prosecutors to bring politically motivated criminal charges.

38 For an overview of criticism, see Evan Mandery, "What Happened to Alan Dershowitz?" *Politico*, May 11, 2018.

critical analysis of my positions.[39] The emails that I receive hourly from cranks and extremists don't surprise me.[40] What does surprise me is that so many serious academics and pundits prefer to attack my motives than to criticize my analysis in a reasoned way.

What also upsets me is that old friends—in New York and Martha's Vineyard—have written to me saying that I have "crossed a line" and they can no longer speak to me. Others have threatened to walk out if I am given a platform from which to express my constitutional views. These fair-weather civil libertarians—who defend only the civil liberties of those whose ideologies they favor—are intolerant of nonpartisan defenders of the civil liberties of their ideological opponents. I joke that I have lost seven pounds on the Trump diet because my wife and I are no longer invited to dinner parties, but my being shunned for expressing politically incorrect legal opinions is a dangerous sign of our increasingly intolerant times. It may be understandable, if still wrong, when immature college students demand "safe spaces" to protect them from views that offend them, but more is expected of mature adults who should be willing to engage with those who express principled positions

---

39   For a representative sample, see Elie Mystal, "Guys, I'm Worried About Alan Dershowitz," *Above the Law*, December 7, 2017.

40   The following are direct quotes from messages I recently received:

"But I wanted you to know personally from me, an American citizen who has no power other than to observe, think, and vote, that I hope with all my heart that you get cancer and die a painful, disgusting death, you fuck, you traitorous fuck.
O.J. was guilty. Trump is guilty. Fuck you, you fucking fucker. Die! Die!
If, above all else, it's all about Jerusalem as the capital, and bombing Iran, and loving Israel to you, just move there! Good riddance. You are a cancer on America, and I hope you get cancer of your own."—Christopher K.

***

"You're a piece of shit for making those comments about obama . . . despite what zionists such as yourself want the rest of us to believe, the world doesn't revolve around jews . . . you're a self-serving disgrace."—Andrew C.

***

"Alan 'Goebbels' Dershowitz.
You'll be remembered as a liar and a phony on the day you die, and then you'll be forgotten by history. Your obit has already been written, like Alfred Nobel's had been."
—Christopher K.

***

"I would ask how you look in the mirror but the answer is that if you call the orangutan as your friend it is that you are a slimy motherfucker! Your a Jew but if there is a hell you are destined to burn in it!"—Howard W.

with which they strongly disagree. I can understand the fear that some people experience from the policies and actions of the Trump administration—some of which I also disapprove of. But the answer to fear should never be repression of unpopular ideas or denial of due process of law.

I hope this short book will provoke debate, not name-calling. The issues I raise are serious and their discussion is essential to democratic discourse. So please respond to my positions. Disagree with me; propose better arguments; defeat me, if you can, in the marketplace of ideas.

So let the debate continue. I am ready to respond to my critics in print, in the media, and in the courts of public opinion. But let's keep the debate civil and on the merits.

Part II:

The Political Case Against Impeaching Trump Doesn't Pass the "Shoe on the Other Foot" Test

―――――

The shoe on the other foot test is a colloquial formulation of a moral principle that traces its roots back to the Bible; the Greek, Roman, and Chinese philosophers; Kant and Mill; and modern political philosophers such as John Rawls. It is simple, elegant, and uncontroversial—at least in theory. Yet it is almost never followed in practice.

The test, which can be applied to every moral argument, is whether the person offering it as a neutral moral principle would make, and/or has made, the same argument when that argument would not serve—or would undercut—his or her interests. These interests might be political or ideological or they might be based on identity—racial, ethnic, religious, or gender. They might also involve sexual preference, national origin, tribal affiliation, family situation, or economic status.

To pass the test, the person offering what purports to be a neutrally principled argument that furthers their interests must satisfy the burden of proving their consistency of principle by demonstrating that they would offer the same argument if it undercut their interests. If the person offering the argument fails the test, the argument itself may not be weakened: the power of a logical argument is not weakened by the hypocrisy of the person offering it. But it weakens—perhaps destroys—the credibility of the person offering the argument.

This is important because those considering the force of an argument often attribute considerable weight to the credibility of the person making it.

Let me offer two examples of arguments that failed the shoe on the other foot test: one from each side of the political divide. The most recent occurred when hundreds of law professors—many quite distinguished and highly respected—sent a petition to the senate and the media urging the rejection of Brett Kavanaugh to be a justice of the Supreme Court. Their argument seemed persuasive on its face: Kavanaugh had shown partisanship and a lack of judicial temperament during his second confirmation hearing when he angrily defended himself against charges of sexual misconduct and accused Democrats of seeking revenge against him for his role in the impeachment of President Clinton. The argument itself was well constructed and strong. What else would you expect from experienced law professors? But what made it even more persuasive was that it was endorsed by *hundreds* of law professors. If exactly the same words had been endorsed by the first thousand people in the Boston phone book (to borrow an example from William Buckley), it would not have carried the same weight.

This observation turns the classic philosophical fallacy *ad hominem* on its head: if a good argument should not be rejected because the person making it is bad, it follows that no argument—good or bad—should be judged by the goodness, brilliance, or credibility of the person offering it. But the reality is that arguments are, in fact, judged by those offering it. Hence the shoe on the other foot test.

So, back to the Kavanaugh petition.

What if it could be proved that most, many, or all the signatories would have refused to offer their compelling argument if the shoe were on the other foot: if the candidate were a gay, liberal woman appointed by a democratic president whose confirmation would assure a progressive majority for years to come. What if this woman had been accused of sexual abuse when she was a teenager and had angrily denied it using language similar to that used by Kavanaugh?

What weight would you give the law professors' Kavanaugh petition if you believed that many of the same professors would have offered precisely the opposite argument—and offered it persuasively as law professors have the ability to do—in the gay woman case? What if they merely would have remained silent and not signed any petition?

Either position would constitute a blatant failure of the shoe test. And those who failed the test would be exposed as hypocrites. I am absolutely certain—because I know many of the signatories—that most would never have signed the identical petition if its target were the gay, liberal woman. I, therefore, accuse them of failing the shoe on the other foot test.

The second example is the majority decision by five Republican Justices in *Bush v. Gore*, back in 2000. I first employed the shoe test in critiquing that decision. I wrote a book entitled *Supreme Injustice* in which I wrote the following:

> This book is about the culpability of those justices who hijacked Election 2000 by distorting the law, violating their own expressed principles, and using their robes to bring about a partisan result. I accuse them of failing what I call the shoe on the other foot test: I believe that they would not have stopped a hand recount if George W. Bush had been seeking it. This is an extremely serious charge, because deciding a case on the basis of the identity of the litigants is a fundamental violation of the judicial oath, to "administer justice without respect to persons. . . ." In this book, I marshal the evidence in support of this charge.
>
> I am convinced—along with many academics, editorial, writers, litigators, and ordinary citizens—that if it had been Bush rather than Gore who needed the Florida recount in order to have any chance of winning, at least some of the five justices who voted to stop the recount would instead have voted to allow it to go forward—that is, they would have failed the shoe on the other foot test.

When I first made this argument in op-eds contemporaneously with the decision, I was roundly condemned by some academics who argued that criticism of the Supreme Court should be limited to the text of the decisions and should not extend to questioning the motives of the justices.

This is how I responded:

> It is understandable why so many academics and lawyers of goodwill would tend to limit their arguments—both in support of and in opposition to a Supreme Court decision—to the face of the opinion and its consistency, or lack thereof, with prior opinions. First, it is difficult to prove an improper motive. Second, to go beyond these traditional modes of criticism is to risk being accused of making an *ad hominem* attack on individual justices, and such personal attacks are regarded as unprofessional. As Professor Cass Sunstein cautioned with regard to this case: "No one should accuse any of the justices of bad faith or trying to ensure that their man gets in."
>
> Well, that is precisely what I am accusing the majority justices of doing. Let me be as clear as I can: The criticism I am making of the

majority justices includes a significant *ad hominem* component. I am not limiting my criticism merely to the intellectual or precedential weaknesses of their arguments. I am accusing them of partisan favoritism—bias—toward one litigant and against another. I am also accusing them of dishonesty, of trying to hide their bias behind plausible legal arguments that they never would have put forward had the shoe been on the other foot. These criticisms are directed at the justices personally, not only at their arguments, though it is the weakness of their arguments—and their inconsistency with prior views expressed by these very justices—that provides the probable cause for probing their motives.

I acknowledged that:

Motive analysis is largely outside the tradition of academic and professional criticism of the Supreme Court, as the admonition from Professor Sunstein suggests. Academics characterize such personal criticism as "the fallacy of *argumentum ad hominem*." And it is a fallacy to try to disprove the correctness of an argument on its merits by leveling a personal attack on the person who offered the argument, since an argument offered by the worst of human beings may nonetheless be correct. But it is equally fallacious to try to defend someone against well-grounded charges of personal dishonesty, bias, or corruption by demonstrating that the argument he made turns out to be correct on its merits.

I then offered an example that proved particularly prescient in light of the subsequent Kavanaugh hearings:

An example of a proceeding at which *ad hominem* criticisms are entirely appropriate is a judicial confirmation hearing. Although different in some respects from an inquiry into whether a particular decision was based on improper considerations, it demonstrates that *ad hominem* inquiry is sometimes probative. The prior opinions of a judicial nominee who is being considered for promotion are obviously relevant, but so are his or her personal characteristics: Does he have a "judicial temperament?" Did he ever commit a crime of "moral turpitude?" Did she ever sit on a case in which she had a conflict of interest (without regard to the intellectual quality of the arguments she made in her decision)? Has he ever based a decision on favoritism toward one litigant or against another?

My two examples—the Kavanaugh petition and the majority decision in *Bush v. Gore*—expose the hypocrisy of important players on both sides of the political divide. Hypocrisy is the coin of the realm when it comes to partisan politics. Consistency has no role in partisan politics. Partisans simply pick sides like sports fans pick teams. They offer whatever argument helps their side, without regard to whether the opposite argument would be offered if the shoe were on the other foot. La Rochefoucauld once quipped: "hypocrisy is a tribute vice pays to virtue." Not so in partisan politics. There is no shame in hypocrisy, no honor in consistency, no credit for principle, no reward for intellectual honesty. Just help your side whatever it takes. That is the world in which we are living.

I am reminded of the story about when President Charles Eliot of Harvard University learned that the Harvard baseball team was winning games because one of its pitchers had learned how to throw a curveball. Eliot called the coach of the team into his office and asked him if that were true. The coach proudly acknowledged his pitcher's mastery of the curveball. President Eliot glared at him and said, "I am told the object of the curveball is to deceive the batter." The coach acknowledged that that was in fact its object. President Eliot then demanded "no Harvard baseball player be allowed ever to throw a curveball. Deception is not a value we teach Harvard men." I am not suggesting that partisan politicians accept President Eliot's anachronistic rules of engagement. But partisan politics has moved so far away from any notion of a single standard that it is impossible to come up with any principle by which to judge the actions of partisans.

To be sure, there is the criminal law; however, as I demonstrated in my book *Trumped Up*, the line between criminal and noncriminal behavior is being challenged by both sides as they seek to weaponize the criminal justice system to their partisan advantage. The threat of impeachment, as I show in this book, has also become a weapon of first choice among partisans on both sides rather than the Constitutional safeguard of last resort intended by the Framers of our Constitution. Nothing is sacred—not the Constitution, not civil liberties, not due process, not the rule of law—when it comes to seeking immediate partisan advantage. Partisans simply don't care if they are justly accused of hypocrisy. They blatantly and willingly fail the shoe on the other foot test in the interest of immediate partisan advantage. They don't even seem to care that they are advocating positions that will establish dangerous precedents that may later come back to haunt their side when the shoe is indeed on the other foot. They want to win now. Let the future be damned.

The upshot of this partisan division is that we have lost the collective capacity to reason together, to argue rationally, to offer compromises, to build bridges and to acknowledge that the other side sometimes has a point. We live in a world of slogans: "lock her up," "impeach," "shout them down," "disrupt their meals," "hurl insults instead of responding to rational arguments."

The partisan divide has become so extreme that it extends beyond politics. When I wrote an article for the *Wall Street Journal* in September of 2018 about the punishment imposed on Serena Williams—loss of a game in her match—for her poor sportsmanship, many of the online comments reflected the political divisions in our nation. I advocated a neutral rule applicable to all sports and all competitors:

> No athletic event—not tennis, basketball, baseball, soccer, hockey, football or any other sport—should be decided by anything other than what the players do in competition.

This new approach would require significant changes in the rules of virtually every sport. No more technical fouls based on mouthing off in basketball. No ejection of players from baseball games for disputing calls. No loss of points or games for smashing rackets or calling an official a thief. No yellow or red cards for screaming obscenities at soccer referees. No penalty box for verbal taunting in hockey. No yardage penalties for touchdown celebrations.

There could still be game-deciding sanctions for hard fouls, beanballs, unnecessary roughness, or other violations that affect games or threaten injury, but not for speech or other expression.

Here are some of the comments:

> Sorry Alan, there was no "injustice" done to Serena Williams. She violated the rules and got what she deserved, unlike Hillary, who was not held to account according to the rules in place. Is that what you are advocating?

. . .

With what we saw in the recent Supreme Court Hearing by the left Dem members this sort of character assassination is real . . . now we just need for them to unleash their MS/13Antifa types upon society.

. . .

Once again in the service to his congenital contrarian nature, Dershowitz demonstrates he is just an every Moron.

. . .

Dershowitz is clearly on a late-innings Reputation Repair Tour of late after disgracing himself back in the OJ days . . .

Sigmund Freud once observed that civilization began the first time a human being hurled an insult instead of a spear. That may be true because physical violence is far worse than verbal assaults. But civilization will not progress until we hurl rational arguments instead of insults. Hurling insults may incite some to hurl spears, or fire guns, or plant bombs.

It is impossible to know which is cause and which is effect, but the growing extremism on both sides of the political spectrum makes nuanced conversation nearly impossible. The extreme right and the extreme left share a common tactic: shutting down their opponents without listening to them. True believers do not need to hear opposing arguments: they know they are right and their opponents are wrong. Neither the extreme right nor the extreme left support free speech as a principle equally applicable to their opponents. Free speech for me but not for thee—that is their tactic.

Many observers have noted that the extreme left is now on the forefront of seeking censorship on university campuses. They ask: when did the change occur? The answer is that there has been no change. The hard-left has never accepted the principle of free speech. Like the hard right, they employ freedom of speech as a *tactic* to help *themselves*. I grew up during the McCarthy era when the hard-left was being censored. So, of course, they advocated free speech—because they were the victims of censorship. The famous Free Speech Movement at Berkeley was another example of free speech for me but not for thee. Mario Savio and other leaders of the Free Speech Movement had no interest in promoting free speech for their political opponents. It was a partisan tactic designed to allow *them* to spread *their* message. Now the hard right is championing free speech on college campuses because they are the current victims of censorship. But don't count on the hard right to support free speech for the hard-left any more than one can count on the hard-left to support free speech for the hard right.

Freedom of speech is a centrist principle, generally supported both by authentic centrist liberals and by authentic centrist conservatives. Liberal centrists generally support free speech for conservative centrists as well as radicals on both sides. Centrist conservatives also generally support free speech for liberals as well as for radicals on both sides.

When I was on the national board of the ACLU back in the 1970s, my fellow board members included liberals and conservatives, democrats and republicans, all of whom had a common commitment to free speech *for me and thee*. We defended the rights of Nazis to march in Skokie, as well as the rights of communists to advocate their pernicious doctrines. We defended the free speech rights of pornographers, perverts, and other ne'er-do-wells. As H. L. Mencken wrote: "The trouble with fighting for human freedom is that one spends most of one's time defending scoundrels. For it is against scoundrels that oppressive laws are first aimed, and oppression must be stopped at the beginning if it is to be stopped at all."

The ACLU has now become part of the problem rather than part of the solution to partisan attacks on freedom of speech. Although the ACLU continues occasionally to represent a high-profile Neo-Nazi or white supremacist, its priorities have shifted away from freedom of speech and due process toward political issues and partisan opposition to President Trump. As I will show later in the book, it now supports and opposes political candidates, referenda, and judicial nominees. Its recent shift has earned it tens of millions of dollars in additional funding from radical leftists who see the ACLU as a weapon to be used against President Trump and the Republican Party. They no longer pass the shoe on the other foot test.

In writing this book, I will be accused—as I was when I wrote *Supreme Injustice*—of engaging in the "fallacy of the argument *ad hominem*": the fallacy that first-year philosophy students learn, namely, that arguments should be judged by their logic and persuasiveness, not by the personal characteristics of the man or woman offering them. To judge the merits of an argument by the person making it is to engage in a logical fallacy called the "fallacy of the argument *ad hominem*." *Ad hominem* is Latin for "of the person."

Having participated in thousands of public policy arguments for more than sixty years, I am convinced that this classic philosophical fallacy is itself a fallacy, especially in the context of public policy. In my experience, the merits and persuasiveness of a public policy argument often depend on who is making it, whether it is consistent with other arguments that person has made when the shoe was on the other foot, and whether it is motivated by partisan or other external considerations.

The shoe on the other foot test is not guilty of violating the fallacy *ad hominem*. It does not argue that the logic of an argument itself is weakened by the weakness of its proponent(s). Indeed, it is a corollary of the fallacy *ad hominem*: to the extent that anyone gives additional weight to an argument because of the credibility of those offering it, those offering it must pass the shoe on the other foot test. If they don't, then no credibility beyond the power of the argument itself should be accorded those offering the argument.

Lawyers and law professors are accomplished at constructing persuasive arguments on all sides of an issue. They are perfectly capable of persuading listeners—and even themselves—of the power of an argument, even if they would make the exact opposite argument if the shoe were on the other foot. In some cases, they have in fact made the opposite argument without shame, embarrassment, or fear of being accused of hypocrisy. Sometimes they make lame efforts to "distinguish" the cases—to show they are not really the same.

Practicing lawyers are, of course, permitted to offer arguments that help their clients even if they have offered inconsistent arguments for other clients in other cases. But judges, professors in their role as teachers, and public intellectuals are not.

So I ask every reader of this book to take the shoe on the other foot test: to look in the mirror and ask yourself—would you be making the arguments you are making if they hurt instead of helped your cause? I ask myself that question before I offer any argument. If I cannot honestly answer yes, I do not make the argument. I ask you to do the same. Be honest with yourself. If the answer is no, and if you continue to offer the arguments as neutral, principled positions, then you have failed the test and are guilty of hypocrisy. I hope you will join me in passing the test and offering only arguments that you would be willing to offer if the shoe were on the other foot.

In the columns that follow, I try to make arguments that would pass the shoe on the other foot test. I make the same arguments I would have made had Hillary Clinton been elected president and been subject to impeachment. I make the same arguments I would have made had a Democratic president nominated a controversial Supreme Court Justice who was accused of sexual misconduct. These arguments are based on neutral principles and objective constitutional analysis. It is up to each reader to decide whether these columns pass the shoe on the other foot test.

In Defense of Equally Applying the Law and Letting Our System Work

The equal application of law is of paramount importance to a functioning democracy. When partisan politics encroaches on the legal system and influences how the law is applied, democracy begins to erode.

Our institutions are far from perfect—and you'll find my recommendations for improving some of those institutions in the following pieces—but our judiciary and our systems of checks and balances must remain above the influence of political tribalism.

That imperative is in danger today, as partisan calls for impeachment blatantly failed the shoe on the other foot test, and created a dangerous precedent of expanding the law to serve political desires. Those who point out this hypocrisy—including myself, who made the same arguments when efforts were undertaken to impeach Bill Clinton and "lock up" Hillary Clinton—are vilified for "taking the other side," rather than praised for defending neutral principles. The pieces that follow highlight where our politics has gotten the best of the law, and what steps we can take to remedy it.

Federal Judge Agrees Nonpartisan Commission Beats Special Counsel[1]

Federal Judge T. S. Ellis, a distinguished jurist from Virginia, has just written an opinion denying former Trump campaign manager Paul Manafort's motion to dismiss the charges against him. Judge Ellis rejected the defense argument that Special Counsel Robert Mueller had exceeded his authority by investigating and prosecuting alleged crimes that preceded the 2016 election and that had little or nothing to do with Russian collusion in the election. But in rejecting this legal attack on the scope of the special counsel, Judge Ellis went out of his way to say that his decision should not be read as approving the appointment of a special counsel.

This is what he wrote:

> [This] conclusion should not be read as approval of the practice of appointing special counsel to prosecute cases of alleged high-level misconduct. Here, we have a prosecution of a campaign official, not a government official, for acts that occurred well before the presidential election. To be sure, it is plausible, indeed ultimately persuasive here, to argue that the investigation and prosecution has some relevance to the election which occurred months if not years after the alleged misconduct. But in the end that fact does not warrant dismissal of the superseding indictment. The Constitution's system of checks and balances, reflected to some extent in the regulations at issue, are designed to ensure that no single individual or branch of government has plenary or absolute power. The appointment of special prosecutors has the potential to disrupt those checks and balances, and to inject a level of toxic partnership into investigation of matters of public importance.

In a footnote, the judge echoed a proposal I made a year ago and had been much criticized by pundits: "A better mechanism for addressing concerns about election interference would be the creation of a bipartisan commission with subpoena power and the authority to investigate all issues related to alleged interference in the 2016 presidential election. If crimes were uncovered during the course of the commission's investigation, those crimes could be referred to appropriate existing authorities within the [Department of Justice]."

The judge concluded his opinion with wishful thinking:

> This case is a reminder that ultimately, our system of checks and balances and limitations on each branch's powers, although exquisitely designed, ultimately works only if people of virtue, sensitivity, and courage, not affected by the winds of public opinion, choose to work within the confines of the law. Let us hope that the people in charge of this prosecution, including the Special Counsel and the Assistant Attorney General, are such people. Although this case will continue, those involved should be sensitive to the danger unleashed when political disagreements are transformed into partisan prosecution.

Although I generally agree with the judge's nuanced assessment of the role for special counsel, I respectfully disagree that our system of checks and balances ultimately depends on the virtue of the individuals who serve in the three branches of government. James Madison, who was largely responsible for devising and defending our unique system of checks and balances, believed that "if men were angels" we would need no government. Nor would we need the cumbersome mechanisms of checks and balances. It is precisely because government officials too often lack virtue, and too often place partisanship over principle, that we need institutional checks. As Madison wrote, "If angels were to govern men, neither external nor internal controls on government would be necessary." But because humans govern other humans, we need "the auxiliary precautions" of institutional checks and balances.

It is for that reason, and not because I distrust Robert Mueller personally, that I oppose special counsels in situations like the current one. The risks alluded to by Judge Ellis, in my view, outweigh the benefits. This does not mean that Judge Ellis was wrong in his legal decision. Just as there is a determinative difference between sin and crime, there is a difference between principled opposition to special counsels and a legal conclusion that this counsel's appointment was unconstitutional or that he exceeded his powers. Since I am not a judge, it is enough for me to join Judge Ellis in his conclusion that a nonpartisan commission would have been "a better mechanism for addressing concerns about election interference."

Jeff Sessions Validates Chant to Lock Up Hillary Clinton[2]

At a Turning Point USA conference in Washington, Attorney General Jeff Sessions laughingly repeated the chant of conservative high school students to "lock her up," referring to Hillary Clinton. He said that he had "heard that a long time over the last campaign." Sessions was referring, of course, to Republican presidential candidate Donald Trump's campaign pledge to appoint a special prosecutor to investigate and charge "Crooked Hillary" with criminal behavior.

To the Justice Department's credit, no special counsel was appointed to investigate Clinton. To the contrary, Trump's own birds came home to roost when the Justice Department appointed, erroneously in my view, a Special Counsel to investigate alleged collusion between his campaign and Russian efforts to influence the 2016 election. This all goes to show just how politicized our criminal justice system has become. Both sides try to criminalize their political opponents. Both sides try to misuse the delicate constitutional mechanism of impeachment for partisan benefit. Both sides are prepared to abandon enduring civil liberties and democratic principles to serve their political ends.

The losers in this race to the bottom are the American people, who are best served by preserving tested neutral principles that should be applied equally to both sides of the political aisle. This is the truth of the shoe on the other foot test, which is simply an application of the golden rule: Do unto Democrats what you would have Democrats do unto you, and vice versa. Almost no one in our hyper-partisan world lives by this rule. Instead, for many Democrats, anything goes as long as it hurts Republicans, especially the president. For many Republicans and Trump voters, anything goes as long as it helps Trump and hurts Democrats.

I have insisted on applying the shoe test and the golden rule to my advocacy of civil liberties and constitutional rights. For this, I have, at different times, been pilloried by both sides and admired by both sides depending on whether my neutral principles hurt or help their partisan causes. Some misunderstand what I am doing. Others know exactly what I am doing, but pretend not to do so in order to condemn me. My position wins me no popularity contests, but neutral civil libertarians do not aspire to popularity. Rather, it is quite the opposite. Our main task is to defend the rights of whoever is most despised and unpopular, especially among our friends and peers at any point in time.

So I will continue to fight against the misuses of criminal law and the impeachment process without regard to who is hurt or helped. My life would be a lot easier right now if Hillary Clinton—for whom I voted—had been elected president and if Jeff Sessions were still in Senate leading the national chant of "lock her up" or "impeach her." I would be making precisely the same arguments with reference to her as I am now making with reference to Trump. The difference is that Democrats would be praising me and Republicans would be condemning me.

Let me be clear that this is not about me. I refer to the reaction to my arguments only to make the larger point about hypocrisy on both sides of the aisle. Even more dangerous than this hypocrisy is the misuse of the law by both sides. We can survive hypocrisy, which may be inherent in partisan politics. But what we cannot survive is establishing dangerous precedents by one side that can be used later against the other side. These dangerous precedents, such as over-criminalization of political differences and stretching the law to fit unpopular targets, lay around like loaded weapons that are capable of being used by anyone in power against the most vulnerable of citizens in this country.

So these are critical issues that affect all Americans regardless of party affiliation. We should all care about the weaponization of the law by those in power or those seeking power. Sessions should be criticized for validating the chant of "lock her up." As attorney general of the United States, he must reflect the utmost neutrality in administering the law. Not only must he do justice, but he must appear to be doing justice. He did not satisfy that appearance by validating the chant of "lock her up."

Trump's Bid to Silence Dissent Violates
Spirit of First Amendment[3]

President Trump recently threatened to strip the security clearances of top former government officials who criticized his performance at Helsinki with regard to Russian president Vladimir Putin. Were Trump to carry out this threat, he would be violating the spirit, if not the letter, of the First Amendment. Such a decision, directed only at those who exercised their First Amendment rights to criticize Trump, might be seen by the courts as punitive government action directed at the content of speech. Even threatening to do so might deter critics from exercising their free-speech rights.

Trump's threat is reminiscent of the decision by General Lewis B. Hershey, who was the director of the Selective Service System during the Vietnam War, to selectively draft critics of the war. In both cases, the government has the authority to act generally by cutting off security clearances or drafting individuals. But it may not have the constitutional power to act selectively against critics who are exercising their rights under the First Amendment.

Were the president to decide to end the security clearances of all former officials, the courts would be confronted with a legal issue similar to the one they faced with regard to the travel ban. In both situations, the president said things that suggest an unconstitutional motive: in the travel case, to ban Muslims; in the clearance matter, to stifle dissent. But then he acted, or would act, in a manner that on its face is constitutional: in the travel case, by not limiting the ban to Muslim countries; and in the clearance matter, by not limiting the cutoff to critics. In the travel case, a closely divided Supreme Court upheld the ban, but there is no assurance it would do so in the clearance matter. The difference is that the travel ban was directed against non-citizens, who have no constitutional rights, so the claim had to be based on a questionable expansion of the prohibition against the establishment of religion. In the clearance matter, the cutoff is directed against American citizens, and their claim would be a core violation of the right to free expression.

The Trump administration would argue that no one has the right to a security clearance. That is true. But even a governmentally granted privilege cannot generally be revoked by government officials as punishment for exercising one's First Amendment rights.

It would be a close case, and you can be sure the American Civil Liberties Union would bring the challenge, despite its recent softness on the First Amendment. It would bring this case because the organization is a big critic of Trump and makes its money bringing lawsuits against his administration. So it's a no-brainer for the partisans who now run what used to be a nonpartisan organization.

All Americans benefit from vigorous dissent, especially from security experts and former government officials. To be sure, some of the current criticism about which Trump is complaining seems partisan and over the top (e.g., accusing him of treasonous behavior in Helsinki), but that is precisely what the First Amendment is designed to protect: unfair and over-the-top criticism. No president should seek to stifle dissent, especially a president who himself is often partisan and over the top. I personally wish both sides would stop exaggerating and provide us with more nuanced exchanges, but the First Amendment doesn't distinguish between good and bad speech. It leaves that to the citizens.

Even if the president's actions were to be ruled constitutional, no president should use his enormous powers over our national security to stifle or deter dissent. So please, Mr. President, do not selectively remove the security clearance of those former government officials who disagree with you. Respond to them in the marketplace of ideas, but don't try to shut down their stalls. This is not about you, Mr. President. Nor is it about your critics. It is about the right of the American people to hear all sides of controversial issues without government officials placing their thumb on the scales of the marketplace of ideas.

Impeaching Rosenstein
May Hurt Trump[4]

The decision by a group of Republicans to seek a bill of impeachment against Deputy Attorney General Rod Rosenstein may well backfire against President Trump. The conservative lawmakers who are seeking to introduce this bill of impeachment have charged Rosenstein with conduct that does not meet the constitutional criteria for impeachment.

As I pointed out in the introduction to this book, the constitutional criteria are very specific: "Treason, bribery, or other high crimes and misdemeanors." These specified crimes do not include the allegations being made against Rosenstein. Accordingly, the Republicans who support this bill of impeachment are implicitly siding with Democrats who argue that Trump can be impeached for noncriminal conduct.

In the introduction, I lay out the history of the impeachment clause and demonstrate, I think quite persuasively, that the Framers intended to limit impeachment and removal to government officials who are tried and convicted by the Senate of the crimes specified in the Constitution. The Framers rejected a proposal allowing removal for "maladministration" or other noncriminal actions or policy differences. Now these Republican lawmakers are taking the Democratic side of this debate, calling for impeachment of Rosenstein for actions that do not fit the specified criteria under the Constitution.

If and when the Democrats regain control of the House, there will surely be efforts to vote a bill of impeachment against President Trump. Proponents of such a bill will argue, as you'll recall Congresswoman Maxine Waters (D-Calif.) and Gerald Ford before her have, that the criteria for impeachment are anything the House votes on, regardless of the words of the Constitution. She said, "Impeachment is whatever Congress says it is. There is no law."

These lawless approaches to impeachment fly in the face of the Constitution. It would be as if senators decided that a two-thirds vote was not necessary for removal, despite the fact that the Constitution explicitly requires such a supermajority. This entire episode demonstrates a point I make in this book and have been making for a long time: namely, that both sides are abusing constitutional criteria for impeachment for reversible partisan advantages. Both sides are abusing the criminal law by stretching it and weaponizing it to target political opponents. Both sides seem to forget that what today may serve their partisan interests will become an enduring precedent that will soon be used by their political opponents against them.

The ultimate losers are all Americans who rely on neutral civil liberties and nonpartisan constitutional protections. Once these civil liberties and rights are weaponized for partisan purposes, they no longer serve the democratic function for which they were intended, namely, requiring the neutral rule of law to govern all actions by federal and state officials.

So, let these Republican lawmakers, who are seeking partisan gain from trying to impeach Rosenstein, look in the mirror and understand the boomerang effect of such shortsighted actions. They should immediately drop any plan to impeach Rosenstein. If they truly believe he improperly refused to comply with subpoenas, they have the option of seeking a contempt citation from a court. The sanction must fit the offense, and the sanction of impeachment does not fit the alleged offense of failing to comply with subpoenas. That is what the contempt power is for.

Among the charges in the proposed bill of impeachment is the allegation that Rosenstein has a conflict of interest because he is a potential witness to any charge of obstruction of justice against the president growing out of his firing of former FBI director James Comey. I agree that Rosenstein does have a conflict of interest, but the proper remedy for this is not impeachment. Rather, there could be a motion to the court to remove him from the investigation based on his conflict of interest.

I am sending a copy of this book to every member of Congress. Let them read the history of the impeachment and removal clause. Let them read *The Federalist Papers*. Let them listen to the debates among those who ratified the Constitution. Most of all, let them read, with great care, the actual words of the Framers. When they do, they will become convinced that it is safer for all Americans, regardless of party affiliation, to reserve the impeachment and removal power for government officials who have committed the crimes designated in the Constitution, rather than using this power for partisan advantage.

Who Leaked the Trump Tape?[5]

Someone leaked the lawyer/client confidential tape containing a conversation between President Donald J. Trump and his lawyer Michael Cohen. A former judge, assigned by the presiding judge to evaluate the seized tapes, reportedly concluded that this conversation was privileged. Yet someone leaked their contents. President Trump's current lawyer, Rudy Giuliani, then waived the privilege as to that tape. He said he never would have waived it had its existence and content not been improperly leaked.

So, the question remains. Who leaked this privileged material? If it was anyone in the Trump camp, there would be no violation of confidentiality, as the privilege belongs to the client, namely Trump, who can waive it. But no one else, most especially his lawyer, may properly waive the privilege. And Giuliani has categorically denied that it was leaked by Trump or anyone on his behalf. Indeed, he has expressed outrage at the leak.

Whom does that leave? Cohen is an obvious suspect, although I am confident that his excellent and experienced lawyer, Lanny Davis, would not have done so. Perhaps Cohen himself, who ran into Michael Avenatti at a restaurant, told him about the tape. We simply do not know.

It is unlikely that any judicial or prosecutorial authority is responsible for the leak, because they would have more to lose than to gain if they were caught.

This again raises the reason that this is important to all Americans, beyond the immediate parties to this taped conversation: it may well discourage clients, patients, penitents, and others from confiding in their lawyers, doctors, priests, and the professionals who promise them confidentiality. Cohen promised confidentiality and yet the world heard what his client confided in him. We know he recorded the confidential conversation without the knowledge of his client. That is bad enough. Then it was deliberately

leaked by someone who must have believed he or she would reap some benefit or advantage from having the public hear it.

We must find out who is the source of this damaging leak—damaging to
all Americans who place their faith in the promise of confidentiality from
the professionals in whom they confide.

It is an ethical violation, subject to serious sanctions including disbar-
ment, for a lawyer to disclose, or cause to be disclosed, privileged conversations. And for good reason. The obligation of a lawyer not to disclose
confidential information is codified in Rule 1.6 of the New York Bar. This
broad rule prohibits, subject to exceptions not present in this case, any knowing disclosure of confidential information. That plainly covers the kind of
conversation we have all now heard in the leaked tape: namely, the discussion between Trump and his attorney as to how to deal with a potential
messy problem. We may not like the subject matter under discussion, but it is
fully covered by the privilege, as the former judge rightly found. That is why
this leak is so difficult to fathom. The risks to the leaker are greater than any
short-term benefit. But the fact remains that the leak occurred, and now it is
imperative that the leaker be exposed and held to account.

This can be accomplished in several ways. Judge Kimba Wood, who is
presiding over the matter, could hold a hearing in which the potential sus-
pects are placed under oath and asked the simple question whether they
leaked the contents of the tape and/or whether they know who the leaker
was. Obviously, people who are willing improperly to leak confidential material may also be willing to lie about it under oath, but the consequences of
lying under oath are greater than leaking, as leaking is not a crime but perjury is.

Notwithstanding the importance of this issue, there seems to be little
interest among the participants in determining who leaked the tape. There
has been no call for an investigation. Perhaps this is because both sides think
they benefited from the leak. I leave that to the public, and eventually the
courts, to determine. What is clear is who was hurt by the leak: all Americans
who rely on confidentiality—which means all of us—were hurt when the
world was allowed to listen to a lawyer/client privileged conversation that no
one except the participants should ever have heard.

An Obstruction Case Against Trump Would Be a Civil Libertarian Nightmare[6]

The *New York Times* has reported that, according to three sources, Special Counsel Robert Mueller is trying to stitch together an obstruction of justice case against President Trump based on his public tweets, TV appearances, conversations with public officials, and other entirely lawful acts. If this is true, it suggests that there is no "smoking gun" or fire, not even any kindling. It suggests that all Mueller seems to have is some dry twigs from which he is trying to build a bonfire. The *New York Times* headline, "Mueller Looking for Obstruction in Trump Tweets," should raise a red flag for all civil libertarians. This is exactly the kind of creative manufacturing of crimes from innocent and indeed constitutionally protected acts that endangers the liberties of all Americans.

Just imagine a prosecutor going through all of your tweets, all of your conversations, and all of your emails in search of a plausible theory of criminality based on a statute such as obstruction of justice. If Mueller manages to cobble together an obstruction of justice case from innocent communications, then this dangerous precedent will lie around like a loaded gun ready to be used by any vindictive prosecutors against any plausible target. That could be you or someone you love. It could be a Democrat or a Republican. It could be a liberal or a conservative.

In the brilliant and increasingly relevant book, *Three Felonies a Day*, the experienced attorney and author Harvey Silverglate describes a "game" prosecutors play. One of them names a known target, and the others scour the criminal code to find three felonies he or she may have committed. If the report is accurate, Mueller and his team may be playing this game with a real live target, namely, President Trump.

I recall a case when the Equal Rights Amendment was pending and the votes of Illinois legislators were essential to secure ratification by that state. A naive young woman approached a legislator and offered a contribution to his campaign in exchange for a commitment that he would do the right thing and vote for equal rights for women. The woman was arrested and charged with attempted bribery under a vague statute.

Civil libertarians were properly outraged in that case. Defenders of Mueller will surely argue that it is common for prosecutors to stitch together innocent conduct to manufacture a crime, especially when the target is a suspected drug dealer, terrorist, or gangster. Tragically, they are right. There are such cases, but there should not be. Many wrongs do not make a right. Moreover, in those cases, the underlying conduct is generally done in secret. Here, Mueller evidently is trying to turn public communications—core First Amendment expressions—into a crime.

The time has come, indeed it is long overdue, for all Americans to take a hard look at broad and ambiguous statutes that empower prosecutors to be "creative." There is a concept in criminal law known as lenity. If there are numerous ways of interpreting a statute, the law requires that it be interpreted in the most reasonably narrow way, so as to avoid empowering prosecutors to target unpopular defendants. Failing to apply this concept to constitutionally protected emails, tweets, messages, and other forms of communication should concern every civil libertarian, even those who are anxious to find legal weapons with which to target President Trump.

Imagine if Hillary Clinton had been elected and a special counsel was trying to stitch together an obstruction case against her for allegedly erasing emails, using her own home server, and taking other ambiguous actions. Democrats would immediately become civil libertarians and denounce such a "witch hunt." Now it is the Republicans who are calling the investigation a "witch hunt." That term may overstate what is happening, but the danger of criminalizing political differences is real.

The problem with turning communications, which by themselves are not criminal, into a criminal obstruction case is that life is lived prospectively while prosecutors look at evidence retrospectively. As the philosopher Søren Kierkegaard put it, "Life can only be understood backwards, but it must be lived forward." In legal terms, this means that isolated statements may have an innocent intention at the time they were made, but when looked at backwards they may appear to be part of a guilty pattern. Even more fundamentally, crime requires both guilty acts and guilty intentions.

There is considerable danger in turning innocent acts, especially constitutionally protected ones, into criminal obstruction based on an intent inferred after the fact from a pattern that may not have been contemplated at the time. This is what Mueller seems to be doing, if the report is accurate. All of us who care about preserving civil liberties and the rule of law should be concerned about this dangerous approach to stitching together a guilty fabric from innocent threads.

Dangers to the First Amendment
If Foreign Campaign Dirt Is Criminal[7]

T he "get Trump at any cost" legal posse has come up with a theory that puts not only the First Amendment at risk, but also the rights of voters to receive information about presidential and other political candidates. According to this theory, the federal election campaign statutes would make it a crime for any candidate to receive information from a foreign source about his or her opponent. The principal statute at issue reads as follows: "It shall be unlawful for (1) a foreign national, directly or indirectly, to make: (A) a contribution or donation of money or other thing of value, or to make an express or implied promise to make a contribution or donation, in connection with a federal, state, or local election."

The language and legislative history of the statute suggest that it was intended to prohibit the solicitation and receipt of cash or other material items of value. Although its words are open to a broad interpretation that would include information of value, to interpret the statute in that way would put it in direct conflict with the First Amendment, which at its core, protects information that political candidates can use to inform the American public about their opponents. If the statute were interpreted to apply to obtaining negative information about an opponent, the following hypotheticals would become reality. Remember these are purely hypotheticals, not based on any facts, intended to make an argument.

A Canadian reporter based in Washington provides information to the Hillary Clinton campaign proving that Donald Trump bribed Canadian officials to secure permits to build a hotel in Montreal. An Israeli green card holder attending an American university discovers that Clinton, while a student at Wellesley College, had joined the Communist Party. Bernie Sanders is given information by a French socialist proving that Clinton and Trump colluded to defeat his primary bid. A Russian lawyer gives evidence that Clinton deliberately destroyed her emails to cover up crimes. A British spy provides information that Trump engaged in improper sexual behavior while in Moscow. An Australian journalist provides a recording of James Comey telling a friend that he purposely reopened the Clinton email probe to defeat her bid for president.

All of these hypotheticals, most of which bear no reality but some of which may come close, would be covered by an interpretation of the statute that brought information within the words "a contribution of money or other thing of value." In each of these hypotheticals, the information is provided by a foreign national. In each of these hypotheticals, the information is at the core of the First Amendment.

Yet, serious academics and other commentators who have joined the "get Trump at any cost" legal posse have argued on national television that the statute prohibits the kind of information that Russians may have wanted to offer the Trump campaign at the Trump Tower meeting. They argue that even if the information was obtained by the Russians lawfully and was not part of a larger "collusion" scheme, the mere gathering of any information from a foreigner—friend or foe—is a criminal violation of campaign laws.

Defenders of the unconstitutionally broad interpretation of this statute might argue that all of the information contained in the above hypotheticals could be given directly to the media, which would then publish it. That may well be true, but if the information was first given to a political candidate or campaign, it could not be transmitted by that candidate or campaign to the media. To do so would be to circumvent the statute by laundering the information through the media. Moreover, under the First Amendment, a candidate would have the right to use or withhold all or part of this information as it best served his or her campaign, rather than giving it to the media. Even if the media published the information, the First Amendment rights of candidates would be violated.

It's worth revisiting the shoe test as a guiding principle here: If President Hillary Clinton were being investigated for violation of campaign finance laws for seeking to obtain negative information about Donald Trump, the American Civil Liberties Union would be up in arms about this obvious violation of the most fundamental principles protecting the freedom of expression of candidates. But since the election of Trump, the ACLU and many other lifelong civil libertarians have failed the shoe on the other foot test. They have applied one standard to Clinton and a quite different one to Trump.

This double standard hypocrisy reflects a broader problem. Throughout the world, civil liberties have been weaponized by both the right and the left in support of their ideological agendas. The standard is "free speech for me but not for thee" instead of free speech and civil liberties for all including opponents. Under any neutral approach to constitutional principles, our campaign laws must not be broadened to deny candidates the right to receive negative information about their opponents.

Is "The Truth" the Truth When
It Comes to Prosecutors?[8]

When Rudy Giuliani stated, perhaps inartfully, that "truth isn't truth," he was getting at a higher—or should I say lower—truth. This is a truth that virtually every experienced defense attorney and prosecutor understands: namely, that prosecutors get to pick which witness—and which "truth"—to believe.

Giuliani was discussing US President Donald Trump's decision whether or not to be interviewed by Special Counsel Robert Mueller. Giuliani made the point that even if President Trump testified truthfully, he could be accused of lying to a prosecutor—a serious felony—if the prosecutor chose to believe witnesses who have provided a different account.

To be specific, President Trump has stated publicly that he was not aware of the Trump Tower meeting between a Russian woman and his son until after it took place. One of Trump's attorneys at the time, Michael Cohen, has apparently said that Trump was aware of the meeting.

President Trump has also stated that he did not ask former FBI Director James Comey to go easy on Michael Flynn. Comey has said that President Trump did.

If President Trump were to repeat these denials in an interview with a prosecutor, he would be walking into a perjury trap even if he truly believed that his denials were the complete truth, and even if he actually were telling the complete truth. All the special counsel needs in order to charge a subject of an investigation with lying to a prosecutor is a single witness willing to contradict the subject. The witness may himself be a criminal who has been squeezed into "singing" in order to save his own skin. The witness may not only be "singing," he may also be "composing," as discussed previously and corroborated by Judge Ellis. Under federal law, the testimony of such a "flipped witness" need not be corroborated in order to secure a conviction.

Because of these realities, most experienced defense attorneys would never allow their clients to get into a swearing contest with a flipped witness, even if the client were telling the absolute truth. That is what Rudy Giuliani meant when he said, in the context of a decision whether to have his client interviewed by the Special Counsel, that "truth isn't truth." Truth may be truth in science (although even scientific truth is subject to challenge and revision), but when it comes to a special counsel, truth is often in the eyes—and ambitions—of prosecutors, who decide which "truth" to believe.

Every experienced defense attorney with whom I have discussed this issue has said that he or she would never advise a client in President Trump's situation to be interviewed by the Special Counsel, even if that interview were limited to a handful of questions. Even one question that results in an answer that is contradicted by one witness would be enough to spring the perjury trap. That is why pundits and commentators who repeatedly pronounce that if President Trump is telling the truth he risks nothing by submitting to an interview are simply wrong. Many former prosecutors who repeat this falsehood in their roles as "expert" commentators know the truth. But in their "anything goes" attitude when it comes to nailing President Trump, they are willing to mislead the public into believing that only witnesses who willfully lie are at risk from an interview.

Traditionally, it has been liberals and civil libertarians who have complained about prosecutors springing perjury traps using questionable flipped witnesses. Traditionally, it has been conservatives and law-and-order types who have defended this tactic. But now that President Trump is in the crosshairs of the Special Counsel, the attitudes have been flipped as quickly as a witness threatened with prosecution.

Hypocrisy abounds on both sides. I, for one, am pleased that Rudy Giuliani, who himself was a tough prosecutor, now understands how this tactic can be used to trap innocent people. I am disappointed, however, that so many liberals, civil libertarians, and defense attorneys are unwilling to criticize this tactic when it is directed at a president of whom they disapprove.

Did President Trump Violate Campaign Finance Laws?[9]

Ever since the news broke that Michael Cohen pleaded guilty to finance laws and swore that candidate Donald Trump directed him to do so, I have been reviewing the morass of rules and laws that govern campaign finance. I have been teaching and practicing criminal law for more than a half century, and yet I have to acknowledge that I am having difficulty understanding the laws as they relate to the allegations made by Cohen against President Trump. But a few things are clear in this case.

A candidate is free to contribute to his or her own campaign. It also is not criminal for a candidate to pay hush money to women whose disclosures might endanger his campaign. So if candidate Trump paid hush money to his two accusers, there would be no violation of any campaign or other laws. To be sure, if he did so for the purpose of helping his campaign, as distinguished from helping his marriage, his campaign would have to disclose any such contribution and failure to do so might be a violation of a campaign law—but the payments themselves would be entirely lawful.

If, on the other hand, Cohen made the payments by himself, without direction from the president, then that would constitute an impermissible campaign contribution from a third party. But if Cohen was merely acting as a lawyer for Trump and advancing the payments, with an expectation of repayment, then it would be hard to find a campaign finance crime other than failure to report by the campaign.

Failure to report all campaign contributions is fairly common in political campaigns in the United States. Moreover, the offense is committed not by the candidate, but rather by the campaign, and is generally subject to a fine. Though it is wrong, it certainly is not the kind of high crime and misdemeanor that could serve as the basis for a constitutionally authorized impeachment and removal of a duly elected president.

Moreover, prosecutors should be reluctant to rely on the uncorroborated word of a defendant who pleaded guilty to lying and defrauding. Thomas Jefferson once observed that a criminal statute, to be fairly enforceable, must be so clear that it can be understood by the average person reading it while running. He did not mean while running for office. He meant that a criminal statute must not be subject to varying reasonable interpretations.

Anyone reading the collection of statutes and regulations that govern elections would immediately conclude, even while sitting, that they do not satisfy this Jeffersonian criteria. Reasonable people can disagree about whether these open-ended laws apply to any of the acts and omissions that Cohen alleged against Trump. An overzealous prosecutor could, of course, stretch the words of the accordion-like statute to target a political enemy, or read it more narrowly to favor a political friend. If the same morass of laws were being applied to a President Hillary Clinton, civil libertarians would be up in arms about their ambiguity.

As a civil libertarian who voted for and contributed to the Clinton campaign in 2016, I am critical as well of efforts to stretch these laws so as to target a president against whom I voted. The guilty plea of Cohen, coupled with the conviction of Paul Manafort, does not make Trump look good politically. He promised the American people to surround himself with the best advisors, but he surrounded himself with too many people who broke the law, even if he himself was not legally complicit. However, the rule of law demands that we distinguish between political sins and federal felonies. As the record now stands, Trump appears to be guilty of political sins but not federal felonies or impeachable offenses.

You would never know that if you just watched those cable television channels that are determined to find crimes and impeachable offenses against President Trump without regard to the law or consideration of civil liberties. Applying the shoe on the other foot test, it's clear there are still large gaps between the plea of guilty of Cohen on the one hand, and crimes or impeachable offenses against Trump on the other. Until and unless those gaps are filled with credible evidence of criminal behavior by the president, his enemies should be cautious about tolling the death knell for this presidency.

Who Is Guarding the Guardians?[10]

Our system of checks and balances is working tolerably well. The courts are reviewing executive orders, striking down some, upholding others. Congress may soon have one chamber controlled by Democrats, empowering it to conduct investigations and hearings regarding the president. The media is doing its job, despite being attacked by the president. So are the academy, religious bodies, the business world, and other mechanisms that are part of our informal checks and balances.

It is not perfect, but no system of governance is ever perfect, as Winston Churchill reminded us when he said, "Democracy is the worst form of government except for all the others that have been tried over time." The same can be said about our imperfect system of checks and balances.

The only institution of government that is not currently being checked is the prosecutorial branch. Although President Trump toyed with the idea of firing Robert Mueller, he will not do so. Nor will he fire prosecutors in the Southern District of New York who are investigating his associates. Indeed, Congress is considering legislation that would insulate prosecutors, especially independent counsels, even further.

It is important for prosecutors to be independent of politics, but prosecutors are not above the law. Prosecutorial abuse has long been rampant throughout the country, as civil libertarians have been pointing out from time immemorial. The Supreme Court has immunized prosecutors from legal liability for many of their excesses because prosecutors are guardians of justice.

Yet, as the Romans asked, "Who will guard the guardians?"

In theory, the attorney general of the United States is supposed to check against prosecutorial abuses by federal prosecutors. But Attorney General Jeff Sessions has recused himself from this entire investigation and his deputy, Rod Rosenstein, is conflicted by his status as a key witness in many obstruction of justice investigations of the president. State prosecutors are subject to even fewer checks, and many of them are elected and play to their constituencies.

The courts, too, are supposed to serve as a check against prosecutorial abuses. Yet when District Judge T. S. Ellis, who presided over the first trial of former Trump campaign chairman Paul Manafort, called out prosecutors for using Manafort as a means to getting their real target, President Trump, Ellis was roundly criticized, including by some civil libertarians. Despite his criticisms of the special counsel, Ellis lacked the power to do much about what he regarded as abuses.

The dangerous reality is that, today, many prosecutors are above the law, even when they engage in prosecutorial misconduct. There is no effective check on their overzealousness. Many of these abuses occur behind the closed doors of a prosecutor's office, in the secrecy of grand jury rooms and in the corridors where secret deals are made with informers. Prosecutorial decisions and actions are among the least transparent of any government officials.

Today, the Special Counsel, the Southern District, the New York attorney general, the Manhattan district attorney, and other prosecutors are targeting President Trump and his associates. Tomorrow they could be targeting Democrats. The day after tomorrow, they could be coming after you. There should be an effective check on prosecutors. It should be a check that does not interfere with their political independence but that makes sure they are not targeting Americans based on politics, or employing prosecutorial tactics that endanger civil liberties.

One check that seems to be working is the inspector general of the Justice Department, whose report on the conduct of former FBI Director James Comey during the campaign was widely seen as fair and objective. But the inspector general's jurisdiction is narrowly defined and his resources are limited. Congress should create a permanent office, outside of politics, staffed by independent experts in legal ethics, prosecutorial tactics, and constitutional law to oversee federal prosecutors around the country and to assure that they are not overstepping their bounds.

Among those serving in such an office might be distinguished former prosecutors such as Robert Morgenthau, professors of legal ethics such as Stephen Gillers, and renowned constitutional lawyers such as Floyd Abrams. Creation of such an office should receive bipartisan support since prosecutorial misconduct has victimized Democrats and Republicans alike. The beneficiaries would be ordinary Americans who today have no recourse against prosecutorial abuses that are often committed below the radar by overzealous prosecutors anxious to advance their careers.

Honest prosecutors are guardians of our liberty but they, themselves, must be subject to nonpolitical oversight and accountability. Without a process for guarding our guardians, our system of checks and balances will remain incomplete.

Should it be Illegal for Prosecutors to "Flip" Witnesses?[11]

Recently President Trump said that "flipping" a witness to incriminate a prosecutorial target "almost ought to be outlawed," saying that individuals who flip are often untruthful.

This statement raises the important question of whether it should be illegal to offer a witness a valuable consideration for providing testimony, as prosecutors allegedly did with Lieutenant General Michael T. Flynn.

Interestingly, it is already illegal for a lawyer to do that—if the lawyer is a defense attorney. If any defense attorney offers a witness an inducement to testify favorably to his client—even if his testimony is 100 percent truthful—that lawyer will be disbarred, prosecuted, and imprisoned. But it is perfectly legal, indeed widely regarded as commendable, for prosecutors to offer major inducements in order to get witnesses to testify against their targets. These inducements include money, freedom from imprisonment, and even life itself.

There are cases in which courts have allowed prosecutors to pay witnesses contingent fees—that is, bonuses—if their testimony results in convictions. There are cases in which prosecutors have threatened to seek the death penalty unless a witness flips against a co-defendant. There are cases in which prosecutors threaten to prosecute wives, children, parents, and siblings of witnesses unless they flip, to offer ten- or twenty-year reductions in sentences in exchange for favorable testimony.

That is why Judge Ellis, who presided over the first Manafort trial, observed that flipped witnesses sometimes have an inducement not only to "sing" but to "compose"—that is, to embellish. Michael Cohen may have been composing when he said through his lawyer, that President Trump knew about the Trump Tower meeting between his son (Donald Trump Jr.) and a Russian. Cohen's lawyer has now, commendably, walked back this accusation.

You might wonder how all this is legal in light of the federal statute that prohibits the payment of anything of value in order to influence the testimony of a witness. Here is what the statute says:

> *Whoever* . . . directly or indirectly, gives, offers, or promises anything of value to any person, for or because of the testimony under oath or affirmation given or to be given by such person as a witness is guilty of a felony. [US Code § 201 (c)(2), emphasis added]

A literal reading of the statute would encompass the offers and threats routinely made by prosecutors to secure the testimony of witnesses. After all, it applies to "whoever," and "any," but the courts have ruled that prosecutors are exempt from the words of the statute. Only defense attorneys and their clients are covered by it, despite the broad language.

Several years ago, a US Court of Appeals applied the language of the statute to prosecutors, raising questions about the entire process of paying witnesses for their testimony. But that decision was quickly reversed by a ruling that continued the exemption of prosecutors from the coverage of the statute.

The only requirement is that prosecutors must inform the judge, jury, and defense attorneys of all payments and promises made to witnesses. But such disclosure would not be enough to exempt defense attorneys or defendants from the criminal penalties provided by the witness tampering statute. This disparity unlevels the playing field of our adversary system of justice.

Civil libertarians and criminal defense attorneys have long been skeptical of the widespread tactics used by prosecutors to intimidate, induce, buy, or rent witnesses. We understand how central this tactic is in the way prosecutors bring cases today. Coupled with the other side of the coin—under which defendants who go to trial receive multiples of the sentence they would have received had they pleaded guilty—these twin tactics explain why so few cases today ever get before a jury: fewer than 10 percent in federal court. It is far more advantageous to cooperate with prosecutors than to challenge them.

Notwithstanding the importance of these tactics, they should raise troubling concerns among anyone concerned with basic fairness.

So, I welcome President Trump's statement about the unfairness of our present system of flipping witnesses, even though I realize it is somewhat self-serving. Would he and his supporters be equally concerned if a special counsel or other prosecutors were using these tactics against his political opponents? Nevertheless, it is important to have these issues raised and debated by all Americans. Today they are being used against Republicans, tomorrow they may be used against Democrats, and every day they are being used against ordinary Americans caught up in our deeply flawed criminal justice system that relies far too heavily on the testimony of flipped witnesses.

Will Mueller Subpoena Trump?
[12]

The long delay by Robert Mueller's team in responding to the Trump legal team's offer to sit down with prosecutors has fueled speculation as to the special counsel's plans. One possibility is that Mueller's team is preparing to subpoena the president and to defend the subpoena against expected constitutional challenge.

Months ago I speculated, paraphrasing *The Godfather*, that the Trump team would be making Mueller an offer he couldn't accept. The purpose behind making such an offer is to allow President Trump to argue that it was Mueller, not he, who turned down the opportunity for a meeting. If that indeed is the tactic, it is likely that Mueller has seen through it and no longer wants to engage in what he regards as a sham negotiation. Mueller may, of course, respond in kind by making the Trump team an offer he knows it can't accept. In either case, the end result may well be a stalemate in the negotiations and no face-to-face meeting between prosecutors and the president.

If that is the end result, then Mueller has several options. The most obvious is that he could subpoena Trump to appear in front of a grand jury. If the president refuses, Mueller can seek a court order. The Trump team would then claim a variety of privileges and the court might well grant some and deny others. The court should, in my view, disallow any questioning of a sitting president about the motives behind actions he took that were authorized by Article II of the Constitution. Allowing the president's motives to be questioned by prosecutors sends us down a slippery constitutional slope, especially in a world where all presidents have mixed motives for their actions.

Presidents have patriotic, partisan, historic, financial, egotistical, and other motives for their actions. Allowing a prosecutor to parse these motives would undercut the authority of every president. So it is likely that a judge would refuse to allow prosecutors to ask a president why he fired or pardoned anyone. The Supreme Court has already suggested that the president's motives in enacting a travel ban do not convert a constitutionally authorized act into an unconstitutional abuse.

But a court might well allow prosecutors to question a president about actions he took before he became president, which are not covered by any privilege. These actions would include paying hush money to accusers, failure to report campaign contributions, and ordinary economic activities. The problem for Mueller is that these actions prior to becoming president are largely within the jurisdiction of the Southern District of New York, which is investigating these matters, not the special counsel.

Trump's team may also try a broadside attack on the power of prosecutors to subpoena a president for any purpose. They could argue that since a sitting president cannot be indicted or tried for alleged crimes, the use of a grand jury is improper. Only Congress may investigate allegedly impeachable offenses. Alternatively, the Trump team might argue that a prosecutor must show extraordinary need to subpoena a sitting president and there is no need to do that in this case because so many other people, including White House counsel Don McGahn, have provided information. Subpoenaing the president to ask him questions to which they already know the answers is a quintessential "perjury trap."

No one can predict how these arguments will resonate with a court. That is why both sides have been cautious in provoking a legal and constitutional challenge. Mueller also has an alternative that would not involve a subpoena. He could simply write a report highlighting the fact that the president has refused to sit down with him, despite statements by Trump that he has nothing to hide. He could use the president's refusal as a building block in a critical report that would be sent to Congress and, ultimately, released to the public.

So stay tuned as the Trump and Mueller teams position themselves for both legal and public relations battles. The Trump team's goal is to have the public see this conflict as largely political, because such a perception would strengthen Trump's base and weaken the credibility of any adverse report. The Mueller team's goal is to have the public see this as an objective legal dispute that is not political in nature but, rather, an application of the rule of law to a controversial president.

In the end, both sides will succeed to some degree in the court of public opinion. But in the court of law, there probably will be a winner and a loser. For now, however, it is too early to know the outcome.

Trump is No Unindicted Co-Conspirator[13]

During Brett Kavanaugh's confirmation hearings, Senator Richard Blumenthal (D-CT) questioned the legitimacy of the judge's appointment to the High Court. Blumenthal said in his opening remarks: "The president of the United States who has nominated you is an unindicted co-conspirator. . . ." Senator Cory Booker has also characterized Trump as "an unindicted co-conspirator."

Following Cohen's guilty plea, pundits across the political spectrum have claimed that since Cohen stated in his allocution that he paid hush money "at the direction of a candidate for federal office," President Trump is now an unindicted co-conspirator.

On Fox News, Jonathan Turley, a law professor at George Washington University, stated that, "If the [prosecutors] believe that what's in this indictment was true, and that he was directed to make this payment . . . then the president just became an unindicted co-conspirator."

Before this claim is repeated so often that people assume it is true, let me state categorically that Donald Trump is *not* an unindicted co-conspirator and that it is *wrong* to characterize him as such. An unindicted co-conspirator is someone against whom a *grand jury* has *found probable cause*, on the basis of *evidence*, that he or she is guilty of being a co-conspirator in a crime. But as far as we know there has been no grand jury indictment in this case, because Cohen *waived* the grand jury and pleaded guilty to an "information" prepared by a *prosecutor*, not a grand jury. An information is used in federal trials generally when a defendant voluntary pleads guilty and waives the right of an indictment by a grand jury. So unless there is a secret indictment against Cohen accusing Trump of being his co-conspirator, Trump cannot be an unindicted co-conspirator.

Moreover, the information against Cohen did not include the allegation by Michael Cohen that he was directed to pay hush money by the candidate.

That self-serving accusation was made by Cohen in his statement to the judge. So it cannot be the basis for a conclusion that Trump is an unindicted co-conspirator.

Unlike President Nixon, who had been named an unindicted co-conspirator in an indictment handed down by a grand jury, President Trump has not been accused by a grand jury indictment of anything thus far. Cohen's guilty plea and allocution cannot turn the president into an unindicted co-conspirator. Only a grand jury can.

Moreover, even if Trump *were* to be an unindicted co-conspirator, civil libertarians should be wary of any such designation.

When President Nixon was named "unindicted co-conspirator" in 1974, I yelled foul, even though I voted against Nixon and was critical of most of his policies. I thought it was unfair to designate the president as an unindicted co-conspirator, since a person in that status has no right to defend himself because he is never brought to trial. I urged the ACLU, on whose board I then served, to challenge this misuse of the grand jury and to protect our political enemy's civil liberties.

Courts have also noted that unindicted co-conspirators have no legal forum in which to defend themselves. In *United States v. Briggs*, 514 F.2d 794 (5th Cir. 1975), the Fifth Circuit Court of Appeals found that a federal grand jury had violated the due process rights of several activists when it named them as unindicted co-conspirators in a plot to disrupt the 1972 Republican National Convention. The court wrote that the due process rights of the alleged co-conspirators were violated and suggested that if the government had probable cause, it should have indicted the co-conspirators instead of naming them in a "presentment." A "presentment" simply names the accused, but is not the basis for a trial. The *Briggs* court wrote:

> A presentment is a foul blow. It wins the importance of a judicial document; yet it lacks its principal attributes the right to answer and to appeal. It accuses, but furnishes no forum for denial. No one knows upon what evidence the findings are based. An indictment may be challenged even defeated. The presentment is immune. It is like the "hit and run" motorist. Before application can be made to suppress it, it is the subject of public gossip. The damage is done.

The injury it may unjustly inflict may never be healed.

United States v. Briggs, 514 F.2d 794, 803 (5th Cir. 1975)

Because of the potential due process violations, federal prosecutors are properly cautioned against identifying people as unindicted co-conspirators. As the US Attorney's Office Manual states:

> In the absence of some significant justification, federal prosecutors generally should not identify unindicted co-conspirators in conspiracy indictments. The practice of naming individuals as unindicted co-conspirators in an indictment charging a criminal conspiracy has been severely criticized in *United States v. Briggs*, 514 F.2d 794 (5th Cir. 1975).
>
> 9-11.130-Limitation on Naming Persons as Unindicted Co-Conspirators

In the rush to weaponize the law against a president they despise, too many Democrats and liberals are becoming incautious about improperly throwing around the loaded accusation of unindicted co-conspirator against President Trump. Unless and until Trump is named or identified in a grand jury indictment as an unindicted co-conspirator, he should not be so characterized.

Those who misuse the term should stop. And when they persist, they should be corrected. Trump is simply not an indicted co-conspirator, and calling him one does not make it so.

Mueller Report and Trump Response Should Be Issued Simultaneously[14]

As Special Counsel Robert Mueller moves toward completing his report, it is important to understand the legal status of such a report and how it should be released and evaluated under the rules governing special counsel.

First and foremost, it must be understood that because it is the report of a prosecutor, it will inevitably be one-sided; all prosecutorial investigations, by their nature, are one-sided. Prosecutors pick the witnesses they will present to the grand jury. Defense lawyers are not allowed to appear with their clients, nor are they allowed to present witnesses who might contradict the prosecutor's case. The prosecutors need not provide exculpatory evidence to the grand jury even if they are aware of it, nor need they interview witnesses who might contradict their narrative. That is why it is generally considered unfair for prosecutors to issue "reports." Normally prosecutors either announce that the subject has been indicted or not, without further comment.

Special counsel and special prosecutors have been allowed more leeway in issuing reports, but this leeway is constrained by rules. The general public is often unaware of the one-sided nature of these reports. Because they are issued by a "special counsel," they carry, in the minds of many people, special weight—weight to which they are not legally, morally, or logically entitled. That is why it is imperative in a high-stakes case like this one that the president's legal team be allowed to issue its own report presenting its side of the case. Basic fairness requires this, and the American public is entitled to judge for itself which side is more persuasive.

There should never be a presumption in favor of crediting the one-sided reports prepared by prosecutors. They have no higher status than an indictment, and remember that even an indictment handed down by a grand jury is not allowed to be considered as evidence of guilt. It is only a charging instrument. A report by a special counsel is as one-sided as an indictment and should be given no greater weight. Like an indictment, it should not undercut the presumption of innocence.

That is why it is so important for the president's legal team to be accorded an opportunity to present its own report, based on its own investigation and its own evidence and its own knowledge of the facts. In order to make the rebuttal presentation fair, the following procedure should be followed:

The Mueller Report should be presented to the Attorney General (or his designee), as required by the rules. A copy should also be provided to the president's legal team. The Attorney General should not allow the Special Counsel's report to be made public (and should take care that it's not leaked) until the president's team has had a chance to review and respond to it. The Attorney General should then issue both reports, so that the media and the general public have a chance to assess them in tandem.

There is no good reason—in law, logic or morality—why the special counsel's report should be issued before the rebuttal is issued. Everybody benefits when both reports are issued simultaneously.

We can anticipate that the Mueller report, if unrebutted, will probably be quite damaging to the president and his associates. No reasonable person should expect an objective, balanced, nuanced report. That is not in the nature of what comes out of a one-sided prosecutorial investigation. I have used the word "devastating" to describe what the President should expect and what his team should be prepared to respond to. Virtually all reports by special counsel and prosecutors—from Kenneth Starr's report on Clinton to Lawrence Walsh's report on Iran-Contra—have been devastating when issued without any rebuttal. No less should be expected from Mueller's report. This doesn't mean that the report will survive a well-documented rebuttal. All it means that standing alone, absent a rebuttal, its impact should not be underestimated.

I don't believe that the Mueller report will actually charge President Trump with any crimes, since collusion—even if Mueller were to conclude that it occurred—is simply not a crime. Nor can constitutionally authorized actions of a president—such as hiring, pardoning, or tweeting—be turned into crimes by stretching elastic statutes. What Mueller will do, if he is smart, is to simply lay out all the facts and try to connect them in the most incriminating way possible. He will try to create a mosaic that makes the president look guilty of political sins, if not federal crimes.

It is important to remember that the witnesses whose information serves as the basis of a prosecutorial report have not been subject to cross-examination. Their accounts may not be entirely credible, but the report can still rely on them. Because the report—if it does not charge indictable crimes—will never be subject to the truth-testing mechanisms of an adversarial trial, its conclusions should not be accepted at face value.

It is not difficult for a prosecutor to construct an incriminating mosaic if there is no contemporaneous rebuttal. The task becomes much more difficult if both sides are heard simultaneously.

The president's lawyer should file a request now with the Justice Department demanding an opportunity to review and respond to the Mueller Report *before* it is released to the public or to Congress. And the Justice Department should grant that reasonable request.[*]

[*]For an analogous situation in Israel, see https://www.haaretz.com/amp/opinion/voters -not-the-police-or-the-courts-should-decide-netanyahu-s-future-1.6718677

On Tolerance, Hyper-partisanship, and our Deteriorating Public Discourse

Democracy necessitates dissent and a fair, tolerant, critical public discourse—it's what America was built upon. But today, dissent is silenced—even criminalized—in favor of confirmation bias, and politics is being pushed to the extremes of the political spectrum. As always, the American people are the real losers.

It is this extremism on both sides, rather than a single politician or president or pundit, that is the greatest underlying threat for our democracy. America has always thrived in the center; we need a mutual disarmament agreement to return to that centrism. I make that case in the columns that follow.

Maxine Waters Does Not Speak For Democrats or Liberals[15]

Congresswoman Maxine Waters (D-CA) recently told her supporters to hound President Trump's cabinet members wherever they find them: "They're not going to be able to go to a restaurant, they're not going to be able to stop at a gas station, they're not going to be able to shop at a department store. The people are going to turn on them, they're going to protest, they're going to absolutely harass them."

Waters does not speak for all Democrats or liberals. Nor do those who threw Sarah Huckabee Sanders out of the Red Hen restaurant. Neither do those who have harassed other members of the Trump administration. But these rude extremists are a symptom of the times. The divisions have gotten so bad that many on both sides refuse to speak or listen to those on the other side. Either you are for Trump or against him, and that is all some people need to know to make judgments about you.

I know this because I have experienced this firsthand on Martha's Vineyard. I am not a Trump supporter nor am I member of the Trump administration. I have strongly and publicly opposed his immigration policies, ranging from the travel ban that was upheld by the Supreme Court to the zero-tolerance policy that led to the separation of parents and children at the border. I oppose other Republican policies as well. I voted for, and contributed handsomely to, Hillary Clinton.

But I have defended Trump's civil liberties, along with those of all Americans, just as I would have defended Hillary Clinton's civil liberties had she been elected and subjected to efforts of impeachment or prosecution. This book could just as easily have been the case against impeaching Hillary Clinton; indeed, I wrote such a book about Bill Clinton, *Sexual McCarthyism: Clinton, Starr, and the Emerging Constitutional Crisis*. I am opposed to appointing a Special Counsel to investigate Hillary Clinton's campaign, and I was against it for Trump. I am a liberal Democrat in politics, but a neutral civil libertarian when it comes to the Constitution.

But that is not good enough for some of my old friends on Martha's Vineyard. For them, it is enough that what I have said about the Constitution might help Trump. So they are shunning me and trying to ban me from their social life on Martha's Vineyard. One of them, an academic at a distinguished university, has told people that he would not attend any dinner or party to which I was invited. He and others have demanded "trigger warnings" so that they can be assured of having "safe spaces" in which they will not encounter me or my ideas. Others have said they will discontinue contributions to organizations that sponsor my talks.

This is all familiar to me because I lived through McCarthyism in the 1950s, when lawyers who represented alleged communists on civil libertarian grounds were shunned. Some of these lawyers and victims of McCarthyism lived on Martha's Vineyard. I never thought I would see McCarthyism come to Martha's Vineyard, but I have. I wonder if the professor who refuses to listen to anything I have to say also treats his students similarly. Would he listen to a student who actively supported Trump? What about one who simply supported his civil liberties?

These childish efforts to shun me because I refused to change my position on civil liberties that I have kept for half a century discourages vibrant debate and may dissuade other civil libertarians from applying their neutral principles to a president of whom they disapprove. But one good thing is that being shunned by some "old friends" on Martha's Vineyard has taught me who my real friends are and who my fair-weather friends were. From a personal point of view, I could not care less about being shunned by people whose views regarding dialogue I do not respect.

But this is not about me, nor is it about Sarah Huckabee Sanders, or Stephen Miller, or Betsy DeVos. This is about the United States of America. It is about our growing intolerance toward opposing views. President Trump certainly bears some of the responsibility for this divisiveness, but Maxine Waters and those who advocate harassing political opponents share much of the responsibility as well. They are both the symptom and the cause of the divisiveness in this country.

I will not change my views as a result of these attempts to ostracize me, but there are some who may remain silent for fear of being shunned. Silence is not my style. Cowardice is not my philosophy. I intend to speak up when I disagree with Republicans, and I intend to speak up when I disagree with Democrats. Right now I am speaking up in disagreement with Maxine Waters. She—like those who shun me on Martha's Vineyard—is part of the problem rather than the solution.

The Hard-Left's Desire to Live in a Political Silo When It Comes to Trump[16]

We live in a world of echo chambers and political silos, in which more and more Americans are reading, watching, and listening only to "facts" and "news" that fit into their preexisting worldview. Truth is no longer the end result of a complex process of learning differing perspectives, arguing about them, keeping an open mind, changing one's mind, and finally arriving at tentative conclusions subject to revision based on changing information. Truth, with a capital T, has become a rigid, fixed dogma, not subject to challenge by untruth. This is especially the case with regard to political truth.

For too many Americans, the political marketplace of ideas should sell only one product, so consumers do not become confused by conflicting ideas. It is almost as if people are swallowing truth pills that deliver the absolute truth into their minds without the need for a learning or truthing process. This is the beginning of a dangerous road to totalitarianism—if not in governance, then in thinking.

Both sides of the political spectrum are increasingly guilty of substituting dogma for discussion. President Trump, with his bully pulpit, surely bears the most responsibility. But the hard-left, with its tactic of harassing and demonizing its political opponents, shares the blame. Neither extreme wants to talk with, or learn from, each other. We are a poorer nation as a result of the death, or at least dearth, of dialogue.

As a liberal academic, my focus is on a new breed of left-wing professors who are criticizing the need for a fully open marketplace of ideas both on and off the campus. They do not see the virtue of wrongheaded views being expressed, especially if they are offensive to those with whom these professors identify. Some academics prefer a world in which each American receives only news that supports his or her preexisting worldview. If this sounds a bit like Fox and MSNBC, that is because this is the direction in which we are going.

Some academics believe that, in the near future, we will be able to swallow a pill before we go to sleep and wake up in the morning speaking foreign languages fluently, without going through the difficult process of learning. I imagine that the next step would be a physics pill, then a history pill, then a politics pill, and finally a truth pill. There will be no alternative pills or antidotes. We would all know everything from pills prescribed by a Dr. Strangelove. Or will it be Dr. Trump who is prescribing the pill?

I have experienced this desire for a singular truth in my defense of Trump's civil liberties and constitutional rights. Although I am a liberal Democrat and a strong supporter of Hillary Clinton, I have made the case against Trump's impeachment and prosecution.

I have controversial views regarding these matters, which I have expressed in numerous articles, media appearances, and books, including this one. I'm the first to admit I may be wrong about some of what I'm arguing. That's why I want to hear differing points of view. I have been persuaded by dialogue to change and refine some of my positions. I welcome more dialogue.

I end the first section this book with the following challenge:

> I hope this will provoke debate, not name-calling. The issues I raise are serious and their discussion is essential to democratic discourse. So please respond to my positions. Disagree with me, propose better arguments, and defeat me, if you can, in the marketplace of ideas. So let the debate continue. I am ready to respond to my critics in print, in the media, and in the courts of public opinion. But let's keep the debate civil and on the merits.

Some radical Trump opponents prefer to cut off dialogue. They see no other side to the issue. Indeed they accuse me—by defending the civil liberties of all Americans, including Trump—of becoming complicit with tyranny in the same way "well-known 20th-century dictators enjoyed the support of public intellectuals."[17] They have urged others to refuse to interact with me intellectually, politically, and personally. Most have refused, including some of my most zealous critics who persist in arguing with me. We continue to learn from each other.

I have likened these efforts to ostracize me to what lawyers who represented accused communists during the McCarthy era went through. These lawyers, too, were ostracized, and their defense of the civil liberties of accused communists was equated with support of communism.

I will continue to defend the civil liberties of all Americans, regardless of party or position. Persuade me why this is wrong by rational argument! I will never subscribe to any media that present only one worldview—even if it is mine. Nor would I take a truth pill if one ever became available. In a democracy, the process of learning is at least as important as the end result.

Zealous Dems Fail to Hear Out Trump's Constitutional Rights[17]

─────

Since *The Case Against Impeaching Trump* has been published, the efforts to silence me have increased. When National Public Radio announced that I would be interviewed about the book, listeners wrote to demand that I not be given a forum on which to express my views. CNN and radio host Michael Smerconish received similar complaints from viewers, as did bookstores featuring the book.

Many people are so upset with President Trump, and for understandable reasons, that they just do not want to hear a constitutional analysis that may help him avoid prosecution or impeachment. Many of the same people would agree with my constitutional arguments if I were making them on behalf of Hillary Clinton had she been elected and Republicans tried to prosecute or impeach her. Indeed, I made similar arguments on behalf of President Clinton during the Ken Starr investigation, and my Democratic friends loved my arguments, and loved me, for making them.

Yet, now that the shoe is on the other foot, everything is different. This has led some of my vociferous critics to accuse me of complicity with evil. One professor has even compared me to German intellectuals who helped bring Hitler to power.

It is pure McCarthyism to equate support for the constitutional rights of a person, or even a president, to complicity in his policies. I oppose Trump's policies on immigration, family separation, Charlottesville, gun control, taxation, and health care. I voted against him, contributed to his opponent, and campaigned for her. Yet, I am accused of being complicit in his policies because I defend his constitutional rights.

This is not the first time McCarthyite tactics have been deployed to try to stop me from defending the constitutional rights of those with whom I disagree. When I was a college student, I stood up for the rights of communists despite my strong opposition to communism. When I was interviewed by *Salon*, the writer went out of his way to thank me for defending his mother, who was a communist. Then, the right-wing McCarthyites accused me of complicity with communism. Today, the left-wing McCarthyites accuse me of complicity with fascism.

To make the point that I would have written the same book had Hillary Clinton been elected president, my publisher produced an alternate cover with the title "The Case Against Impeaching Clinton." My publisher also produced a special cover for Martha's Vineyard, which is a plain brown paper cover with the real title in tiny print, so people could secretly read it in the beach without being accused of complicity.

All this may sound humorous or petty, especially when people on Martha's Vineyard focus on parties or other social events, about which I could care less. They also focus on the fact that the *New York Times* has four stories about me in the space of a week, despite the reality that I did not ask for these stories but rather just responded to requests from reporters.

Focusing on these petty aspects masks a much larger problem that efforts to silence me are a symptom of the dangerous time in which we live. These days, debate is being stifled on university campuses in the name of political correctness, a term coined by the Stalinist regime. Even the ACLU is now placing free speech and due process lower in its priorities than other partisan issues that earn the organization more contributions.

That is why, despite the attacks and efforts to silence me, I will continue to speak up on behalf of the democracy our Framers laid out and the civil liberties of all Americans in this country, including our president. As I argue in the introduction to the first section of this book: "If a controversial president is denied constitutional protections, then any citizen can be denied constitutional protections. That is why this issue is so important to all Americans."

That is why we should begin listening to each other, should welcome dissenting views, should demand that the marketplace of ideas be kept open, and should act with civility toward each other, even if we disagree.

Coarseness, Bigotry, and Threats on Both Sides of Trump Divide[18]

It is widely reported in the media that President Trump and his supporters have "coarsened" the dialogue and resorted to name-calling and personal attacks, rather than reasoned discourse. There certainly is some truth in this accusation, but it also is true that many of President Trump's opponents have contributed to this coarsening and name-calling.

Both extremes have rejected nuanced dialogue and opted for gutter accusations, false comparisons, gross exaggerations, and even threats. The emails, messages, and tweets directed at me reflect this—a disturbing nation-wide trend that transcends any individual. If I am receiving these curses and threats, so must many other people on all sides of the political spectrum. So this op-ed is not about me. It is about those who send these messages and what they say about today's America.

The verbal attacks on me for defending President Trump's civil liber-ties—as I would be defending Hillary Clinton's civil liberties, had she been elected—fall into several categories: bigotry (ageism, anti-Semitism), threats and curses, false comparisons to Hitler and other dictators, false personal accusations (that I am being paid or blackmailed by President Trump) and, finally, just simple nastiness.

Let's begin with ageism. Rather than criticizing my ideas, many emails call me "senile," "old and feeble" and "impotent." The CFO of a large com-pany who boasts that he has only one employee "over 50" says "You're tired and it's time for retirement," and demands that I "move aside, old man." Another one demands that I "shut the f--- up old man."

Then there is the anti-Semitism, anti-Israel extremism.

One email that begins by calling me "a piece of s---" continues with the following: "Despite what Zionists such as yourself want the rest of us to believe, the world doesn't revolve around Jews." Another says that alleged support for President Trump is "all about Jerusalem as the capital, and loving

Israel to you, just move there." It wishes "with all my heart that you get cancer and die a painful, disgusting death, you f---, you traitorous f---," and ends with "Die! Die!" Yet another accused me of saying what I say for "the Money" and accusing my "home country," Israel, of being like the "f------ Nazis." He ends his email by acknowledging that "I don't like Jewish people."

Then there is a lawyer, with twenty-five years of experience, who calls me "a despicable, unethical, lying scum bag" and ends with "Your [sic] a Jew, but if there is a hell, you are destined to burn in it." Finally, an email supporting Cynthia Nixon says, "f--- Israel," and continues: "The only thing the average American ever got from our 'relationship' with that country was an early death on 9/11."

Then there are the anti-Trump extremists who compare Trump to Hitler and compare those of us who defend his civil liberties to those who brought Hitler to power.

One email addresses me as "Alan 'Goebbels' Dershowitz." Another accuses me of being just like the "public intellectuals" who facilitated Hitler's rise to power. (Comparing Trump to Hitler is a form of soft Holocaust denial: If Trump is Hitler, there were no gas chambers, death camps, or killing fields in the Third Reich.)

Most disturbing are the threats and curses. One email warns me to be very careful, threatening to "arrange a woman to start accusing me." Another says "we the people will make sure" that I die "for supporting an act of treason." It goes on to say "F--- you and F--- Trump you F------ Trump loving commie. . . . I piss on you boy." Another urges me to "put a bullet in your head . . . kill yourself and do us all a favor." An educated woman told people that if she saw me she would "stab me through the heart."

Nor are these crude attacks directed only at me. They are directed at my family as well, using words like "You and your family members are evil and disgusting." A female family member received an email calling her an "entitled bitch" with "no f------ heart."

Strangers come up to me and to my family, cursing and threatening. A friend is insisting that I should have armed security.

I also receive crude emails from Trump supporters, though not nearly as many. Here is one representative missive:

So we're all now waiting for Jew communist Ruth Bader Ginsburg to soon enough drop dead. Like John McAsshole. No joke. I'm soooo sick of Democraps and other assortments, flavors of Soviet socialists by whatever name . . . Communists Nancy Piglosi, Maxine [Black Racist] Waters, or Jewish Chucky Cheese Schumer—no, no, no!!!) That now I foresee the final twilight of commies infecting our governmental institutions. Yes!! Bring it on! Love Trump!!

This is what is happening to America—from both sides. Many of the anti-Trump zealots are as crude, ageist, anti-Semitic, and threatening as pro-Trump extremists.

It is important to point out—as many already have—these negative characteristics when they emanate from Trump supporters. It is equally important to expose them when they come from Trump opponents. So I will continue to collect and publish bigoted communications that I receive from both sides.

How the Hard-Left Only Helps the Republicans and Donald Trump[19]

The hard-left is helping Republican candidates and Donald Trump in numerous ways. First and most obviously, by running candidates such as those in the Green Party, the hard-left siphons off votes that otherwise would go to Democrats. Third parties may well have cost the Democrats the 2000 and 2016 presidential elections, because the Green Party siphoned off enough votes to make the difference in crucial states.

Green Party supporters argue that their voters would not have come out to vote if they had to choose between Democrats and Republicans, so they claim that they have not siphoned off any votes from Democrats. While this may be true of some extremists who see no difference between Democrats and Republicans, it certainly is not true of many core voters attracted to the environmental policies of the Green Party, but who would most certainly vote and, if they did, would vote for Democrats.

Then there are the off-the-charts extremists like Susan Sarandon who actually prefer to see Republicans such as Donald Trump elected over Democrats such as Hillary Clinton. Her absurd argument is that a Trump presidency will bring revolution more quickly than would a Clinton presidency. Fortunately for America, these extreme revolutionaries represent a tiny fraction of the electorate across the country.

Another way the hard-left helps Republicans and President Trump is through their exaggerations and gutter tactics. The claim by Rosie O'Donnell that Trump stole the 2016 election only emboldens his base with the denial of his victory. Her rhetoric, and that of others like her, turns off centrist voters and shifts some of them to the Republican camp. So do the constant personal attacks by people like "Morning Joe" Scarborough and Mika Brzezinski, who recently devoted significant airtime to talking about the size of Trump's fingers. The reality that Trump himself engages in similar attacks does not diminish the negative impact of gutter tactics.

The attacks on Trump administration officials in restaurants and other public places also turns off centrist voters who cast ballots for Democrats in the past but who are deeply offended by tactics they associate with supporters of the hard-left. If Republicans manage to hold on to one or both chambers of Congress in the midterms, it will be at least in part because of wounds inflicted on the Democratic Party by extremists on the hard-left. The highly publicized candidacies of Democratic socialists such as Alexandria Ocasio-Cortez and Cynthia Nixon surely will drive many centrist voters out of the party. The election of Keith Ellison as deputy chairman of the Democratic National Committee has alienated moderates who remember his close association with Louis Farrakhan.

Is there anything the Democrats can do before the midterms to bolster their chances of winning one or both houses? I think there is. The Democratic Party should appoint centrist liberal leaders to positions of authority within the party and should emphasize the centrist liberal policies that have been the key to their success since the days of Franklin Delano Roosevelt. We are a country of centrists and one of the few in the Western world that has never had successful communist or fascist parties.

America thrives at the center. Reasonable voters can disagree about whether centrist liberalism or centrist conservatism is best for the country. That is what most previous elections have been about. But, now the extremes in both parties are advocating hard-left and hard-right positions that do not serve the interests of average Americans.

The Democrats need more centrist liberal candidates like Bill Clinton and fewer socialist candidates like Bernie Sanders. Young people may be energized by extremism, but in the end they simply do not vote, at least not in the numbers that are expected of them. The Democrats cannot count on "flash in the pan" extremists to energize young voters. They need centrist candidates who appeal to all segments of the party.

There are such candidates out there. Some may not be widely known, at least not yet. Remember that Bill Clinton was an unknown governor of Arkansas just months before he won the Democratic nomination for president. The Democrats should not abandon the center, despite their loss with a moderate candidate in 2016. Democrats can win by attracting centrists of all ages, ideologies, and backgrounds. Moving to the hard-left is a guarantee of failure, both in the short term and the long term.

Immigrants Who Change America
Are Its Lifeblood[20]

L aura Ingraham's attack on illegal, and in some cases legal, immigration
harks back to a time when my forebearers and hers immigrated to this
great country, and were accused of changing it for the worse.

Here is what Ingraham said:

> [In] some parts of the country, it does seem like the America we
> know and love doesn't exist anymore. Massive demographic changes
> have been foisted on the American people. They're changes none of
> us ever voted for, and most of us don't like. . . . Both illegal and in
> some cases legal immigration, which, of course, progressives love.

When my Jewish Polish grandparents came to America at the end of the
19th and beginning of the 20th century, many white Protestants whose fore-
bears had been here for generations complained that these "different" immigrants were turning America into a country they didn't "know and love." To
be sure, my grandparents were different. They spoke a different language.
They looked a little bit different. They were poor. They were uneducated in
the ways of America. They worshiped differently. And they voted Democrat.
But despite these differences, or even because of them, they and their fellow
Eastern European immigrants loved America, and they and their descendants contributed greatly to our nation's success in the twentieth and twenty-
first centuries.

Ingraham's forebearers came from Poland and Ireland. The anti-Polish
and anti-Irish sentiments in this country were widespread. Discrimination
against Polish and Irish immigrants was pervasive. Yet their descendants,
too, have contributed significantly to the success of this great country.

These are a few of the many individuals caught up in President Trump's
dragnet.

I went to Brooklyn College, a free public university, where virtually all of my classmates were the children or grandchildren of immigrants. Like my brother and me, most were the first in their family to attend college. Even when I graduated first in my class from Yale Law School, and was editor in chief of the *Yale Law Journal*, and a future Supreme Court law clerk, I was turned down for a job by thirty-two out of the thirty-two Wall Street firms to which I applied. So were some of my Irish and Polish classmates. These firms wanted white Protestants of British and German stock, who they regarded as "the real Americans." We had to go to work for smaller law firms that were open to the children and grandchildren of immigrants.

Now some of these same descendants of immigrants—like Laura Ingraham, Stephen Miller, and Steve Bannon—are trying to close the door to broad legal immigration because they don't like how the current immigrants look, speak, vote, and raise their families. It reminds me of the Russian immigrant comedian Yakov Smirnoff, who had a humorous bit in which he would be standing in front of the Statue of Liberty thanking her for welcoming him to this great country, and then, as he was leaving, he turned back to Ms. Liberty and shouted, "Now please keep the rest of those damn immigrants out."

Nor would "merit" immigration assure us the kinds of immigrants who would contribute significantly to our country. It is impossible to judge the future merits of potential immigrants who are deprived of educational and other opportunities. Previous immigrants who have changed the country for the better would never have passed any so-called merit test. Many came from what President Trump would regard as "shithole" countries. When my grandparents came here, all of Eastern Europe was characterized that way, and look at what these immigrants have contributed to our country.

It is a cliché to say that we are a nation of immigrants, but the cliché is so true. Every year, the *New York Times* runs a full page that shows the faces and contributions of immigrants to America. They have contributed to medicine, technology, economics, literature, law, philanthropy, and so much else. It is hard to imagine an America without immigrants who look, speak, and think differently than the original American colonists.

It is reasonable to try to control our borders against massive illegal immigration, even despite the reality that illegal immigrants, too, have contributed to America. My own grandfather illegally secured false affidavits from neighbors in order to rescue twenty-nine of our relatives from the Holocaust. He got these neighbors to sign false affidavits about their need for religious functionaries in nonexistent basement synagogues. Though himself a lawful man and a grateful immigrant, he was willing to break the law to save lives. One of those he saved became the chairman of the engineering department of Columbia University. Another became a prominent rabbi in Los Angeles. Their children and grandchildren continue to contribute greatly to the economy and culture of this diverse country.

This is not intended to justify lawlessness and illegal immigration, except in the most extreme cases like the Holocaust, when racist barriers to immigration precluded Jews from escaping Hitler's gas chambers. But it is to respond to Ingraham's point that "both illegal, and in some cases, legal immigration" have changed our country. Yes, immigration has changed our country, mostly for the better. To be sure, some illegal immigrants, and even some legal immigrants, do not contribute to our country. But that is true as well of *Mayflower* descendants (our first immigrants).

So please, Laura Ingraham, be more tolerant of differences—even lack of "merit," as some would define it—that immigrants bring to this country. You are I are both the product of these differences.

Kavanaugh, the Presumption of Innocence, the Court of Public Opinion, and the Integrity of Our Institutions

The process of nomination to the Supreme Court has become increasingly partisan in recent years, but came to a head when the Republicans refused to move forward with President Barack Obama's nomination of brilliant centrist judge Merrick Garland. The partisanship reached its nadir then and in the subsequent hearings regarding Judge Brett Kavanaugh, during which both sides offered arguments that failed the shoe on the other foot test—that is, their arguments would surely have been different had the nominee been of a different political orientation.

The politicization of the Supreme Court, intended to be the necessary nonpartisan institution to provide integral checks and balances in our democracy, is yet another manifestation of the underlying problems in our culture and government. As I'll show in these pieces, hasty convictions in the court of public opinion now take precedent over the presumption of innocence, and our democratic institutions are suffering gravely for it.

A Self-Inflicted Wound to
Judicial Independence[21]

M any on the left claim they are worried that the Trump administration will destroy the independence of the judiciary by appointing judges who will support the right-wing agenda. They have a point, but if they are indeed concerned with judicial independence—as distinguished from furthering their own partisan agendas—they should be equally concerned about a recent recall of a judge in California.

Judge Aaron Persky was recalled because he showed leniency in sentencing a Stanford student who was convicted of raping "Emily Doe." Both the convicted man, Brock Turner, and the victim had been drinking at a fraternity party, and he had sex with her while she was apparently unconscious. Because he was a first offender and himself inebriated, the probation department recommended that the Stanford freshman receive a non-prison sentence. Judge Persky sentenced Turner to six months in jail and three years of probation.

This sentence caused outrage among many feminists and a demand for the judge's recall. Reasonable people can certainly disagree about whether the sentence was too lenient, but reasonable people often disagree about particular sentences, with liberals often criticizing sentences as being too harsh.

Yet, demanding a recall of a judge because of disagreement with a particular sentence has institutional implications that transcend a single case. The campaign to recall Judge Persky was led by a feminist law professor from Stanford named Michele Dauber, who argued that Judge Persky was too lenient in his sentence and that she wanted to send a message to other elected judges.

Opponents of the recall included prosecutors and judges, who argued, "It certainly appears the goal is to teach judges, all judges, some lessons: If you want to keep your job as a judge, keep an eye on media reports of public sentiment when you are exercising your sworn duty to sentence a defendant in light of the law and the facts."

Professor Dauber succeeded in recalling Judge Persky but, in doing so, she and those who voted for the recall inflicted a deep wound on judicial independence. Today, they recalled a judge who made a ruling against their agenda. Tomorrow, this recall will energize extremists from the right to recall judges who make rulings supporting the left-wing agenda.

California has already experienced a successful right-wing effort to remove liberal judges. Back in 1986, Chief Justice Rose Bird and Associate Justice Cruz Reynoso were voted out of office because of their opposition to the death penalty and their support of other liberal agenda issues. We are likely to see more recalls and contested judicial elections now, organized by extremists on both sides.

The sad reality is that the last thing extremists want is judicial independence. What they want is judges who will do their bidding, who will support their agenda, and who will vote their side. In an age when nearly everybody picks a side and supports it without regard to neutral principles of justice or civil liberties, the danger to judicial independence comes equally from the left and the right.

The difference is that the left needs judicial independence more than does the right. This is because independent judges are supposed to defend the rights of the disenfranchised, the weak, the discriminated against, and those who cannot prevail in our majoritarian political system. No judge has ever been removed from office for being too tough on crime, for imposing excessive sentences, or for siding with prosecutors. The recall is a right-wing tool that now has been sharpened by the hard-left.

So the decision to recall Judge Persky may benefit the extreme left in the short run, but it hurts liberals and progressives in the long run. But extremists always demand immediate gratification and rarely look to the long-term implications of the damage they are doing. The ultimate losers will be African Americans, Hispanic Americans, Native Americans, and other minorities who too often are treated unfairly by our legal system.

Allow Fordham law professor John Pfaff to have the last word:

The recall will make judges more aggressive, and in ways that will never be neatly confined to the issues in the Turner and Persky cases. More people will be sent to prison, and that increase won't make us safer. Since a majority of people in prison are black or Hispanic, the impact of this toughness will fall disproportionately on minorities. For those hoping to see the United States become a less punitive place, the recall's success is disappointing.

It All Depends on What Kind of Conservative Trump Chooses[22]

President Trump will clearly replace Supreme Court Justice Anthony Kennedy with a conservative who appeals to the president's base. The real question is what kind of conservative justice he nominates.

The two key words in assessing the president's nominee to replace Justice Anthony Kennedy are *stare decisis*. This ancient Latin phrase, which means let the decision stand, represents a conservative approach to judging: that precedent imposes constraints on judicial innovation. Put another way, that judicial innovation should be balanced against the need to maintain stability in our legal system. The Supreme Court, unlike the lower courts, is not technically bound by stare decisis. As the late Justice Antonin Scalia frequently pointed out, his oath of office required him to apply the Constitution, not the decisions of his predecessors on the bench if those past decisions were wrong.

But all judicial nominees, whether liberal or conservative, will always throw a bone to stare decisis. They will claim, quite correctly, their legal system depends on stability, certainty, and predictability. But they will also point out that the law must sometimes change to suit the times. So the questioning of these potential nominees must be more probing and substantive. They should be asked about the criteria they apply in determining whether to be bound by past decisions.

There are two basic types of conservative justices. The first defers to stare decisis. Such a justice might say, "I would have decided *Roe v. Wade* differently if I had been a justice back in 1973, but since that decision has been on the books for forty-five years, I will not overturn it." Such a justice might say something similar about more recent decisions concerning gay rights and gay marriage. That is one kind of conservative justice the president might pick.

But there is another kind of conservative justice in the vein of Scalia. This freewheeling kind of justice, with less respect for stare decisis, might well vote to overrule *Roe v. Wade* and other landmark cases, regardless of how long they have been on the books.

If the president were to nominate a conservative who rejects stare decisis, the court would then have these three factions. The conservatives would be divided into two camps, one that followed precedent and the other that did not. (Obviously these would be matters of degree, since no one always follows precedent and no one always ignores it.) These conservatives might vote very differently on particular cases.

The third faction would be comprised of the court's current liberals who likely would vote along with those conservatives who supported stare decisis, to ensure that old precedents are not easily overruled.

These positions on stare decisis may influence President Trump's decision on whom to nominate, especially the candidates' views on *Roe v. Wade*. Today, liberals want to use stare decisis to preserve *Roe v. Wade,* gay marriage, and other iconic liberal decisions of the past. Many conservatives would like to see these decisions overruled. The new nominee, as guided by his or her respect for precedent, will be forced to take a position on these issues. *Roe v. Wade* will be at the forefront.

The conservative view can fall into several categories: The first is that *Roe v. Wade* was wrong when decided, it is wrong now, and it should be overruled. President Trump has suggested that he expects his nominee to take that position, but any such nominee may have difficulty being confirmed because at least two Republican senators opposed reversing *Roe v. Wade*.

The second position is that *Roe v. Wade* was wrong when decided but it has been the law for forty-five years, and the nation has come to rely on it as governing law. Accordingly, it should not be overruled, but nor should it be expanded. This is the most likely position that a successful nominee might take.

Then there is the extreme position, hinted at by Justice Clarence Thomas: Not only is there no right for a woman to have an abortion, but it is unconstitutional for the state to allow abortion, since abortion violates the right to life of the fetus. Such a radical view would dramatically change both constitutional law and politics in America, but the Supreme Court's decision interpreting the second amendment granting the personal right to own guns also reversed long-standing precedents and changed the nature of law and politics in our country. It is unlikely that any nominee with such an extreme view concerning abortion could be confirmed, if he or she acknowledged that they would vote to prevent states from keeping abortion legal.

President Trump would be well advised to select a justice who believes in precedent and who would not overrule *Roe v. Wade* and gay rights cases. Overruling *Roe v. Wade* would end up hurting conservatives in national elections.

The majority of Americans strongly support a woman's right to choose, perhaps with some limitations. Because of *Roe v. Wade*, elections are not referenda on this important right. For that reason, many moderately conservative women feel comfortable voting for a Republican president and senators. But if these moderate conservatives came to believe that a vote for Republicans is a vote against the right of their daughter, sister, or niece to obtain a necessary abortion, they might well change their vote.

This may not be as true for centrist Republicans who support gay rights and gay marriage. But many such Republicans do support these rights, and the fear of losing them might turn them against the Republican Party. President Trump also will be better off with a united conservative group on the high court, one that is not divided by their views on precedent.

Finally, true conservatives should place considerable importance on precedent, because conservatism espouses stability, respect for the past, deference, and judicial restraint. Freewheeling judges who disregard precedent can quickly become judicial activists who substitute their own views for those of the executive, legislature, and the Constitution.

This is an important time for the Supreme Court. It is quickly becoming a politicized institution, and many of its votes can be predicted by looking at party affiliation. That was certainly true of *Bush v. Gore*, in which the justices voted their politics rather than the constitutional views they had previously espoused. Partisan decisions diminish the power of the court.

As *The Federalist Papers* observed, the Supreme Court is the "least dangerous branch" of our government because it has neither the purse nor the sword with which to enforce its decrees. It depends entirely on its credibility and the trust placed in it by American citizens.

The appointment of a Supreme Court justice is one of the most important functions a president can perform. The Senate behaved abysmally and, in my view unconstitutionally, when it refused to consider President Obama's nomination of Merrick Garland, a brilliant centrist judge.

Senate Republican leaders said they would refuse to consider and process any nomination regardless of its merits that President Obama submitted near the end of his term. The Democrats may well try to play the same game, but they don't have the votes to carry it out. They should still rigorously question any Supreme Court nominee in order to determine his or her views on the importance of precedent.

President Trump will get his nomination through the Senate if he picks from the list provided to him by the Federalist Society. The judges on this list are all conservatives with high levels of qualification. But he can act as a statesman, rather than a politician, if he selects a nominee who strongly believes in following precedent, especially in cases where American citizens have come to rely on prior decisions in regulating their lives.

So the next several months may be a civics lesson for all Americans as we observe the president making his decision about whom to nominate, and we watch senators make their decision as to whether they confirm the nominee. We need such a lesson because the vacancy that occurred when Justice Scalia died provided an object lesson in politics trumping decency and constitutionality, as Senate Republicans violated their duty to advise and consent by refusing even to consider any nominee put forward by President Obama in his last year. Let us hope that the process of replacing Justice Anthony Kennedy will provide a more ennobling lesson for all Americans.

Let the president and the Senate perform their constitutional duties, and let the public evaluate them on how well they perform these duties. This is the ultimate check and balance that our Constitution demands.

The SCOTUS Confirmation Process
Has Gotten Out of Hand[23]

The Framers of our Constitution would be turning over in their graves if they could see what happened to their words "with the advice and consent of the senate."

Now senators neither advise nor consent to Supreme Court nominations. They politicize, delay, demonize, obscure, fabricate, and discredit what should be a nonpartisan process of assuring that the most qualified lawyers serve on our highest court. Instead we have come to expect votes that are cast largely along party lines.

It was not always what it has now become. Even in the recent past, highly qualified but controversial nominees—such as Antonin Scalia and Ruth Bader Ginsberg—were confirmed with hardly any dissents. No more.

There is enough blame to go around. Republicans point to the Bork rejection (which resulted in the Kennedy nomination) and the Clarence Thomas "high-tech lynching." Democrats point to the Republican refusal even to consider former President Barack Obama's nomination of the highly qualified and centrist Merrick Garland. They also point to the fact that President Trump has "outsourced the selection process to the Federalist Society."

Whoever is to blame, the real victims are the American people who have been denied the constitutional protection of a legitimate confirmation process.

Focusing on the current confirmation battle over Brett Kavanaugh, some Democrats showed their disdain for the process by carrying signs opposing President Trump's nominee even before the nomination was made. They left the name blank and filled it in only after the president nominated Judge Kavanaugh. Others have taken the view that they would never confirm any nominee whose name was on the list provided by the Federalist Society.

A story from the past is worth recalling. When the great Justice Oliver Wendell Holmes retired, President Herbert Hoover asked his attorney general to supply him a list of ten names to fill the seat of this great justice. The list contained nine Republican names, but at the bottom was the name of one Democrat—a great New York judge named Benjamin Cardozo. When Hoover saw the list, he reportedly said to his attorney general, "It's a great list but you have it upside down. Cardozo's name should be on the top because he is the most distinguished sitting judge in the US." The attorney general reportedly responded that Cardozo was a Democrat, a Jew (there was already one Jew on the Supreme Court, Louis Brandeis), and a New Yorker, and his appointment would not serve the political interest of the president or his party. But Hoover nominated Cardozo, who served with distinction on the high court.

Today such a nomination would be unthinkable. Generally, presidents still look for high-quality nominees, but among the many who are so qualified they demand a nominee who will toe their ideological line, be acceptable to their base, and generally promote the interests of their party. That is not what the Framers contemplated.

The Supreme Court is supposed to be above politics. It is supposed to serve as a check and balance against the two political branches of government. It is supposed to be nonpartisan. The votes of justices are not supposed to be based on ideological or partisan considerations. The Framers would be livid at the 5-4 party line vote in *Bush v. Gore*. They would have been equally livid if there were a 5-4 partisan vote in favor of a Democratic president. Partisan votes are supposed to take place in Congress, not in the chambers of our highest court.

It may be too late to restore the integrity of the confirmation process. We are in the age of tit-for-tat political reprisals. The Democrats say that the Republicans stole the Merrick Garland nomination, so the Democrats want to try to steal the Kavanaugh nomination. They will almost certainly fail, but not before they have further tarnished the confirmation process.

It will take a statesman rather than a politician in the Oval Office to change this dynamic. A great president will someday nominate the most distinguished lawyer in the country, without regard to party ideology or other political considerations. All presidents claim that they are doing this. Former President George H. W. Bush told the American public that Clarence Thomas was the most qualified person in American to serve on the high court. No one, probably not even Clarence Thomas, believed that. But he, too, was confirmed, largely along party line votes.

Justice Kavanaugh is extraordinarily well qualified by his educational and academic background and judicial history. He should be given a hearing and asked probing questions about his judicial philosophy and his approach to constitutional construction and precedent. Senators should approach this process with an open mind. Before I finally make up my own mind, I will be listening carefully to his answers.

Six Rules for the
Ford-Kavanaugh Hearings²⁴

——————

It's not surprising that each side of the Christine Blasey Ford/Brett Kavanaugh he said/she said dispute is seeking different procedures. This is an adversarial, high-stakes confrontation between a male Supreme Court justice nominee and his female accuser. Reasonable people could disagree about the appropriate procedural steps, but there are basic rules that must be followed for hearings of this kind to be fair.

Rule 1: No one should presume that either party is lying or telling the truth. There is no gender-based gene for truth telling. Some women tell the truth; some women lie. Some men tell the truth; some men lie. Without hearing any evidence under oath, and subject to cross-examination, no reasonable person should declare Ford, a psychology professor, to be a victim or federal judge Kavanaugh to be a perpetrator. Nor should anybody declare the opposite. The issue is an evidentiary one and evidence must be heard and subject to rigorous cross-examination, preferably by an experienced and sensitive female litigator.

Rule 2: The accuser must always testify first, and be subject to cross-examination. The accused must then be allowed to respond to the accusation and also be subject to cross-examination. In the bad old days of the Inquisition, the accused was required to testify first without even knowing the grounds of the accusation. The rule of law in the United States had always been the opposite. The accuser accuses first and the accused then has an opportunity to respond to all accusations.

Rule 3: Political considerations should not enter into he said/she said decision making. Investigators, including FBI background checkers, must take as much time as necessary to get as close to the truth as possible, without regard to whether this helps the Democrats or the Republican or particular candidates. There should be no deadlines designed to influence the midterm elections. Both sides should be given as much time as is reasonable to make their cases and no decision should be made until each side has had that opportunity, which should include the power to subpoena witnesses.

Rule 4: Everybody must be willing to accept the shoe on the other foot test. The same rules that would apply if a liberal Democrat had been nominated by a liberal Democratic president must be applied to a conservative Republican candidate nominated by a Republican president. There can't be one rule for the left and a different one for the right. The rule of law must apply equally in all situations.

Rule 5: The standard for proving a serious sexual allegation must be high. In a criminal case, the evidence must prove the crime beyond a reasonable doubt. To quote Blackstone, it is "better ten guilty go free than one innocent be wrongly convicted." That standard must vary with the consequences to both sides. On university campuses, for example, the standard for proving a charge of sexual assault that could result in expulsion should be close to proof beyond a reasonable doubt, perhaps "clear and convincing evidence."

But it should never be "a mere preponderance of the evidence," because that means no more than a fifty-one percent likelihood that the sexual assault occurred. Under that low preponderance standard, forty-nine out of every one hundred people convicted may well be innocent. That is far too high a percentage.

What about when the issue is suitability to serve a lifetime appointment on the Supreme Court? The consequences of an erroneous decision are high on all sides. A nominee rejected for a false allegation of sexual assault will suffer grievous reputational and career consequences. But so will the woman whose accusations are deemed untruthful. There is also the consequence of having a Supreme Court justice serve for many years if he was a sexual assailant.

On balance, the standard for accepting a serious allegation of sexual assault should be higher than proof by a mere preponderance. It should come close to clear and convincing evidence, especially if the allegation is decades old and the nominee has lived an exemplary life ever since. But senators should cast their votes based on a total assessment of the candidate's suitability.

Rule 6: No material information should be withheld from either side. Each side should have a full opportunity to examine inculpatory, exculpatory, or otherwise relevant material that may have an impact on the truth-finding process.

Doubts should be resolved in favor of disclosure because Ford came forward voluntarily with her accusation, thus waiving any right to privacy. Kavanaugh too has waived his privacy rights by being a candidate for the Supreme Court, and any information relevant to his activities, even thirty-six years ago, should be disclosed.

If these neutral rules are followed, the process may end up being fair to both sides. All Americans have a stake in the fairness of this process and no one should compromise the basic rules of fairness and due process that have long been the hallmarks of the rule of law.

How to Decide Who to Believe in
Kavanaugh, Rosenstein Drama²⁵

Increasingly, we are living in a world of "he said/she said," "she said/she said," "he said/he said." These conflicts are being played out not in the courts of law, where established rules govern, but rather in the court of public opinion where political predispositions seem to rule. Some people seem to believe that there are gender-based truth genes. They believe women because they are women, or men because they are men. Others seem to believe there is a politically based gene for truth telling. They believe Republicans lie and Democrats tell the truth, and vice versa.

The issues are far more complex. First, there is a continuum of truth telling. Some people have photographic memories and remember everything precisely as events occurred. Most of us have selective memories in which our biases determine what we remember and what we forget. Accordingly, many people truthfully misremember; that is, they believe that what they are remembering is true, even if the video camera would show something different.

In the last several days, these issues have emerged in two different but somewhat related contexts. The first is the direct, dramatic conflict between the several women who have accused Supreme Court nominee Brett Kavanaugh of sexual misconduct and Kavanaugh's categorical denials. The second involves Rod Rosenstein's categorical denial of a *New York Times* story reporting that he had discussed invoking the 25th Amendment against President Trump and surreptitiously wearing a wire during a meeting with the president.

Several years ago my son, who is a film producer, and I worked on an idea for a script in which a "she said/he said" encounter played out in court. Each participant testified quite differently about the recollections of the event. What she remembered constituted sexual assault, while what he remembered constituted a consensual sexual encounter. Reminiscent of the great film *Rear Window*, our plot had a teenage voyeur secretly recording the encounter from his window across from where the event occurred.

Only at the end of the trial, after both sides testified to diametrically opposite perceptions, did the young man come forward with his video, which conclusively demonstrated that the recollections of both were imperfect and that the situation was far more nuanced and subject to multiple interpretations. I suspect that this fictional account reflects reality as often as reconstructive memories do.

Far too many people, including senators from both parties, have immediately invoked gender stereotypes: Women never lie. Men often lie. Men are assailants. Women are victims. There is absolutely no scientific basis for any of these conclusions. An entire academic area of pseudoscience has arisen in a phony effort to prove that women claiming sexual assault are always, or almost always, truthful. I have studied and taught the subject for decades and I have seen no authoritative study that comes close to establishing a gender-based predisposition for truth telling or lying in the context of sexual assault.

The so-called empirical arguments in support of these highly politicized conclusions are so deeply flawed as not to warrant serious consideration. Yet they prevail in the media and on both sides of the political spectrum. A predisposition toward lying, truth telling, memory reconstruction, memory failure, and other aspects of reporting the past are completely individualized. People must be judged individually and not by gender, political affiliation, or ideology.

Beyond the testimony of the individuals involved in a "she said/he said" controversy, there is circumstantial evidence that can support either side. Circumstantial evidence itself can, of course, be based on true or false recollections, but sometimes there is objective circumstantial evidence, such as the entries in Brett Kavanaugh's yearbook. But inevitably, such evidence is subject to multiple interpretations. A life well lived as an adult is not conclusive proof of the absence of misbehavior as an adolescent.

The corollary of this truism is that adolescent behavior is not necessarily a predictor of adult behavior. Should a man in his fifties be judged by what he may or may not have done or said in his teen years? Should that depend on the nature of his teenage activities? Should doubts about whether allegations about teenage improprieties occurred be resolved by looking at the life lived thereafter? These and other probing questions must be asked after we hear testimony from all accusers and the accused. A great deal is at stake, because this is a lifetime appointment and because the accusations against Kavanaugh, if untrue, can be life-destroying.

The stakes are far lower when it comes to whether to believe Rod Rosenstein or the *New York Times*. There is little doubt that Rosenstein will not serve beyond the midterm elections. Whether he resigns or is fired, his career in the Justice Department is over. The issue is whether he remains on between now and the midterm elections and whether he plays any continuing role in the Mueller investigation and in the decision about how to deal with the report that Mueller's team will write. These are important but somewhat transitional issues that will be resolved by political considerations.

We may never know whether Rosenstein seriously raised the prospect of a 25th Amendment coup d'état—and that's what it would have been if any effort had been made to remove President Trump under the 25th Amendment. That amendment was intended to deal with a president like Woodrow Wilson, who suffered a debilitating stroke, or a president like Ronald Reagan, who was shot. It was never intended to allow a palace coup under which members of a cabinet could remove a president who they believed was behaving improperly or even erratically.

That's what elections are for, and that is why we have our system of checks and balances in place. We live in an age where truth itself has become so politicized that we lack basic rules for arriving at objective conclusions. This is a dangerous phenomenon and we should pay far more attention to its implications for our system of governance.

Burden Is on Avenatti to Show Proof,

or Face Consequences[26]

Michael Avenatti, whose judgments have proved questionable so many times, may be right in demanding a thorough investigation of his client's outrageous claims of multiple gang rapes participated in and witnessed by a young Brett Kavanaugh.

These claims, typical of Avenatti, seem so incredible on their face that even partisan Democratic senators have generally stayed away from them. Yet, if they are true, they are not only disqualifying for Judge Kavanaugh to become an associate justice of the Supreme Court, but they should result in criminal prosecutions of anyone and everyone who allegedly drugged young girls and subjected them to systematic gang rape on multiple occasions.

The affidavit laying out these allegations is so deeply flawed and so filled with gaps that it would be easy for any experienced cross-examiner to raise doubts about the credibility of the affiant. One critical question is why this young woman would repeatedly return to parties where she claims to have witnessed gang rapes of drugged women. Yet since the charges are so serious, further investigation is warranted.

But there is one condition that should be imposed before an investigation is conducted: The accuser should have to waive her lawyer-client privilege with Avenatti so that investigators can determine how much of her affidavit and how many of her claims were originally her own, and how many, if any, may have been "improved upon" by her conversations with her highly partisan lawyer or others.

If she is telling the truth, she should have no reason for not waiving the privilege. If she is lying, then there is no privilege anyway, since the crime-fraud exception would take it outside of the privilege. She should be asked how she got in contact with Avenatti, who first introduced the term "gang rape" into the conversation, and whether she intended the information she conveyed to Avenatti to be made public.

Both Avenatti and his client should be questioned by the FBI as well as by Senate investigators. If Avenatti wants the truth to come out, let him place no barriers to fair inquiry.

So, the ball is now in the court of Avenatti and his client. Let her appear on television if he wants to try the case in the court of public opinion, but don't allow her to hide behind privilege. Moreover, Avenatti has another option: he can demand a criminal investigation by local authorities in Maryland, because Maryland law has no statute of limitations for the kind of rape he and his client have accused Judge Kavanaugh of committing.

The current situation is untenable—for Kavanaugh, for his accusers, and for the American public. An accusation as serious as gang rape simply cannot be allowed to sit out there uninvestigated. Kavanaugh and his accuser are both entitled to a full investigation. If the investigation establishes that the accusations are true, there should be serious consequences for Kavanaugh. But if the investigation proves that the allegations are made up of whole cloth, or if Avenatti did not properly investigate them before making so serious an accusation, there should be consequences for both Avenatti and his client.

These allegations are simply too extreme to be left to the court of public opinion, where people believe what they want to believe and where puffery and wild, unsubstantiated accusations often serve as a substitute for proof.

So the burden is now on Avenatti to file a formal complaint with the Maryland authorities. Put your client on television and allow her to answer all questions about her accusations and your role in bringing them forward, and be prepared to pay the consequences if it turns out that you or your client have defamed a man innocent of these crimes.

Now that the Senate Judiciary Committee has voted to send the nomination to the floor of the Senate and to allow a week of further investigation, there is no excuse for not thoroughly, fully investigating this charge along with others. The public, Congress, and law enforcement are entitled to know whether accusers are telling the truth or are committing perjury for partisan or other ideological reasons. The stakes are high. The resources for a thorough investigation are there. Let the process move forward for a fair resolution for all concerned.

This Is No Mere "Job Interview" ²⁷

Until Judge Brett Kavanaugh was accused of horrible crimes—sexual assault, lewd conduct and even gang rape—his confirmation hearings could fairly, if not entirely accurately, be characterized as a "job interview." The burden was on him to demonstrate his suitability to serve on the Supreme Court. He apparently met that burden in the eyes of a majority, a partisan one to be sure, and seemed on the way to getting the job.

But now everything has changed. So should the burden of persuasion. The behavior of which Judge Kavanaugh has been accused is so serious and devastating that it requires a high level of proof before forming the basis for his rejection. There is an enormous and dispositive difference between a candidate's rejection on ideological grounds, as was the case with Robert Bork, and rejection on the ground that he has committed crimes warranting lifetime imprisonment rather than a lifetime appointment.

Being on the Supreme Court is a privilege, not a right. But being disqualified based on a false accusation of a crime would be a violation of the fundamental right to fairness. Some will argue that the issue of Judge Kavanaugh's ideological and professional qualifications should be merged with the sexual allegations and that doubts should be resolved against a lifetime appointment.

In some cases that would be a plausible argument. But it is too late for that kind of nuanced approach now, because these accusations have received worldwide attention. Judge Kavanaugh is on trial for his life. At stake are his career, his family, his legacy, and a reputation earned over many decades as a lawyer and judge.

If he is now denied the appointment, it will be because he has been depicted as a sexual predator who deserves contempt, derision, and possible imprisonment. He may no longer be able to teach law, coach sports, or expect to be treated respectfully. He could be forced to resign his current judicial position, because having a "convicted" rapist on the bench is unseemly. For these reasons, he now has the right—perhaps not a legal right, but a right based on fundamental fairness—to have the charges against him put to the test of clear and convincing evidence or some standard close to that.

The court of public opinion is different from a court of law, but it too is an important court. Wouldn't anyone rather be convicted in a court of law of drunken driving—also a serious crime—than convicted in the court of public opinion of being a serial sex predator? Many would even rather go to prison for a year on drunken driving charges than be labeled a sexual predator for life. In a nation dedicated to fairness and due process, explicit constitutional rights often serve as a metaphor and guide in the kind of basic fairness we demand even in nonlegal proceedings. That model should operate here as well.

Had Judge Kavanaugh been rejected on ideological or professional grounds before these sordid accusations were leveled, he could go back to his life, as Robert Bork did. But if the Senate fails to confirm him now, his life will never be the same.

Some would argue that if Judge Kavanaugh is now confirmed in the face of these serious accusations, it will have an equally damaging effect on the life, reputation, and credibility of his accusers. That is false. Even if he is confirmed, those accusers will be treated as heroes by the many people who believe them. It will not have close to the impact on them that a failure to be confirmed will have on Judge Kavanaugh. The best evidence of that is Anita Hill, who has gone on to a distinguished career as an academic, writer, commentator, and feminist. The stakes are simply not comparable.

I don't know whether Judge Kavanaugh is guilty, innocent, or somewhere in between. I don't know whether he told the truth, the whole truth, and nothing but the truth. Judge Kavanaugh wouldn't have been my candidate of choice for the Supreme Court. I am a liberal Democrat who believes Republicans improperly denied Judge Merrick Garland a seat on the high court.

But this is no longer about who would make the best Supreme Court justice. It is about the most fundamental issues of fairness this country has faced since the McCarthy era, when innocent people were accused of trying to overthrow the government and had their lives ruined based on false accusations while being denied all semblance of due process or fairness. The American Civil Liberties Union stood strong against McCarthyism by demanding due process and hard evidence. But the ACLU now argues that "unresolved questions regarding credible allegations of sexual assault" be resolved against the accused nominee.

We have come a long way since McCarthyism, but we now live in an age that risks a new form of sexual McCarthyism. We must not go to that even darker place. The best way of assuring that we don't is to accord every person regardless of his status the kind of fundamental fairness we would expect for ourselves if we were accused.

What If Kavanaugh Were a Liberal Muslim Accused of Terrorism?[28]

As a law professor for half a century, I tested the consistency and strength of my students' arguments by constructing thought experiments in the form of challenging hypothetical cases—we called them hypos. So let's construct one to test the arguments being offered in the Kavanaugh case.

A thought experiment: President Hillary Clinton nominates the first Muslim American to the Supreme Court. Let's call him Amir Hassan. Republicans oppose him and accuse him of being a judicial activist. Then several witnesses place him at a mosque at which terrorism was advocated. He claims he went there to hear all sides of the issue. One witness places him in a terrorism training camp but that account is not corroborated. One final witness identifies him as the man who planted the bomb that blew off his leg at a demonstration. He categorically denies any association with terrorism.

How would the Senate, the media, American Civil Liberties Union (ACLU), and the public deal with these accusations?

The answer seems clear: the sides and arguments would be largely reversed. The shoe would be on the other foot and the hypocrisy of double standards would be exposed for all to see.

Surely the ACLU would not be arguing, as they have in the Kavanaugh case, that doubts should be resolved in favor of guilt. Radicals would not be insisting that terrorism survivors must always be believed as to identification. My left-wing colleagues would not point to the anger displayed by the possibly falsely accused nominee as proof of his disqualifying injudicious temperament.

To the contrary, the ACLU would be demanding due process, a presumption of innocence, and a high burden of proof before so serious a charge could destroy a life, a family, and a career. My colleagues would be defending the righteous anger of a falsely accused victim of ethnic prejudice.

The identity politics accusations would not be directed against old white men, but rather against those who would stereotype Muslims as terrorists. The *Jewish Forward* would not be featuring an article entitled "Is Amir Hassan every Muslim man?" as it is now featuring an article entitled "Is Brett Kavanaugh every American man?"

Many right-wing Republicans would now be making arguments similar to those being made by their left-wing Democratic colleagues in the Kavanaugh case. This is just a job interview, not a trial. Believe terrorism survivors. There is no burden of proof; mere suspicion is enough to deny a possible terrorist a lifetime appointment to the Supreme Court. Look how angry he is, demonstrating a lack of judicial temperament.

Hypocrisy is the coin of partisanship. It affects both sides. It may be better than simply not even caring whether people think you're being fair. As Francois de La Rochefoucauld once put it: "Hypocrisy is the homage vice pays to virtue."

It is precisely because of the pervasiveness and apparent acceptance of hypocrisy that I insist on applying the shoe on the other foot test to all aspects of politics, law, morality, and lives. It drives my colleagues and friends crazy when I challenge them to pass the test. Few are willing to take it. Even fewer pass it.

Applying that test to the Kavanaugh case doesn't provide a perfect resolution. But it does supply some guiding principles. Ask yourself what you would be thinking and saying about my Muslim American hypothetical thought experiment. One's first instinct is to try to distinguish the cases: rape is not like terrorism; stereotyping a Muslim American as a terrorist is different than stereotyping a privileged white man as a rapist; rape survivors are more reliable witnesses than terrorism survivors; the burden of proof should be higher for proving terrorism than rape.

None of these distinctions are compelling in the context of a Supreme Court confirmation process. They are makeweights designed to weaken the force of the shoe on the other foot test and to justify the hypocrisy of shifting arguments when it is your ox that is being gored.

So now back to Kavanaugh. The test for him should be the test that would have been demanded had the first Muslim American been nominated to the Supreme Court by a Democratic president and been accused of engaging in terrorism as a seventeen-year-old.

A full investigation, a fair process of judgment, no presumption of truth telling by alleged victims, no presumption of guilt against the nominee because he has so much to lose, a standard of guilt that varies with the seriousness of the accusations, and no identity political stereotypes as substitutes for hard evidence. These and other neutral rules should be applied to this case and every case going forward. Only then could we be confident in the fairness of the outcome.

No One Won During the
Brett Kavanaugh Confirmation[29]

When the votes have been counted and Brett Kavanaugh has been confirmed to serve on the Supreme Court, one conclusion will be clear: no one won.

One wonders how Brett Kavanaugh would now answer the following question: If you had it to do over again, would you rather never have been nominated, not having been accused of serious sex crimes, and continue to serve on the DC Circuit? Or would you do it all over again, knowing the outcome? I don't know how he would answer the question, but it would not be self-evident.

Clarence Thomas has served on the Supreme Court after a bruising confirmation fight, but the accusations against him were far less serious than those directed against Kavanaugh. Despite his narrow confirmation victory, he did not win: his reputation remains in tatters and he will probably not be allowed to continue to teach at Harvard.

The same question could be put to Dr. Christine Blasey Ford: Knowing what she now knows, would she have gone public with her accusations and endured the scorn, mockery and attacks, including from President Donald Trump? I suspect her answer would be yes, despite the fact that she did not succeed in defeating Kavanaugh's nomination. But one cannot be certain, especially in light of the fact that she did not intend for these accusations to become public until it became clear to her that the media was on to the story. So she didn't win.

The Democratic senators, many of whom came out against the nomination as soon as it was made but then doubled down following the sexual accusations, came off looking partisan, petty, and oblivious to the civil liberties and due process considerations at stake in this case. They did not win.

The Republican senators seemed desperate to rush the case to a vote in order to sit Kavanaugh on the Court before the midterm elections. They appeared to be more interested in political gain than truth, and their decision to hire a special counsel to question the witnesses backfired badly both legally and politically. Despite the narrow vote in support of the nomination, the Republicans did not win.

The ACLU has lost whatever shred of credibility it still had, following its abandonment of its principles in the interest of funding from leftists who couldn't care less about neutral civil liberties. Its insistence that suspicion of sexual wrongdoing was enough in the confirmation battle to put it on the wrong side of our basic rights. The ACLU has won financially but has lost its way.

The media, as has become typical, divided into roaring camps, one of which argued that Kavanaugh could do no wrong while the other argued that he could do no right. A handful of journalists reflected the complexity and nuance of the situation facing the senate, but they were rare. Much of the media lost its credibility.

Another big loser is the #MeToo movement, some of whose leaders have overstated its case by denying the possibility that some women willfully lie in a calculated manner in order to gain material benefits including money, fame, and revenge. Michael Avenatti's decision to publicize the highly questionable claims of gang rape made by his client, Julie Swetnick, has done enormous damage to the movement. There is no compelling evidence that Swetnick—who is two years older than Kavanaugh, lived in a different neighborhood, and traveled in different social circles—ever even laid eyes on Kavanaugh. She blatantly contradicted her sworn statement in a television interview in which she changed the facts dramatically.

It is certainly possible, though we may never know, that she simply made up the story of whole cloth. Yet radical #MeToo'ers have demanded that we accord her the same credibility that we appropriately afforded Professor Ford because "survivors don't lie." Some, of course, do. Some are not survivors at all. Others may have survived sex assaults but not by the person they accuse. There is no sex-linked gene for telling the truth or lying. The credibility of the #MeToo movement has suffered a loss.

But the biggest losers were, of course, the American people and the future of the nomination and confirmation processes as spelled out in our Constitution. The Framers never intended this kind of a media circus with partisanship trumping principle. The upshot will be that fewer qualified candidates will allow their names to be put forward if they know that by doing so their high school actions will be examined, their yearbook entries scrutinized, and their reputations subjected to search and destroy missions. This means that we have all lost.

So what have we learned from this debacle? That the process of nominating and confirming justices has become flawed beyond immediate repair. We need to change the process. I recommend that the executive, legislative, and judicial branches appoint a blue-ribbon commission to look into new ways, consistent with the broad outlines of the Constitution, to nominate and confirm judges, especially justices. More investigation should be done before the nomination is made, and a process for ongoing and discreet investigation should be established to assure there are few surprises. The system will never be perfect, but we can do better. Everybody lost this time. We must not repeat our mistakes.

Should Kavanaugh Be Stopped from Teaching at Harvard Law School?[30]

Now that Brett Kavanaugh's nomination to the Supreme Court has been confirmed, many law students are demanding that he be punished by ending his teaching career at Harvard Law School.

This effort reminds me of the time when I was a student in Brooklyn College in the 1950s, witnessing professors who were fired because it was suspected they might have been communists years earlier. It didn't matter whether they were innocent or guilty. Being suspected was enough to make them unsuitable to teach students, especially if they had pleaded the Fifth Amendment or angrily condemned the Un-American Activities Committees of Congress.

Now, flash forward sixty-five years as Harvard Law students and some faculty demand that Kavanaugh, who had taught with distinction since 2008, no longer be allowed to do what he loves and what many students loved. When Kavanaugh was nominated to the Supreme Court, Harvard Law School was exuberant in its praise of his teaching. Dean John Manning thanked Kavanaugh for his "superb teaching" and "generosity, dedication, and collegiality he has shown our community." A group of more than eighty former students sent a letter to the Senate Judiciary Committee, attesting that "[we] may have differing views on political issues surrounding the confirmation process, but we all agree on one thing: Judge Kavanaugh is a rigorous thinker, a devoted teacher, and a gracious person."

After the accusations of sexual assault emerged, "hundreds of Harvard Law Students walked out of class . . . to protest Kavanaugh" demanding that he be barred from teaching, according to *The Crimson*. It also reported that students at a viewing party of the Kavanaugh testimony "applauded" and "burst out in cheers," when Kavanaugh lamented the fact that these allegations may prevent him from teaching again. Harvard Law School has announced that Kavanaugh would not teach in winter term 2019. Although

Harvard claims that it was Kavanaugh who decided, before he was confirmed, not to teach next semester, there can be little doubt that whoever made the decision, it was influenced by the student demands that he not be allowed to continue teaching.

Despite his lack of tenure, there is a long tradition at Harvard Law School to encourage judges to continue to teach in the winter term if they satisfy the general academic criteria and receive excellent student evaluations. I do not know Kavanaugh, though I encountered him once or twice in the faculty lunchroom. This is not so much about Kavanaugh as it is about a new form of McCarthyism that is quickly descending on university campuses and spreading throughout the country.

Nor has this successful effort to end Kavanaugh's teaching career based on neutral or objective standards that are equally applicable to all suspected serious crimes, regardless of the political or ideological backgrounds of the teacher.

Recall that former terrorists, some of whom were convicted of causing or intending the deaths of innocent people, are now teaching at several American universities. Consider the cases of former Weather Underground members Kathy Boudin and Bill Ayers. Boudin was convicted of complicity in the murder of police officers, served her term, and is now a member of the faculty and co-director of the Center for Justice at Columbia University. Ayers, who has boasted of his past association with terrorism, recently retired from a faculty position at the University of Illinois at Chicago. I am aware of no efforts to deny them their teaching positions. Had Boudin been a left-wing male who had completed a prison term for sexual assault, I'm certain that many of the same students who now oppose Kavanaugh teaching at Harvard Law School would be demanding the right to take a course from the convicted terrorist. Is what Kavanaugh been accused of—whether truthfully or falsely—really worse than participating in the murder of innocent people? How can this double standard be tolerated by thoughtful students and faculty members? Do we really want to distinguish between alleged crimes committed by people of the left and people of the right?

Before a teacher is terminated on grounds such as those at issue in the Kavanaugh case, neutral and objective standards equally applicable to all must first be established. There cannot be *ad hoc* decisions based on mob rule and political correctness demands of the day. These standards have not been met in the Kavanaugh case. He should be invited to continue to teach. I would understand if he declined the offer, but fairness demand it should be his decision to make. Students should, of course, have the right to refuse to attend his class for any reason or no reason, but as long as there are students, no matter how few, who wish to learn from him, they should be accorded the opportunity to do so—regardless of other students might think.

ACLU's Opposition to Kavanaugh Sounds Its Death Knell[31]

Now that Brett Kavanaugh has been confirmed, it is appropriate to look at the damage caused by the highly partisan confirmation process. Among the casualties has been an organization I have long admired.

After *Politico* reported that the ACLU is spending more than $1 million to oppose Judge Kavanaugh's confirmation to the Supreme Court, I checked the ACLU website to see if its core mission had changed—if the ACLU had now officially abandoned its non-partisan nature and become yet another Democratic super PAC. But no, the ACLU still claims it is "nonpartisan."

So why did the ACLU oppose a Republican nominee to the Supreme Court and argue for a presumption of guilt regarding sexual allegations directed against that judicial nominee?

The answer is as clear as it is simple. It is all about pleasing the donors. The ACLU used to be cash-poor but principle-rich. Now, ironically, after Trump taking office, the ACLU has never become so cash-rich yet principle-poor. Before Donald Trump was elected president, the ACLU had an annual operating budget of $60 million dollars.

When I was on the ACLU National Board, it was a fraction of that amount. Today it is flush with cash, with net assets of over $450 million dollars. As the ACLU itself admitted in its annual report ending 2017, it received "unprecedented donations" after President Trump's election. "Unprecedented" it truly has been: the ACLU received $120 million dollars from online donations alone (up from $3 to $5 million during the Obama years).

The problem is that most of the money is not coming from civil libertarians who care about free speech, due process, the rights of the accused, and defending the unpopular. It is coming from radical leftists in Hollywood, Silicon Valley, and other areas not known for a deep commitment to civil liberties. To its everlasting disgrace, the ACLU is abandoning its mission to follow the money. It now spends millions of dollars on TV ads that are indistinguishable from those of left-wing organizations, such as MoveOn, the Democratic National Committee, and other partisan groups.

ACLU's "reinvention in the Trump era" was reported on by the *New Yorker*:

> In this midterm year . . . as progressive groups have mushroomed and grown more active, and as liberal billionaires such as Howard Schultz and Tom Steyer have begun to imagine themselves as political heroes and eye presidential runs, the ACLU, itself newly flush, has begun to take an active role in elections. The group has plans to spend more than $25 million on races and ballot initiatives by [midterm] Election Day in November.
>
> Anthony Romero, the group's executive director, told me, "It used to be that, when I had a referendum I really cared about, I could spend $50,000."

This new strategy can be seen in many of the ACLU's actions, which would have been inconceivable just a few years ago. The old ACLU would never have been silent when Michael Cohen's office was raided by the FBI and his clients' files seized; it would have yelled foul when students accused of sexual misconduct were tried by kangaroo courts; and it surely would have argued against a presumption of guilt regarding sexual allegations directed against a judicial nominee.

Everything the ACLU does today seems to be a function of its fundraising. To be sure, it must occasionally defend a Nazi, a white supremacist, or even a mainstream conservative. But that is not its priority these days, either financially or emotionally. Its heart and soul are in its wallet and checkbook. It is getting rich while civil liberties are suffering.

There appears to be a direct correlation between the ACLU's fundraising and its priorities. When the ACLU's national political director and former Democratic Party operative Faiz Shakir was asked why the ACLU got involved in the Kavanaugh confirmation fight, he freely admitted, "People have funded us and I think they expect a return." Its funders applaud the result because many of these mega-donors couldn't care less about genuine civil liberties or due process. What they care about are political results: more left-wing Democrats in Congress, fewer conservative justices on the Supreme Court, and more money in the ACLU coffers.

When I served both on the National and Massachusetts Boards of the American Civil Liberties Union, board members included conservative Republicans, old-line Brahmans, religious ministers, schoolteachers, labor union leaders, and a range of ordinary folks who cared deeply about core civil liberties. The discussions were never partisan. They always focused on the Bill of Rights. There were considerable disagreements about whether various amendments covered the conduct at issue.

But no one ever introduced the question of whether taking a position would help the Democrats or Republicans, liberals or conservatives, Jews or Catholics, or any other identifiable group. We cared about applying the constitution fairly to everyone, without regard to the political consequences.

As the *New Yorker* described these more innocent times: the ACLU ". . . has been fastidiously nonpartisan, so prudish about any alliance with political power that its leadership, in the 1980s and 1990s, declined even to give awards to like-minded legislators for fear that it might give the wrong impression."

Those days are now gone. Instead, we have a variant on the question my immigrant grandmother asked when I told her the Brooklyn Dodgers won the World Series in 1955: "Yeah, but vuz it good or bad for the Jews?" My grandmother was a strong advocate of identity politics: all she cared about was the Jews. That was sixty-three years ago.

The questions being asked today by ACLU board members are: Is it good or bad for the Left? Is it good or bad for Democrats? It is good or bad for women? Is it good or bad for people of color? Is it good or bad for gays?

These are reasonable questions to be asked by groups dedicated to the welfare of these groups but not by a group purportedly dedicated to civil liberties for all. A true civil libertarian group transcends identity politics and cares about the civil liberties of its political enemies, because it recognizes that this is the only way that civil liberties for everyone will be preserved.

But today too few people are asking, "Is it good or bad for civil liberties?"

The Shoe Test in the Media
and Foreign Relations

Widespread failure of the shoe on the other foot test is not a phenomenon constrained to domestic politics and news; the same double standard is proliferating in our foreign relationships, finding its way through the extremist media to a receptive public. It manifests sharply in demonizers of Jews and the nation-state of Israel, who make demands not made on other peoples or nations and therein miserably fail the shoe test.

This deserves to be brought to light and criticized, regardless of the perpetrator. I do so in the following writings.

Biased Media Complicit as Hamas Sends Women, Children to Front Line[32]

If this were the first time that Hamas deliberately provoked Israel into self-defense actions that resulted in the unintended deaths of Gaza civilians, the media could be excused for playing into the hands of Hamas. The most recent Hamas provocations—having forty thousand Gazans try to tear down the border fence and enter Israel with Molotov cocktails and other improvised weapons—are part of a repeated Hamas tactic that I have called the "dead baby strategy."

Hamas's goal is to have Israel kill as many Gazans as possible so that the headlines always begin, and often end, with the body count. Hamas deliberately sends women and children to the front line, while their own fighters hide behind these human shields.

Hamas leaders have long acknowledged this tactic. Fathi Hammad, a Hamas Member of the Palestinian Legislative Council, stated as far back as 2008:

> For the Palestinian people, death has become an industry, at which women excel, and so do all the people living on this land. The elderly excel at this, and so do the mujahideen and the children. This is why they have formed human shields of the women, the children, the elderly, and the mujahideen, in order to challenge the Zionist bombing machine. It is as if they were saying to the Zionist enemy: "we desire death like you desire life."

Hamas used this tactic to provoke two wars with Israel in which their fighters fired rockets from civilian areas, including hospitals, schools, and mosques. When Israel responded, it tried its best to avoid civilian casualties, dropping warning leaflets, calling residents of potential targets, and dropping nonlethal noise bombs on the roofs of houses that were being used to launch rockets and store explosives. Inevitably, some civilians were killed, and the media blamed Israel for these deaths, despite the precautions it had taken.

The same was true when Hamas built terror tunnels used to kidnap Israeli civilians. The entrances to these tunnels were in civilian areas as well, including mosques and schools. Using their own civilians as human shields while targeting Israeli civilians, is a double war crime. Yet, the media generally focuses on Israel's reaction to these war crimes rather than Hamas' war crimes.

The cruel reality is that every time Israel accidentally kills a Gaza civilian, Israel loses. And every time Israel kills a Gaza civilian, Hamas wins. Israelis grieve every civilian death its army accidentally causes. Hamas benefits from every death Israel accidentally causes. That is why it encourages its women and children to become martyrs.

Calling this the "dead baby strategy" may seem cruel, because it is cruel. But don't blame the messenger for accurately describing this tactic. Blame those who cynically use it. And blame the media for playing into the hands of those who use it by reporting only the body count and not the deliberate Hamas tactic that leads to one-sided body counts.

It is true that Gaza is in a desperate situation and that it is wounded. But the wound itself is self-inflicted. When Israel ended its occupation of the Gaza—removing every single soldier and settler—Gaza could have become the Singapore on the Mediterranean. It is a beautiful area with a large seacoast. It received infusions of cash and other help from Europe. Israel left behind agricultural equipment and hothouses. But instead of using these resources to feed, house, and educate its citizens, Hamas built rockets, terror tunnels, and Molotov cocktails. It threw dissenters off the roof and murdered members of the Palestinian Authority who were willing to recognize Israel and negotiate with it.

Hamas rejects the two-state solution or any solution that leaves Israel intact. Its only solution is violence, and the events at the fence these past days are a manifestation of that violence. Would any country in the world allow forty thousand people, sworn to its destruction, knock down a border fence and attack its citizens living peacefully near the border? Of course not. Could Israel have done more to reduce casualties among those trying to breach the border fence? I don't know, and neither do the legions of arm chair generals that are currently criticizing Israel for the steps it took to prevent a catastrophe among the residents of Kibbutzim and towns that are proximate to the border fence.

One thing is crystal clear: Hamas will continue to use the dead baby strategy as long as the media continues to report the deaths in the manner in which it has reported them in recent weeks. Many in the media are complicit in these deaths because their one-sided reporting encourages Hamas to send innocent women and children to the front line.

Perhaps Israel could do a better job in defending its civilians, but it is certain that the media can do a better job in accurately reporting the Hamas strategy that results in so many innocent deaths.

There is a marvelous cartoon that illustrates the difference between Hamas and Israel. It shows an Israeli soldier standing in front of a baby carriage with a baby in it, shielding the baby. Then it shows a Hamas terrorist standing behind a baby carriage with the baby in it, using the baby to shield him. This cartoon better illustrates the reality that is occurring at the Gaza fence than most of the "objective" reporting by the media.

NBC Demonizes John Bolton, Gatestone[33]

When I was growing up, organizations that expressed any views at all similar to those expressed by communist groups were called "communist fronts." Anyone who defended on the grounds of civil liberties the right of communists to express their hateful ideology was labeled a "commie-symp."

All decent people railed against this coerced, "politically correct" guilt-by-association because it endangered freedom of speech, freedom of association, basic fairness, and especially truth.

But today a similar tactic of defamatory character assassination against people with whom one disagrees, particularly conservatives, is being employed by elements of the left, including some in the mainstream media.

Consider the recent attack by Heidi Przybyla of NBC News against the recently appointed National Security Advisor, Ambassador John Bolton, and an organization whose board he chaired before that, Gatestone Institute. The headline of the hit piece is, "John Bolton Chaired Anti-Muslim Think Tank." Nothing could be further from the truth.

Przybyla wrongly described Gatestone an "anti-Muslim think tank" presumably because it published some articles about Muslim "no-go zones" in parts of Europe. The existence of certain areas in Europe that are unsafe for non-Muslims is widely debated as "politically incorrect" in the European media. It is well established that visible Jews—wearing kippahs or other indicators of their religion—have been attacked. Two weeks ago, a non-Jew apparently trying to discredit such rumors by wearing a kippah was attacked on a Berlin street.

Others have been attacked as well. Even German Chancellor Angela Merkel, a vocal supporter of mass migration, has commented on this troubling situation. According to the *Daily Express*, Merkel warned that, "There cannot be any no-go areas . . . where people are afraid to go, but such places are a reality."

For some Gatestone writers to have participated in this debate does not make Gatestone "anti-Muslim." It makes them pertinent.

Even a cursory look at Gatestone's website shows that its writers and scholars include numerous Muslims, such as the prominent journalists Amir Taheri; Khaled Abu Toameh; President of the American Islamic Forum M. Zuhdi Jasser; Salim Mansur, and Raheel Raza—among others.

Many of Gatestone's articles are, in fact, pro-Muslim—advocating human rights and civil liberties for all Muslims—including Palestinians and Iranians.

Przybyla also claims that Gatestone is somehow in the pocket of Putin's Russia based on the following "fact," "NBC news found at least four instances of known Russian trolls directly retweeting from the Gatestone account."

The fact that Russian trolls may have retweeted a handful of Gatestone articles means nothing, especially as Dan Abrams's Law and Crime website independently confirmed 267 retweets of MSNBC's Joy Reid. As the noted journalist Daniel Greenfield wrote, "Four times vs. 267 times. If getting retweeted 4 times makes you a Russian spy, NBC must be the Kremlin." Everything on the Internet is public information; anyone is free to read or tweet about it. One cannot post material labeled, "except for Russians."

If Przybyla's accusations sound familiar to those of us who lived through the thought police of the McCarthy era, it is because they are so similar. Blaming an organization for those who read or circulate its material is McCarthyesque defamation. Attributing to an organization all the views of those who are invited to debate controversial issues is McCarthyesque demonization.

Let John Bolton be judged by his own statements and actions, for which he needs no defense from me. But let not the media indulge in the discredited tactics of guilt-by-association, distortion, and outright deceit based on ideological or political differences.

I am a frequent op-ed contributor to Gatestone and often speak at its events. I also proudly serve on its board. I find Gatestone to be refreshingly centrist. Gatestone encourages dialogue between the center left, represented by people such as former Sen. Joe Lieberman and myself, and people from the center right represented by speakers such as John Bolton and the eminent historian Victor Davis Hanson.

I am scheduled to speak at an event with Ayaan Hirsi Ali, who, based on her own personal experiences of female genital mutilation and forced marriage, has expressed views about abuses committed by some Muslims against other Muslims in the name of Islam.

These discussions are always informative and serious. I disagree with some of what I hear and read at Gatestone events and in its publications, but that is true of every organization of which I am aware. Przybyla wrenches out of context a few points of view that to her seem controversial, and not only attributes them to the organization but makes it appear as if these views are the only ones the organization represents.

The answer to deception and falsehoods has always been truth. I urge everyone who has read Przybyla's misrepresentation to go to the Gatestone website and read a wide array of its extensively substantiated articles. Then everyone can judge for themselves. Is Gatestone an "anti-Muslim think tank?"

Or, is it an open-minded institute that encourages diverse views on a wide range of pressing subjects? Then you can answer Groucho Marx's famous rhetorical question, "Who are you going to believe—me or your lying eyes?"

Chomsky Calls Russian Interference
a Joke—and Guess Who He Blames?[34]

Noam Chomsky has gone off the deep end once again. This time he claims that in "most of the world" the issue of Russian interference in US elections is "almost a joke." The real villain, according to him, is, of course, Israel—as it almost always is with Chomsky. According to the world's "top public intellectual," Israeli intervention in US elections "vastly overwhelms anything the Russians may have done." His proof of this absurd and false charge is that Israeli Prime Minister Benjamin Netanyahu gave a speech in front of Congress "with overwhelming applause." Only on Planet Chomsky would it be worse for the Prime Minister of an American ally *openly* to accept an invitation from the Speaker of the House to address Congress about an issue of mutual concern, than for Russian agents *surreptitiously* to try to manipulate voters by false social media campaigns, hacking emails, and other illegal actions.

Chomsky simply fails to understand how democracy is supposed to work. Transparency and public accountability are the cornerstones of democracy. Prime Minister Netanyahu's very public opposition to Obama's Iran Deal—a deal opposed by most members of Congress and most Americans—was just as consistent with democracy as Winston Churchill's public demands for the United States to help Great Britain fight the Nazis.

American presidents, as well as Israeli prime ministers, seek to influence the policies and electoral choices made by their allies. That, too, is part of democracy. The United States has pressured Israel to stop building settlements; Israel has pressured the United States to be more aggressive in preventing Iran from developing a nuclear arsenal. This, too, is part of democracy.

The American Israel Public Affairs Committee (AIPAC) is an American organization that lobbies on behalf of American support for Israel. Lobbying is as American as apple pie.

What is un-American, and what is undemocratic, is for secret agents working surreptitiously on behalf of Vladimir Putin's Russia to commit numerous crimes, for which several of its agents have been indicted, in an effort to influence American elections without transparency or public accountability.

Chomsky is smart enough to understand this, but his willful blindness toward anything involving Israel leads him to make the kind of false comparative statement that no intellectual should ever make. Again, only on Planet Chomsky would Russia's continuous efforts improperly to intervene in American elections would be characterized as "almost a joke." Only on Planet Chomsky Israel's open, transparent, and democratic efforts to have America support its security be deemed worse than Russia's crimes. But such blindness is to be expected from Chomsky when it comes to anything regarding Israel, Jews, or anti-Semitism.

Remember this is the same man who defended the so-called "research" of the notorious Holocaust-denier, Robert Faurisson. Not only did Chomsky defend Faurisson's phony research, but he denied that Faurisson—who is a notorious Jew-hater—had said anything that qualifies as anti-Semitic. Here is what Chomsky wrote:

> I see no anti-Semitic implications in denial of the existence of gas chambers, or even denial of the Holocaust. Nor would there be anti-Semitic implications, per se, in the claim that the Holocaust (whether one believes it took place or not) is being exploited, viciously so, by apologists for Israeli repression and violence. I see no hint of anti-Semitic implications in Faurisson's work.

Chomsky, who is a prominent linguist, knows nothing of the meaning of language in context. Holocaust denial is quintessentially anti-Semitic, because it falsely accuses the Jews of fabricating stories of the murder of six million Jews.

Experts understand that there are different kinds of intelligence. Chomsky may be intelligent when it comes to linguistics, but his statements regarding Israel, Russia, and the Holocaust are simply counterfactual. There is no other word for his bizarre views, if he actually believes them. If he does not, then there is another word that aptly describes his statements: bigotry.

If Britain Wants To Show Its "Moral Backbone," It Must Reject Jeremy Corbyn[35]

I was recently interviewed by British public news broadcaster Channel 4 about Donald Trump. Host Matt Frei asked me what he likely intended to be a rhetorical question: "Where is the moral backbone of America these days?"

I responded: "Well, where is the moral backbone of Great Britain to have as the head of the Labour Party a virulent anti-Semite, a virulent hater of Jews and the nation-state of the Jewish people? Don't lecture us about our political system as long as you have Jeremy Corbyn, who may potentially become the next Prime Minister. Shame on Great Britain for letting that come to pass."

Frei responded that Corbyn "would be rejecting all these accusations." That should have been the end of the matter, with each having made our point. But no, Frei felt it was necessary to apologise to his viewers—when I was off-air—for what I had said. "And our apologies for those unexpected remarks from one of our guests about the Labour leader Jeremy Corbyn," he said, "who as we've reported many times consistently and robustly denies allegations of anti-Semitism."

In a rebroadcast, Channel 4 cut the discussion of Corbyn. It wrote an email to me explaining that it is obligated under the rules to present "the other side of the story" whenever there is "a significant allegation being made." Yet Channel 4 doesn't apologize or present the "other side" when it accuses Trump of misconduct which he denies.

Why the double standard? Why not let viewers decide for themselves whether my characterisation of Jeremy Corbyn is correct? So let me present my case. I invite a response by Corbyn. In a widely accepted definition, adopted by the US State Department and its British counterpart, anti-Semitism includes:

> Accusing the Jews as a people, or Israel as a state, of inventing or exaggerating the Holocaust ... applying double standards by

requiring of it a behaviour not expected or demanded of any other democratic nation . . . drawing comparisons of contemporary Israeli policy to that of the Nazis. Accusing Jewish citizens of being more loyal to Israel . . . than to the interests of their own nations.

Corbyn's statement and actions meet these standards. Corbyn has taken part in events with Dyab Abou Jahjah, a Lebanese militant who rails against "Jew-worship" and calls homosexuals "Aids-spreading faggots," according to the *National Review*. He also argued against the expulsion from Britain of Raed Saleh, a leader of the Islamic Movement in Israel, who claims Jews were behind the 9/11 terrorist attacks. In 2012 Corbyn invited him to take tea with him on the terrace at Parliament, saying Saleh "is far from a dangerous man. He's a very honored citizen; he represents his people extremely well."

Corbyn has also been accused of donating money to Deir Yassin Remembered, founded by self-proclaimed Holocaust denier Paul Eisen. Corbyn denies having any knowledge of Eisen's views but has acknowledged that he attended one of DYR's events as recently as 2013.

At another conference, Corbyn said "Zionists . . . don't understand English irony," despite "having lived in this country for a very long time, probably all their lives."

In this context, Corbyn seemed to be using the term "Zionists" to apply broadly to British Jews. This same conference also featured a speaker who blamed Israel for the 9/11 attacks. Britain's former Chief Rabbi, Jonathan Sacks, has accused Corbyn of having given "support to racists, terrorists, and dealers of hate who want to kill Jews and remove Israel from the map" and said his remarks about Zionists not being sufficiently British is "the language of classic pre-war European anti-Semitism."

Corbyn called former Israeli Foreign Minister Tzipi Livni, an advocate of the two-state solution, "a war criminal" while calling terrorist groups Hamas and Hezbollah "friends"—a comment which he later claimed he regretted making. While condemning Israel for human rights violations, Corbyn has praised human rights violators such as Venezuela, Cuba, and Iran.

After the death of former Venezuelan President Hugo Chávez, Corbyn described him as "someone who stood up, was counted, was inspiring. . . ." Following the death of Fidel Castro, Corbyn praised the Cuban dictator's "heroism" and called him "a champion of social justice." He has also praised Iran for "tolerance and acceptance of other faiths, traditions, and ethnic groups in Iran."

Corbyn seems to have little interest in the human right of Kurds, Chechens, Tibetans, and other groups. Is he more interested in the Palestinians largely because their alleged oppressors are Jewish? I don't recall hearing Corbyn complain when Palestinians are oppressed by Jordan or by Hamas.

To be sure, Israel does not have a perfect human rights record. No country does. But singling out Israel for condemnation while praising some of the worst human rights violators and ignoring violations against people at least as oppressed as the Palestinians is applying precisely the sort of double standard against the nation-state of the Jewish people the UK and the US have recognised as anti-Semitic.

Corbyn's actions paint a foreboding picture for British Jews as well as Anglo-Israeli relations should Corbyn become prime minister. It may come as no surprise then that the leading Anglo-Jewish newspapers called a potential Corbyn administration an "existential threat" to Jewish life in the UK and warned that "the [Labour] party that was, until recently, the natural home for our community has seen its values and integrity eroded by Corbynite contempt for Jews and Israel."

Let the good people of Britain show the moral backbone of that great country by rejecting Corbyn and the bigotry he has supported.

Why Did the Clintons Share the Stage With Farrakhan?36

Imagine President Trump being invited to speak at the funeral of a white singer who he admired (say, Ted Nugent, if he were to pass) and seeing that David Duke was on stage in a place of honor, he remained and gave a speech. Well, President Clinton gave a speech in the presence of Louis Farrakhan at the funeral for Aretha Franklin. Hillary Clinton was sitting off to the side but did not speak.

Why would President Clinton, a good man and a friend of the Jewish people, do this? There are several possible answers. First, he was taken by surprise at Farrakhan's presence and didn't want to do anything to disrupt the service. But the shoe on the other foot question remains: Would he have acted similarly if it had been Duke rather than Farrakhan?

Second, Clinton doesn't believe that refusing to sit alongside a bigot is the proper response to bigotry. Again the shoe on the other foot question remains: Would he sit alongside Duke?

Third, Clinton doesn't regard Farrakhan as comparable to Duke. But that is simply wrong. Farrakhan is a blatant anti-Semite with an enormous following. Finally, Farrakhan's anti-Semitism is not considered as serious a problem as Duke's white supremacy. But without getting into comparisons of bigotry, anti-Semitism is a serious and growing problem.

Farrakhan is at least as bigoted as Duke. This is a man who only last year called Jews members of the "Synagogue of Satan" and claimed that Jesus called Jews the "children of the devil." Farrakhan is also a homophobe claiming that Jews are "responsible for all of this filth and degenerate behavior that Hollywood is putting out turning men into women and women into men." In the past, Farrakhan delivered similar remarks claiming that "when you want something in this world, the Jew holds the door" and calling Adolf Hitler "a very great man." He's also a racist claiming a few years ago that "white people deserve to die."

Many younger people on the left may not know the extent of Farrakhan's bigotry, or they may condone it by claiming he did a service for African American communities. For example, Tamika Mallory, cofounder of the Women's March, called Farrakhan a "GOAT," or greatest of all time, and Congressman Keith Ellison, deputy chairman of the Democratic National Committee, once called him a "role model for black youth."

Earlier this year, a photo of Barack Obama smiling with Farrakhan taken in 2005 emerged. (Although I supported President Obama, both in 2008 and 2012, I would not have campaigned as enthusiastically for him had I known then about this suppressed photograph.) Ellison, who may become Minnesota's next attorney general, later distanced himself from Farrakhan but, like Mallory, claimed that Farrakhan's contribution to African American empowerment is "complex." Would we accept this kind of complexity and nuance if a white singer's family had invited Duke?

Liberals need to make unequivocally clear that the Democratic Party tent will never be big enough for anti-Semites and anti-Americans like Farrakhan, just as Republicans need to do the same with sympathizers of the alt-right. There are not "good people" on the side of anti-Semitism, any more than there are "good people" on the side of white supremacy.

There is no place for a double standard when it comes to anti-Semitism. Black anti-Semitism should not get a pass on account of the oppression suffered by so many African Americans. Neither should "progressive" tolerance of anti-Semitism of the kind shown by Bernie Sanders backing Jeremy Corbyn, the anti-Semite leader of the British Labour Party who may well become the next prime minister of America's closest ally.

Just contrast the Aretha Franklin memorial service with the controversy surrounding the decision of the *New Yorker* to invite Steve Bannon for what promised to be a critical conversation with the magazine's editor, David Remnick. After many prominent liberals, such as Judd Apatow, Jim Carrey, and Patton Oswalt, announced that they would not attend lest they "normalize hatred," Bannon was disinvited. Chelsea Clinton tweeted, "For anyone who wonders what normalization of bigotry looks like, please look no further than Steve Bannon being invited by both @TheEconomist & @NewYorker to their respective events in #NYC a few weeks apart."

To that I would add, look no further than the Clintons sharing the stage with Farrakhan. I hope they will take this occasion to distance themselves from, and strongly condemn, Farrakhan's anti-Semitism.

Refusing Study in Israel Is a
Bitter Lesson in Discrimination[37]

Imagine a white university professor telling a highly qualified African American student that he refused to recommend her for a year-abroad program to an African country because he disapproved of the way that country treated its white minority. That professor would be ostracized, boycotted, reprimanded, disciplined, or fired.

Well, now the shoe is on the other foot: a left-wing professor at the University of Michigan, John Cheney-Lippold, has refused to recommend a highly qualified Jewish student for study in Israel. How do we know she was qualified? Because the professor already had initially agreed to give her a recommendation. Then he noticed that she wanted to study in Israel, with whose policies he disagrees. So he withdrew his offer to recommend her based on his support for the boycott of Israeli universities.

This pernicious boycott tactic is designed to cut off all academic, scientific, cultural, and other contacts with only one country: the nation-state of the Jewish people. Many who support singling out Israel will actively encourage academic contacts with Russian, Cuban, Saudi, Venezuelan, Chinese, Belarusian, and Palestinian universities despite the horrid human-rights records of these undemocratic countries and the discriminatory policies of their universities. Israel is one of the world's most democratic nations, with one of the best human-rights records and among the freest, most diverse universities. Yet it is the only target of this bigoted academic boycott. And the Boycott-Divestment-Sanctions (BDS) tactic applies only to Jewish Israelis, not Muslims.

This hypocritical professor probably would not hesitate to recommend his student to universities that discriminate against gay and transgender, women, Jewish, or Christian students. Israeli universities do not discriminate against anyone; on the contrary, they have affirmative-action programs for Muslim and black students. They are on the forefront of scientific, technological, and medical innovations which benefit the entire world and would be set back by boycotts.

Defenders of Professor Cheney-Lippold will argue that he has the "academic freedom" to decide who to recommend and who not to recommend. But even his defenders would have to agree that if his decision to refuse to recommend a particular student was based on improper factors—such as race, gender, sexual preference, or religion—academic freedom would not protect him against charges of discriminatory action. The question, therefore, is whether refusing to recommend a student for a year abroad in Israel constitutes a permissible or impermissible basis.

The answer rests on the shoe on the other foot test. If a university would allow a professor to refuse to recommend a student to an African country, to a Muslim country, or to a communist country, then it might be permissible to refuse to recommend her to a Jewish country. It is more than ironic that many of the same radical leftists who would support Professor Cheney-Lippold's discriminatory action have strongly opposed President Trump's travel ban, precisely because it focused on Muslim-majority countries—many of which are among the most discriminatory human-rights offenders and facilitators of terrorism. Yet they would support a ban against a Jewish country that does not discriminate and that fights terrorism within the rule of law.

His defenders also argue that Israel sometimes disallows Palestinian Americans from joining academic programs at Israeli universities. But Muslim countries bar women, gays, Israelis, and Jews from attending their universities. Yet Professor Cheney-Lippold would probably not hesitate to recommend a Muslim student to spend a year at such a Muslim university.

Academic freedom may permit a professor to advocate a boycott against Israeli (or any other) universities, misguided as that may be. But it does not permit a professor to actually discriminate against one of his students based on invidious factors. A teacher must treat all of his students fairly and equally, without regard to their religious, political, or ethnic views or identities. Just as academic freedom would permit a racist, sexist, homophobic, anti-Muslim, or anti-Jewish professor to express his bigoted views outside the classroom, so too academic freedom would protect Professor Cheney-Lippold for expressing anti-Israeli views—but it does not protect him from discriminating against a student who has different views.

The University of Michigan has issued a response and must now decide what its policy is, and what it will be going forward, with regard to professors of either the radical left or the alt-right who act on their bigotry by refusing to recommend qualified students to universities in countries with whose actions they disagree.

Whatever policy the university adopts must be equally applicable to all universities in all countries. The University of Michigan is a public university which, unlike private universities, may have more legal constraints on their actions. It must adopt a fair policy for this and future cases that does not allow professors to discriminate against students based on invidious factors. Shame on Professor Cheney-Lippold for allowing his wrongheaded political views to override his academic and legal obligation not to discriminate against students who disagree with him.

Impeachment Is Not the Answer

I've shown that the proposed impeachment of Donald Trump and now Brett Kavanaugh aren't legally viable; rather, impeaching them sets a precedent that is dangerous for all Americans and is a pointed manifestation of the perversion of our country's discourse, the importance that political gain has taken on, and the push toward the political extremes that continues to widen.

Impeachment would be the ultimate failure of the shoe on the other foot test.

We must look to solutions. Rather than impeachment proceedings that will drag on for two years, we must strive to re-democratize our dialogue, to condemn the current criminalization of politics and weaponization of law, to move our conversation back toward the centrist values of tolerance and non-violence in which America thrives. We must put down our arms and do what is best for the American people.

Democrats, Don't Try To
Conduct a Revenge Inquisition[38]

The confirmation disaster surrounding Justice Brett Kavanaugh, whose appointment to the Supreme Court was approved by the Senate on a 50-48 vote Saturday, has done much damage to our country and its institutions. And the damage may well continue if Democrats regain majority control of the House and conduct a revenge inquisition against the new associate justice.

Because I am a liberal Democrat, I want to see the House flipped to my party as an important check and balance between the executive and legislative branches. But what I don't want to see is a Democratic House abuse its authority by conducting vengeful impeachment proceedings against Kavanaugh.

I have no problem with an objective, preferably bipartisan, inquiry into how to improve the confirmation process. There is much that can be done to make it better. But an investigation of thirty-six-year-old charges against a sitting justice would be an abuse of the powers of Congress.

Such an investigation would simply be partisan payback for Kavanaugh's confirmation. Nor is it likely to produce much new information about what did or did not happen in house in Maryland in about 1982, when Christine Blasey Ford alleges Kavanaugh sexually assaulted her when they were both in high school. Kavanaugh has denied sexually assaulting Ford or anyone else.

As to impeachment, no sitting Supreme Court justice has been impeached and removed. One was impeached by the House more than two hundred years ago on completely partisan grounds, but ultimately not removed from office by the Senate.

It is unlikely that Congress has the power to impeach a sitting justice for alleged offenses he may or may not have committed while a private citizen and a teenager. It would be the first time in American history any impeachment went back that far and focused on such adolescent conduct.

Democrats may try to move it forward by alleging that the grounds for impeachment include perjury committed by nominee Kavanaugh in his testimony at his Senate Judiciary Committee confirmation hearing. Before his Supreme Court confirmation, Kavanaugh was a sitting judge on the US Circuit of Appeals for the District of Columbia subject to the impeachment power of Congress.

But that would be a ploy, somewhat akin to the phony perjury grounds used to impeach President Clinton. Democrats were outraged when Republicans used perjury as a surrogate for sexual improprieties. They should be similarly outraged if their colleagues seek to use perjury as a pretext for relitigating old charges of sexual misconduct against Kavanaugh.

But when it comes to revenge politics, hypocrisy is the coin of the realm. And don't expect consistency from zealots in either party.

The time has come to move forward and not look backward. Let Justice Kavanaugh assume the bench. If his conduct on our nation's highest court is a continuation of his conduct as an appeals court judge, we can expect conservative rulings coupled with excellent judicial demeanor.

It would not surprise me—indeed, it would please me greatly—if the experiences that Kavanaugh has gone through in the Supreme Court confirmation process increase his sensitivity with regard to due process, freedom of expression, and other civil liberties.

Judges often reflect their own histories and experiences, both good and bad. A sensitivity to rights often grows out of a recognition of wrongs one has experienced. We have seen that with liberal justices in the past, such as Thurgood Marshall, Ruth Bader Ginsburg, Sonia Sotomayor, and perhaps to some degree with Clarence Thomas. We may well see it with Justice Kavanaugh.

So let's hope that if the Democrats regain control of the House in the midterm elections Nov. 6, they will act as an appropriate check and balance on the other branches rather than as a revenge-driven Javert, the villain of *Les Misérables*, obsessed with righting past wrongs rather than preventing future ones.

Finally, if the Democrats spend the next month running against Justice Kavanaugh, they will alienate many centrist voters who are sick and tired of partisan gamesmanship and want to see a return to the day when members of both houses of Congress can work together in the interest of all Americans—even those who vote against them. This may sound unrealistic in our age of hyper-partisanship, but one can hope.

Justice Kavanaugh Should Not Be
Impeached or Investigated[39]

N ow that the Democrats are about to gain control of the House of
Representatives, some radical elements within the Democratic Party
are suggesting that Justice Brett Kavanaugh should be impeached, or at the
very least that he should be investigated by a committee controlled by
Democrats. A left-wing political action committee has garnered close to two
hundred thousand names on a petition to impeach the newly confirmed
Justice. Representative Jerrold Nadler, who will head the House Judiciary
Committee, promised to investigate Kavanaugh's alleged misconduct:

> If he is on the Supreme Court, and the Senate hasn't investigated
> (Kavanaugh), then the House will have to. We would have to inves-
> tigate any credible allegations of perjury and other things that hav-
> en't been properly looked into before.

These would be a serious mistake, both legally and politically.

A sitting justice cannot be impeached and removed for alleged conduct
he committed decades ago when he was seventeen years old. This would
seem beyond dispute. But taking a page from the Republican playbook in the
Bill Clinton impeachment, some Democrats are saying that Kavanaugh can
be impeached for the testimony he gave about those long-past events. That,
too, would be constitutionally dubious. First, he was not a sitting justice
when he gave that testimony. He was a judge on the United States Court of
Appeals. So he would have to be impeached and removed from that office.
But he no longer serves in that office. Zealots might argue that he can be
impeached and removed as a Justice of the Supreme Court for perjury committed during his confirmation hearing to serve on the High Court. That is
somewhat more plausible but it, too, is a stretch.

Moreover, it would be virtually impossible to prove that Justice

Kavanaugh committed perjury—that is, willfully lied about a material fact. Even if he was wrong—even if Professor Christine Blasey Ford truthfully testified about what happened years ago—it is highly likely that Kavanaugh did not remember what Ford claims happened. If that were the case, his testimony would not be perjurious. Nor would it be perjury for him to have a different recollection of his drinking habits than the recollection of some of his classmates. Perjury is difficult to prove, especially regarding decades old events.

Let's recall that modern attempts to impeach Supreme Court Justices have been directed against liberal members of the Court: Chief Justice Earl Warren and Justice William O. Douglas. These efforts never went anywhere because they were transparently political. So, too, would current efforts by the Democrats to manufacture a case for impeachment against a justice who they oppose on ideological grounds. But they would establish a terrible precedent that could come back to haunt liberal justices and Democrats. Remember what happened when foolish Democrats employed the "nuclear option" to eliminate the supermajority rule for confirming judges.

I worked hard on behalf of Democratic candidates to assure that at least one house of Congress is under the control of the opposing party. A divided Congress is an important check and balance against one-party rule. But the Democrats risk weakening their power if they foolishly prioritize impeachment, investigations, and revenge over legislative priorities that could help the American public. We need more bipartisan legislative efforts and fewer hyper-partisan show trials or investigations.

Impeachment is a constitutional remedy of last resort, deliberately made difficult by our Framers. Impeaching and removing a president is, of course, the most extreme step that Congress could take, but impeaching a justice who has been confirmed by the Senate comes close. It would be a flagrant abuse of power for the Democratic majority to act in so unconstitutional, unwise, and shortsighted a manner. But in this age of hyper-partisan politics nothing should surprise us.

Leaders of the Democratic Party seem to understand this, but some soon to be Committee chairs seem ready to deploy their newly found power to gain headlines and appeal to the immediate gratification of their base. The leadership should restrain these impulses and look to the future instead of trying to investigate past sins of those with which they disagree. Justice Kavanaugh has been hearing arguments on the high court. Soon he will deliver his first opinions. Let's put recriminations behind us and judge him on his actions as a justice, not on allegations of his past behavior.

Don't Seek Partisan Advantage
from Pipe-Bomb Arrest[40]

The arrest of Cesar Sayoc Jr. for the flurry of pipe bombs directed against liberal and left-wing icons leaves many questions unanswered. It does seem to put to rest the conspiracy theory of a "false flag" operation organized by the hard-left to demonize the hard-right or the Trump administration. But we still don't know whether the pipe bombs were intended to kill or merely to frighten. The FBI has determined that these bombs were not "hoax devices," but they have not disclosed whether they were capable of lethally exploding.

Either way, the perpetrator must be condemned in the strongest of terms and tried for serious crimes.

The entire episode brings back painful memories of the Weathermen and other radical left-wing groups who planted bombs in the 1970s. The Weather Underground and other radical groups targeted universities, army bases, police officers, banks, and other establishment places and people. The death toll was considerable and the fear was palpable. At about the same time, the Black Panthers, the Symbionese Liberation Army, and other radical leftist groups terrorized the United States.

So far, no one has tried to glorify the person responsible for the recent pipe bombs. Although President Trump has condemned the perpetrator, it would not be surprising if some right-wing extremists took perverse pleasure and pride in the attacks on the left-wing icons.

This is different from how some on the left glorified the Weather Underground, Black Panthers, and other hard-left terrorists. Left-wing lawyers, who would never defend an accused right-wing terrorist, rushed to represent them; prominent leftists contributed to defense funds and attended fund-raising parties. Films, books, plays, and articles sought to understand the motives of these young murderers.

Years later, Barack Obama befriended Bill Ayers and Bernardine Dohrn, who had been active members of the Weathermen and supporters of violent terrorism. Both Ayers and Dohrn were invited to teach at major American universities, as was Kathy Boudin, who had served a long prison term for participating in a terrorist-inspired robbery that resulted in the deaths of two policemen and one armored-truck guard and seriously injured a second guard. It is difficult to imagine any American university appointing a right-wing terrorist, even one who had served his term and claimed to be rehabil-itated. It is fair to say that public attitudes by some on the left were somewhat sympathetic to left-wing terrorists.

Tragically, we have seen violent terrorism in the US on both sides of the political spectrum. In the nineteenth and early twentieth centuries, the Ku Klux Klan was a violent terrorist group with significant support from politi-cal figures and ordinary citizens. During the first decades of the 20th cen-tury, left-wing anarchists planted bombs and engaged in other forms of violence that killed many innocent people. More recently, hard-left violence was directed at Republican congressmen as they practiced for a charity base-ball game, wounding several people, including Rep. Steve Scalise of Louisiana. A threatening letter claiming it contained ricin was sent to Sen. Susan Collins (R-Maine) because she voted to confirm Brett Kavanaugh to the Supreme Court, and other hard-left threats were directed against prominent Republicans.

The extreme right and the extreme left both have a penchant for lawless-ness, violence, and terrorism. It is ahistorical to identify such terrorism only with either the hard-right or the hard-left, though partisans always seem to do that when it serves their short-term ideological interests.

The hard-right and the hard-left share in common a disdain for the law, an intolerance toward those with whom they disagree, a distrust of dialogue, and a willingness to use despicable means to achieve what they believe are desirable ends.

All Americans should condemn terrorism, regardless of its source—but conservatives have a special obligation to condemn right-wing terrorism, just as liberals have a special obligation to condemn left-wing terrorism. No one should be given a pass. It is not that conservatives are responsible for right-wing terrorism, or that liberals are responsible for left-wing terrorism. The point is that hard-right terrorists often falsely claim to be acting on behalf of the conservative agenda; similarly, left-wing terrorists sometimes falsely claim to be acting on behalf of the progressive agenda. It is too easy for con-servatives to condemn left-wing terrorism and for liberals to condemn

right-wing terrorism. Both sides have to disassociate themselves from violence on *their* side of the political spectrum.

In the days to come, we will learn more about the alleged perpetrator and
his motives. For now, it is enough to applaud law enforcement for the arrest
it made, and for all decent Americans to avoid the temptation to try to secure
partisan advantage from this frightening episode.

Shootings, Bombs Reflect a Deerper Malady[41]

The cowardly shootings—in a synagogue, in a black church, and on a baseball diamond—along with the mailed pipe bombs, are extreme manifestations of a deeper, more pervasive attack on American values of tolerance, reasoned discussion, and non-violence.

The core constitutional and political values of our nation are currently being challenged in many places and by many people, but most dangerously by students and faculty leaders on university campuses. These values include the free and open exchange of ideas, the right to hold and express views that offend some listeners, and the value of the marketplace of ideas as a means of discerning truth; the very value of truth as an end in itself; the need for diversity of ideas; due process and the presumption of innocence for those accused of misconduct, especially sexual misconduct; individual rather than identity accountability; and other traditional hallmarks of liberal democracy and barriers to tyranny.

In place of these proven protections, many students and faculty are insisting that freedom of speech is part of patriarchal privilege designed to preserve the status quo; that truth is identity-based and variable; that evidence is in the eye of the beholder; that they know their Truth—with a capital T—and need hear no others; that due process is a tactic for requiring the oppressed to prove their victimization; that identity politics must displace individualism; that intersectionality—the academic construct that teaches that all oppressed groups share common oppressors—demands group accountability; and that democracy and liberty are themselves constructs of hegemonic white, male, hetero Western autocracy.

Most frightening is the claim by some academics that violence is an acceptable tactic of change if democratic institutions do not produce the desired results.

This is the current *lingua franca* of much academic discourse, not only on the campus but in many classrooms, including required courses—and the attack is spreading beyond the campus to extremists on all sides of the political and ideological spectrum. Centrist liberalism and conservatism—which share a strong commitment to the core values under attack—are being marginalized by extremists who used to dwell on the margins of politics, academia, and the media.

The political center is shrinking, as many on the left move away from liberalism toward misnamed "progressivism," which often espouses many regressive, intolerant elements, and as the right moves toward populism, the alt-right, and outright white supremacy.

This is a worldwide trend, manifested by the rise of both the hard-left and hard right. Jeremy Corbyn in Great Britain represents the hard-left in this trend, as do some recently elected Democratic politicians in our own country. The trend toward the hard right is represented by nationalistic leaders in Hungary, Poland, Greece, Austria, and other European countries, as well as by some extremist Republican politicians.

In the US, we are blessed with a constitutional system of checks and balances that constrains the excesses of either extreme, but the most important check always remains with the people. As the great Judge Learned Hand wisely reminded us many decades ago: "Liberty lies in the hearts of men and women; when it dies there, no constitution, no law, no court can save it."

Our system of checks and balances transcends legal institutions—executive, legislative, and judicial. It includes extra-legal institutions, such as the academy, the media, business, religion, science, and technology. When President Trump decided to separate families at the border, these institutions coalesced to say, "No, that's not what Americans do. You went too far." And President Trump backed off—not enough, but to a considerable degree.

The concerning question is whether the current trends toward extremism and intolerance are wounding liberty in the hearts of our future leaders, and whether we have the capacity to treat these wounds before they fester and become fatal.

Some of the media, too, has prioritized ideology over truth, opinion over reporting, pandering over challenging. One-sided news "analysis" appears on the front page of the *New York Times* right next to selective reporting (all the news that fits our narrative). Fox, CNN, and MSNBC report the same facts differently. The media has become as adversarial as our legal system, but without judges (who are also becoming more adversarial). The ACLU, which long protected civil liberties in a nonpartisan, neutral manner, has now become part of the problem, prioritizing left-wing partisanship over neutral civil liberties.

History has generally blessed this nation with an absence of powerful, influential extremes. We never had the kind of large fascist and communists parties that plagued Europe in the 1920s and 1930s. To be sure, there were regional extremists such as the Klan, which exercised considerable power in some parts of the country for decades, but they were always peripheral and transient to governance. When Europe responded to the post–World War I depression with Nazism and communism, we responded with the New Deal. To be sure we had right-wing McCarthyism, but a Republican president stood up to that potential tyrant and he flamed out.

Now we are experiencing its mirror image: left-wing McCarthyism. But where are the Democratic leaders willing to stand against the intolerance of the hard-left?

President Trump was justly criticized for not condemning, more forcefully, white supremacists who falsely claimed to be speaking in his name. So, too, must Democratic leaders be criticized for not condemning more forcefully those who distort liberalism into intolerant radicalism. So, too, should academic leaders condemn those who misuse their academic license to propagandize rather than educate, who tell their students what to think rather than teaching them how to think for themselves.

Too many mainstream Democrats have remained silent—some, even complicit—with the anti-Semitic, anti-gay incitements of Louis Farrakhan, and some of his bigoted followers on university campuses; he has considerable influence on many young people in the inner cities. And too many mainstream Republicans have remained silent—some, even complicit—with alt-right neo-fascists who preach xenophobic hatred against "the other."

Pipe bombs, synagogue and church shootings, the targeting of congressmen playing baseball—all are dangerous, extreme symptoms of a deep underlying sickness in our body politic. But the underlying causes include a growing intolerance on both sides of the political spectrum. That such intolerance is being taught to our future leaders who are now university students should frighten us even more than the shootings and pipe bombs.

The good news is that there is pushback from some students and faculty. The bad news is that it is coming mostly from the very conservatives who have been victimized by hard-left intolerance, and it therefore appears self-serving.

It is imperative that centrist liberals and conservatives join together in a coordinated, non-partisan effort to regain the spirit of liberty so essential to democratic governance. That is the best response to violent acts of hatred.

Both Sides Are Failing the
Shoe on the Other Foot Test

If it is true that President Trump wanted to order the Justice Department to prosecute Hillary Clinton and James Comey, then President Trump not only failed the shoe on the other foot test, but he also nearly shot himself in the foot. President Trump has rightfully railed in opposition to weaponizing the criminal justice system against political opponents when *he* is the target, but now it seems that he was willing to weaponize the Justice Department against *his* political opponents. Fortunately, wiser heads prevailed and former White House counsel Donald McGahn persuaded the president that he might be abusing his power if he targeted his political enemies.

History shows that past presidents went after their political enemies: most notably, John Adams ordered the prosecution of members of the opposition party under the notorious Alien and Sedition Acts; Thomas Jefferson demanded the prosecution of Aaron Burr; Abraham Lincoln prosecuted copperheads; John Kennedy (and his brother, who was attorney general) tried to get Roy Cohn. The system worked and most of the political prosecutions failed, but that didn't make it right. The criminal justice system must not be used to even scores, to score political points, or to further the interests of a political party.

Both parties have been guilty of trying to weaponize the criminal justice system. Some Democrats want to investigate and possibly prosecute Ivanka Trump for using her personal email for government business. As the *Guardian* put it: "What goes around comes around." The chant "lock her up" cuts both ways.

Former FBI director James Comey was right in concluding that Hillary Clinton's sloppiness in using a private email server should not be prosecuted. (He was wrong in how he handled the entire matter.) Neither should Ivanka Trump be prosecuted for her far less serious violation of rules that many government officials, from both parties, seem to ignore. There must be *one law* for both parties and for those in power and out of power. And that law should require that criminal prosecution be a last resort against only clear violations of narrowly defined criminal statutes. This means that President Trump should not be accused of "collusion," which is simply not a crime. Nor should he be accused of obstruction of justice for exercising his constitutional authority to fire, pardon, or exercise control over the Justice Department (though it may be wrong to do so, *wrong* is not the same as *criminal*). It also means that neither Hillary Clinton nor James Comey should be prosecuted for political sins that do not rise to the level of crime.

The same is true of impeachment. President Bill Clinton should never have been impeached for his Oval Office misconduct or his testimony about his sex life. Nor should President Trump be impeached for noncriminal political sins. Neither should Justice Brett Kavanaugh be impeached for what he is accused of doing as a teenager and his subsequent testimony about it. The threat to impeach is today being thrown around like a baseball after a strike-out. Maxine Waters wants to impeach Vice President Pence just because she doesn't like him, and the Democrats have a majority in the House. Some Republicans want to impeach Rod Rosenstein (who should be recused but not impeached), while some Democrats want to impeach acting Attorney General Matthew Whittaker because they object to his interim appointment. The promiscuous and partisan threat of impeachment will only politicize and delegitimize that important safeguard, and make it difficult to employ when it is really and properly needed.

Criminalization of political differences and impeachment are double-edged swords. When they are unsheathed against one party, they can and will be deployed against the other party. The shoes are always on both feet. So the shoe on the foot test is not only a moral imperative; it is a pragmatic caution. The mirror image of the Golden Rule is that what you do unto others, they will surely do unto you—especially in this age of amoral, hyper-partisan, anything-goes, tit-for-tat, weaponization of our legal system.

So we need mutual disarmament: a commitment from both sides to resolve political differences politically—at the ballot box—and not through the misuse of criminal law and impeachment.

Conclusion

Part II

WILL THE MUELLER INVESTIGATION PROVIDE A BASIS FOR IMPEACHMENT?

B ased on the public record, the Mueller investigation does not seem to be providing a factual or legal basis for impeaching President Trump.

The recent guilty plea of Michael Cohen for lying represents the dominant trend in Mueller's approach to prosecution. The vast majority of indictments and guilty pleas obtained against Americans by Mueller have not been for substantive crimes relating to his mandate: namely, to uncover crimes involving illegal contacts with Russia. They have involved indictments and guilty pleas either for lying or for financial crimes by individuals unrelated to the Russia probe. If this remains true after the filing of the Mueller report, it would represent a significant failure on Mueller's part. It would also fail to provide a basis for impeaching the president.

Mueller was appointed special counsel not to provoke individuals into committing new crimes, but rather to uncover past crimes specifically involving alleged illegal coordination between the Trump campaign and Russian agents. No one doubted that Russia attempted to influence the 2016 election in favor of Trump and against Hillary Clinton. But Mueller's mandate was not to prosecute Russians or to point the finger at Vladimir Putin. His mandate was to uncover crimes committed by the Trump campaign with regard to Russia's attempts to influence the election.

It was always an uphill battle for Mueller, since collusion itself is not a crime. In other words, even if he could show that individuals in the Trump campaign had colluded with Russian agents to help elect Trump, that would be a serious political sin but not a federal crime. Even if Mueller could prove that members of the Trump team had colluded with Julian Assange to *use* material that Assange had unlawfully obtained, that, too, would not be a crime. What would be a crime is something that no one claims happened: namely, that members of the Trump campaign told Assange to hack the Democratic National Committee before Assange did so. Merely using the product of an already committed theft of information is not a crime. If you don't believe me, ask the *New York Times*, the *Washington Post*, the *Guardian*, and other newspapers that used material illegally obtained by Assange with full knowledge that it was illegally obtained. Not only did they use information from Assange, but also from Chelsea Manning and from the stolen *Pentagon Papers*. The First Amendment protects publication by the media of stolen information. It also protects use of such information by a political campaign, since political campaigns are also covered by the First Amendment.

It is important to note that Special Counsel Robert Mueller does not have an unrestrained power to ferret out political sin, to provoke new crimes, or to publish conclusions about non-criminal activities that may be politically embarrassing to the president. His mandate, like that of every other prosecutor, is to uncover past crimes. In Mueller's case, those crimes must relate to Russia. He also has the authority to prosecute crimes growing out of the Russia probe, but that is collateral to his central mission. In the end, Mueller should be judged by how successful he has been in satisfying his central mission. Judged by that standard and based on what we now know, he seems to be an abysmal failure.

Perhaps more will come out when his report is published, but it is unlikely that he uncovered anything dramatically new with regard to allegations that the Trump campaign acted illegally in an attempt to help Russia undercut Hillary Clinton's campaign. Even if the report alleges uncharged criminal behavior, it must be remembered that many of the allegations in the report will likely be based merely on un-cross-examined evidence. Some of that evidence seems to come from admitted liars, who have pleaded guilty for lying. These liars would make poor witnesses in an actual criminal or impeachment and removal trial, but if their evidence serves as a basis for conclusions reached in the Mueller report, then these conclusions may seem more credible than they actually are. We must, of course, wait for the publication of the Mueller report before reaching any final judgments, but if the Mueller report merely catalogs all the guilty pleas and indictments achieved thus far for lying and unrelated financial crimes, and tries to build a case of guilt by association around them, the American public will be justly critical of the process.

Some members of the Democrat-controlled House may nonetheless try to use the report to begin impeachment proceedings. Maxine Waters called for the impeachment of both President Trump and Vice President Pence even before the report was completed. But, hopefully, wiser heads will prevail and impeachment will not be undertaken.

There is, of course, the possibility—however slight—that Mueller may come up with smoking gun evidence of impeachable crimes. Unless that occurs, we would all be far better off without a constitutionally questionable impeachment process that would further divide an already fractured nation. The case for impeaching President Trump has not been made, so it should not be pursued.

Notes

Part I

1. Dershowitz, Alan. "The Partisan Shoe Is on the Other Foot." *The Hill*, August 12, 2017. http://thehill.com/blogs/pundits-blog/the-administration/346307-opinion-dershowitz-the-partisan-shoe-is-on-the-other
2. Dershowitz, Alan. "When Politics Is Criminalized." *New York Times*, November 28, 2017. https://www.nytimes.com/2017/11/28/opinion/politics-investigations-trump-russia.html
3. Dershowitz, Alan. "The Criminalization of Politics." *Newsmax*, January 24, 2018.
4. Dershowitz, Alan, interviewed by Tucker Carlson. *Tucker Carlson Tonight*, FOX News Channel, May 31, 2018.
5. Dershowitz, Alan. "A Partisan Rush to Prosecute Trump." *The Boston Globe*, July 20, 2017. https://www.bostonglobe.com/opinion/2017/07/20/partisan-rush-prosecute-trump/rDTQDUPZBKLx1Fr218WpUP/story.html
6. Dershowitz, Alan. "Why Donald Trump Can't Be Charged with Obstruction." *Macleans*, December 14, 2017. https://www.macleans.ca/opinion/why-trump-cant-be-charged-with-obstruction/
7. Dershowitz, Alan. "'Corrupt Motive' as the Criterion for Prosecuting a President." *Gatestone Institute*, June 20, 2017. https://www.gatestoneinstitute.org/10556/corrupt-motive-as-the-criterion-for-prosecuting
8. Dershowitz, Alan. "Dershowitz: Ruling Shows I'm Right on Trump and Corruption." *The Hill*, July 17, 2017. http://thehill.com/blogs/pundits-blog/the-administration/342301-opinion-alan-dershowitz-ruling-shows-im-right-on-trump
9. Dershowitz, Alan. "No One Is Above the Law." *The Hill*, December 15, 2017. http://thehill.com/opinion/judiciary/363387-no-one-is-above-the-law
10. Dershowitz, Alan. "Donald Trump Has Congressional Immunity. Yes or No?" *Macleans*, December 19, 2017. https://www.macleans.ca/opinion/donald-trump-has-congressional-immunity-yes-or-no/
11. Dershowitz, Alan. "Rod Rosenstein Should Not Be Fired, but Should He Be Recused?" *The Hill*, February 5, 2018. http://thehill.com/opinion/judiciary/372373-rod-rosenstein-should-not-be-fired-but-should-he-be-recused
12. Dershowitz, Alan, interviewed with Bob Bauer by Chuck Todd. *Meet the Press*, NBC, April 1, 2018.
13. Dershowitz, Alan. "Dershowitz: Why Did Mueller Impanel a Second Grand Jury in DC?" *The Hill*, August 7, 2017. http://thehill.com/blogs/pundits-blog/the-administration/345602-opinion-dershowitz-why-did-mueller-impanel-a-second

14. Dershowitz, Alan. "Flynn Plea Reveals Weakness, Not Strength of Mueller Probe." *Newsmax*, December 4, 2017. https://www.newsmax.com/alandershowitz/fbi-kis-lyak-new-york-times/2017/12/04/id/829716/

15. Dershowitz, Alan. "Alan Dershowitz: Trump Doesn't Need to Fire Mueller—Here's Why." FOX News, December 18, 2017. http://www.foxnews.com/opinion/2017/12/18/alan-dershowitz-trump-doesnt-need-to-fire-mueller-heres-why.html

16. Dershowitz, Alan. "Desire to 'Get Trump' Risks Death of Civil Liberties." *The Hill*, April 21, 2018. http://thehill.com/opinion/white-house/384252-desire-to-get-trump-risks-death-of-civil-liberties

17. Dershowitz, Alan. "Does the President Have the Right to Expect Loyalty from His Attorney General?" *Gatestone Institute*, September 20, 2017. https://www.gatestoneinstitute.org/11038/does-the-president-have-the-right-to-expect

18. Dershowitz, Alan. "Alan Dershowitz: The Nunes FISA Memo Deserves More Investigation. Time for a Nonpartisan Commission." FOX News, February 2, 2018. http://www.foxnews.com/opinion/2018/02/02/alan-dershowitz-nunes-fisa-memo-deserves-more-investigation-time-for-nonpartisan-commission.html

19. Dershowitz, Alan. "Trump Is Right: The Special Counsel Should Never Have Been Appointed." *The Hill*, March 21, 2018. http://thehill.com/opinion/white-house/379372-trump-is-right-the-special-counsel-should-never-have-been-appointed

20. Dershowitz, Alan. "Alan Dershowitz: The President Has a Special Obligation to Condemn the Racist Right." *Wall Street Journal*, August 22, 2017.

21. Dershowitz, Alan. "Alan Dershowitz: Enough with the Anti-Trump McCarthyism!" *Forward*, April 18, 2018. https://forward.com/opinion/letters/399063/alan-dershowitz-enough-with-the-anti-trump-mccarthyism/

22. Dershowitz, Alan. "Dershowitz: Targeting Trump's Lawyer Should Worry Us All." *The Hill*, April 10, 2018. http://thehill.com/opinion/judiciary/382459-dershowitz-targeting-trumps-lawyer-should-worry-us-all

23. Dershowitz, Alan. "For ACLU, Getting Trump Trumps Civil Liberties." *The Hill*, April 12, 2018. http://thehill.com/opinion/white-house/382886-dershowitz-for-aclu-getting-trump-trumps-civil-liberties

24. Dershowitz, Alan. "'Firewalls' and 'Taint Teams' Do Not Protect Fourth and Sixth Amendment Rights." *Gatestone Institute*, April 11, 2018. https://www.gatestoneinstitute.org/12154/donald-trump-michael-cohen

25. Dershowitz, Alan. "Alan Dershowitz: We Need a New Law to Protect Lawyer-Client Communications." *The Hill*, April 13, 2018. http://thehill.com/opinion/judiciary/383017-we-need-a-new-law-to-protect-lawyer-client-communications

26. Dershowitz, Alan, interviewed with Mimi Rocah and Dan Abrams by George Stephanopoulos. *This Week with George Stephanopoulos*, ABC, April 22, 2018.

27. Dershowitz, Alan. "The Epic Struggle for Michael Cohen's Soul and Testimony." *The Hill*, April 23, 2018. http://thehill.com/opinion/judiciary/384440-the-epic-struggle-for-michael-cohens-soul-and-testimony

28. Dershowitz, Alan. "Federal Judge Rightly Rebukes Mueller for Questionable Tactics." *The Hill*, May 7, 2018. http://thehill.com/opinion/judiciary/386508-federal-judge-rightly-rebukes-mueller-for-questionable-tactics

29. Dershowitz, Alan. "Trump's Better Off Litigating than Testifying." *USA Today*, May 3, 2018. https://www.usatoday.com/story/opinion/2018/05/03/donald-trump-better-litigating-testifying-alan-dershowitz-editorials-debates/34524873/

30. Dershowitz, Alan, interviewed by Chuck Todd. *Meet The Press*, NBC, May 5, 2018.

31. Dershowitz, Alan, interviewed with Dan Abrams by George Stephanopoulos. *This Week with George Stephanopoulos*, ABC, May 20, 2018.

32. Dershowitz, Alan. "Can Trump Pardon Himself? The Answer Is No One Actually Knows." *The Hill*, June 4, 2018.

33. Dershowitz, Alan, interviewed by Chuck Todd. *Meet The Press*, NBC, June 5, 2018. https://www.msnbc.com/mtp-daily/watch/dershowitz-i-guarantee-no-president-will-pardon-himself-1248883267941

34. Dershowitz, Alan, interviewed by Harris Falkner. *Overtime*, FOX News, June 11, 2018.

Notes

Part II

1. Dershowitz, Alan. "Federal Judge Agrees Nonpartisan Commission Beats Special Counsel." *The Hill*, June 29, 2018. https://thehill.com/opinion/judiciary/394793-federal-judge-agrees-nonpartisan-commission-beats-special-counsel

2. Dershowitz, Alan. "Jeff Sessions Validates Chant to Lock up Hillary." *The Hill*, July 25, 2018. https://thehill.com/opinion/judiciary/398732-jeff-sessions-validates-chant-to-lock-up-hillary-clinton

3. Dershowitz, Alan. "Trump's Bid to Silence Dissent Violates the Spirit of the First Amendment." *The Boston Globe*, July 25, 2018. https://www.bostonglobe.com/opinion/2018/07/25/trump-bid-silence-dissent-violates-spirit-first-amendment/czPW9wyCBsSwkxIvvB5dvJ/story.html

4. Dershowitz, Alan. "Impeaching Rosenstein May Hurt Trump." *The Hill*, July 26, 2018. https://thehill.com/opinion/white-house/398994-impeaching-rosenstein-may-hurt-trump

5. Dershowitz, Alan. "Who Leaked the Trump Tape?" *Gatestone Institute*, July 26, 2018. https://www.gatestoneinstitute.org/12767/who-leaked-the-trump-tape

6. Dershowitz, Alan. "An Obstruction Case Would Be Civil Libertarian Nightmare." *The Hill*, July 27, 2018. https://thehill.com/opinion/judiciary/399205-an-obstruction-case-against-trump-would-be-civil-libertarian-nightmare

7. Dershowitz, Alan. "Dangers to the First Amendment If Foreign Campaign Dirt Is Criminal." *The Hill*, August 13, 2018. https://thehill.com/opinion/judiciary/401521-dangers-to-the-first-amendment-if-foreign-campaign-dirt-is-criminal

8. Dershowitz, Alan. "Is 'The Truth' the Truth When It Comes to Prosecutors?" *Gatestone Institute*, August 20, 2018. https://www.gatestoneinstitute.org/12896/is-the-truth-the-truth-when-it-comes-to

9. Dershowitz, Alan. "Did President Trump Violate Campaign Finance Laws?" *The Hill*, August 22, 2018. https://thehill.com/opinion/judiciary/403072-did-president-trump-violate-campaign-finance-laws

10. Dershowitz, Alan. "Who Is Guarding the Guardians?" *The Hill*, August 27, 2018. https://thehill.com/opinion/judiciary/403836-who-is-guarding-the-guardians

11. Dershowitz, Alan. "Should It Be Illegal for Prosecutors to 'Flip' Witnesses?" *Gatestone Institute*, August 29, 2018. https://www.gatestoneinstitute.org/12935/flipping-witnesses

12. Dershowitz, Alan. "Will Mueller Subpoena Trump?" *The Hill*, August 31, 2018. https://thehill.com/opinion/white-house/404526-will-mueller-subpoena-trump

13. Dershowitz, Alan "Donald Trump Is Not an Unindicted Coconspirator." *Boston Globe*, September 7, 2018. https://www.bostonglobe.com/opinion/2018/09/07 /donald-trump-not-unindicted-coconspirator/BSTHmaIPpmOzRAHP7EyS2H /story.html

14. Dershowitz, Alan. "Don't Let Mueller's Report Go Unanswered" December 2, 2018. https://www.wsj.com/amp/articles/dont-let-muellers-report-go-unanswered -1543786233

15. Dershowitz, Alan. "Maxine Waters Does Not Speak for Democrats or Liberals." June 27, 2018. https://thehill.com/opinion/civil-rights/394346-maxine-waters-does -not-speak-for-democrats-or-liberals
    Shanahan, Mark. "The Martha's Vineyard Crowd Strikes Back at Alan Dershow-itz." *Boston Globe*, July 4, 2018. https://www.bostonglobe.com/lifestyle/names/2018 /07/03/the-martha-vineyard-crowd-strikes-back-alan-dershowitz-for-his-defenses -trump/ykxKWa6erCQsSUsbcrFURO/story.html

16. Dershowitz, Alan. "The Left's Desire to Live in a Political Silo When It Comes to Trump." *Boston Globe*, July 6, 2018. https://www.bostonglobe.com /opinion/2018/07/06/the-left-desire-live-political-silo-when-comes-trump /OAS3UzM31pSTrnTWsJ3z7M/story.html

17. Dershowitz, Alan. "Zealous Dems Fail to Hear Out Trump's Constitutional Rights." *The Hill*, July 12, 2018. https://thehill.com/opinion/judiciary/396783-zealous-dems -fail-to-hear-out-trumps-constitutional-rights

18. Dershowitz, Alan. "Coarseness, Bigotry and Threats on Both Sides of Trump Divide." *The Hill*, August 2, 2018. https://thehill.com/opinion/campaign/400092 -coarseness-bigotry-and-threats-on-both-sides-of-trump-divide

19. Dershowitz, Alan. "How the Hard-Left Only Helps the Republicans and Donald Trump." *The Hill*, August 9, 2018. https://thehill.com/opinion/campaign/401127 -how-the-hard-left-only-helps-the-republicans-and-donald-trump

20. Dershowitz, Alan. "Immigrants Who Change America Are Its Lifeblood." *Boston Globe*, August 16, 2018. https://www.bostonglobe.com/opinion/2018/08/16 /immigrants-who-change-america-are-its-lifeblood/M6Aam5KzgBwls5aFiTyYhK /story.html

21. Dershowitz, Alan. "A Self-Inflicted Wound to Judicial Independence." *The Hill*, June 13, 2018. https://thehill.com/opinion/judiciary/392133-a-self-inflicted -wound-to-judicial-independence

22. The combined text of this piece appeared originally in two separate articles: Dershowitz, Alan. "It All Depends on What Kind of Conservative Trump Choos-es." *The Hill*, June 28, 2018. https://thehill.com/opinion/judiciary/394577-it -all-depends-on-what-kind-of-conservative-trump-picks
    Dershowitz, Alan. "Replacing Justice Kennedy: What Kind of Conservative Will President Trump Pick?" *Gatestone Institute*, June 29, 2018. https://www .gatestoneinstitute.org/12615/replacing-justice-kennedy-what-kind

23. Dershowitz, Alan. "The SCOTUS Confirmation Process Has Gotten Out of Hand." *Gatestone Institute*, July 13, 2018. https://www.gatestoneinstitute.org/12696 /the-scotus-confirmation-process-has-gotten-out

24. Dershowitz, Alan. "Six Rules for Conducting Ford-Kavanaugh Hearings." *Boston Globe*, September 22, 2018. https://www.bostonglobe.com/opinion/2018/09/22/six

-rules-for-conducting-ford-kavanaugh-hearings/ceJUeP97WOmIcKquyMIhzO
/story.html

25. Dershowitz, Alan. "How to Decide Who to Believe in Kavanaugh, Rosenstein Drama." *The Hill*, September 25, 2018. https://thehill.com/opinion/judiciary /408391-how-to-decide-who-to-believe-in-kavanaugh-rosenstein-drama

26. Dershowitz, Alan. "Burden Is on Avenatti to Show Proof, or Face Consequences." *The Hill*, September 28, 2018. https://thehill.com/opinion/judiciary/409032-burden -on-avenatti-to-show-proof-or-face-consequences

27. Dershowitz, Alan. "This Is No Mere 'Job Interview.'" *Wall Street Journal*, September 30, 2018. https://www.wsj.com/articles/this-is-no-mere-job-interview-1538313919

28. Dershowitz, Alan. "What If Kavanaugh Were a Liberal Muslim?" *Jerusalem Post*, October 4, 2018. https://www.jpost.com/Opinion/What-if-Kavanaugh-were-a -liberal-Muslim-accused-of-terrorism-568696

29. Dershowitz, Alan. "No One Won During The Brett Kavanaugh Confirmation." *Newsweek*, October 6, 2018. https://www.newsweek.com/alan-dershowitz -kavanaugh-confirmation-no-one-won-1156713

30. Dershowitz, Alan. "Should Brett Kavanaugh Be Stopped from Teaching at Harvard Law School?" *Boston Globe*, October 8, 2018. https://www.bostonglobe.com /opinion/2018/10/08/should-brett-kavanaugh-stopped-from-teaching-harvard -law-school/BxMas12xnUEiZh7UePv41N/story.html

31. Dershowitz, Alan. "ACLU's Opposition to Kavanaugh Sounds Its Death Knell." *Gatestone Institute*, October 6, 2018. https://www.gatestoneinstitute.org/13087 /aclu-opposition-to-kavanaugh-sounds-its-death

32. Dershowitz, Alan. "Biased Media Complicit as Hamas Sends Women, Children to Front Line." *Newsmax*, May 16, 2018. https://www.newsmax.com/alandershowitz /hamas-israel-palestinians-terrorism/2018/05/16/id/860711/

33. Dershowitz, Alan. "NBC Demonizes John Bolton, Gatestone." *Gatestone Institute*, May 10, 2018. https://www.newsmax.com/alandershowitz/hanson-islam-muslims -przybyla/2018/05/09/id/859415/

34. Dershowitz, Alan. "Chomsky Calls Russian Interference a Joke–Blames Guess Who?" *Gatestone Institute*, August 3, 2018. https://www.gatestoneinstitute .org/12799/noam-chomsky-russian-interference

35. Dershowitz, Alan. "If Britain Wants to Show Its 'Moral Backbone,' It Must Reject Jeremy Corbyn." *Evening Standard*, September 7, 2018. https://www.standard.co.uk /comment/comment/if-britain-wants-to-show-its-moral-backbone-it-must-reject -jeremy-corbyn-a3930311.html

36. Dershowitz, Alan. "Why Did Clinton Share the Stage with Farrakhan?" *The Hill*, September 7, 2018. https://thehill.com/opinion/civil-rights/405520-why-did-clinton -share-the-stage-with-farrakhan

37. Dershowitz, Alan. "Refusing Study in Israel Is a Bitter Lesson in Discrimination." *The Hill*, September 21, 2018. https://thehill.com/opinion/education/407647 -refusing-study-in-israel-is-a-bitter-lesson-in-discrimination

38. Dershowitz, Alan. "Kavanaugh and Impeachment–Democrats, Don't Try to Conduct a Revenge Inquisition." Fox News, October 6, 2018. https://www.foxnews.com /opinion/alan-dershowitz-kavanaugh-and-impeachment-democrats-dont-try-to -conduct-a-revenge-inquisition

39. Dershowitz, Alan. "Justice Kavanaugh Should Not Be Impeached or Investigated." *The Hill*, November 21, 2018. https://thehill.com/opinion/judiciary/417849-justice -kavanaugh-should-not-be-impeached-or-investigated

40. Dershowitz, Alan. "Avoid Temptation to Seek Partisan Advantage from Pipe Bomb Arrest." *The Hill*, October 26, 2018. https://thehill.com/opinion/national -security/413410-avoid-temptation-to-seek-partisan-advantage-from-pipe-bomb -arrest

41. Dershowitz, Alan. "Shootings and Bombs Reflect the Attack on Our Democratic Values." October 29, 2018. https://thehill.com/opinion/judiciary/413722-shootings -and-bombs-reflect-the-attack-on-our-democratic-values